Media, Culture
and Catholicism

Media, Culture and Catholicism

Paul A. Soukup, editor

Sheed & Ward
Kansas City

Sheed & Ward™ is a service of The National Catholic Reporter Publishing Company.

Library of Congress Cataloguing-in-Publication Data

Media, culture, and Catholicism / edited by Paul A. Soukup.
        p.   cm. — (Communication, culture & theology)
   Includes bibliographical references and index.
   ISBN: 1-55612-769-3 (alk. paper) ISBN 978-1-55612-769-4
   1. Mass media in religion—United States. 2. Mass media—Religious aspects—Catholic Church. 3. Christianity and culture—United States. 4. Catholic Church—United States. I. Soukup, Paul A. II. Series.
BV652.97.U6M43 1996
261.5'2'08822—dc20
                                                       96-26535
                                                           CIP

Published by: Sheed & Ward
               115 E. Armour Blvd.
               P.O. Box 419492
               Kansas City, MO 64141-6492

To order, call: (800) 333-7373

Table of Contents

Media, Culture, and Catholicism

A quick look at the attitudes of Catholics towards the mass media, particularly the electronic mass media, reveals ambivalence at best and confusion at worst. Fundamentally, the situation arises from an uncertain search by individuals and institutions for a way to deal theologically, pastorally, and administratively with a mass-mediated culture. Most agree that the Church should do something in communication; some readily embrace the electronic media; some treat them with distrust and suspicion; and others would welcome media sympathetic to the Church. Each view finds support in a particular vision of Church and communication.

This is not to say that the Church avoids involvement with the mass media. Here, for example, is a partial list of Church communication. Each year the United States Catholic Conference (USCC) uses an annual Communication Day collection to fund close to $2 million of national communication projects: print and electronic public service campaigns in support of family life and prayer; documentary films and video on Church life; radio programs supporting faith; multi-language programming aimed at evangelization; telecommunications connections linking dioceses and Church organizations; and other more specialized materials. The USCC supervises lobbying efforts in support of Church positions regarding communication. The USCC also provides an office of media relations and supports the National Catholic News Service. In all this, the USCC regards communication as a ministry, part of a "public dialogue of faith" (Administrative Board, 1986, p. 8).

Local dioceses participate in communication as well. Many actively support a Catholic press. Others form the Catholic Television Network, a loose group that produces and airs educational programming for Catholic schools using an ITFS [Instructional Television Fixed Service] system. For budget reasons, others restrict communication to broadcasting the Mass. Some dioceses have little more than a part-time press officer.

Professional associations, particularly the Catholic Press Association and Unda (Catholic broadcasting and allied communicators), link independent publishers and producers of religious materials; these tend to regard communication as a ministry as well as a job. The organizations work to provide support and some training for their members while they encourage greater Church involvement in the mass media. Religious communities—the

Franciscans, Maryknoll, the Paulists, the Daughters of St. Paul, etc.—as well as non-profit and for-profit corporations publish and produce materials.

Others, primarily those in Catholic education, have promoted media education as a means to teach children the workings of the mass media in the United States. Because their aims include developing a critical consciousness about the media, they are more likely to question the assumptions underlying communication in the Church.

Not all members of the Church are as open to the mass media. Some criticize the commercialism, materialism, sexuality, violence, and apparent bias; they ask whether the Church should have anything to do with communication.

But in today's information age, an age defined by the mass media and growing at a nearly exponential rate through information technologies, Church efforts seem uncertain, if not inadequate. Bishops and other Catholic leaders, religious communicators, and church members do not seem to have fully engaged this era of mass communication and information revolution. Few realize its impact; fewer still note the larger problems of information, access, and democratization of communication—particularly from our First World vantage point. Those who wish to act find that they can barely influence much less control the course of events. In the face of the wide cultural influence of the mass media, religious values seem threatened. Church members, as well as church leaders, are ambivalent about the media: We love the media while we hate them; we depend on them even while we condemn their shortcomings.

This situation and the list of Church activities in communication demonstrates what the essays in this volume spell out in greater detail: the competing claims that face the Church and communication. Is mass communication a good thing for the Church? Does it lead to greater or lesser authority in the Church's teaching? Should communication have a national coordinating body or is it better left to individuals? Is communication another ministry of the Church? Or should the Church purchase what it needs as it needs? More seriously, has contemporary communication undermined the very nature of local communities?

One reason for the uncertainty in the search for ways to deal theologically, pastorally, and administratively with mass-mediated culture and communication reflected in these questions is the lack of precision with which we approach the issue of communication. The essays in this volume illustrate and respond to the uncertainty. They also offer a path through it that might clarify matters. First, the essays criss-cross the complexity of both the media themselves and the attitudes that characterize how the Church responds to the media. Second, these essays propose a number of different ideas about culture, the Church's place in the culture, and the media's interaction with both. Finally, the essays remind us that the Church itself is not monolithic either in its communication or in its description.

The Media

The questions posed earlier might be rephrased in terms of basic attitudes or stances towards religion and communication. People might judge the mass media negatively, positively, or neutrally: Each judgment would result in a particular course of action for the Church and the mass media. Similarly, people might define the action of the mass media differently—as a social or political forum or as a tool. To understand the relation between the Catholicism and the mass media in America better, one needs to take these positions into account. Each has something to offer and each asks valid questions. Briefly, here are five common positions.

First, despite the Church's positive statements about communication (*Inter Mirifica, Communio et Progressio, Aetatis Novae*), many religious people have a deep-seated distrust of the mass media, fearing their corrupting influence on society. By no means is this outlook restricted to the Church; popular culture and its expressions in music, film, or television leave many skeptical and prompt others to actively campaign against them. To those following this perspective, the mass media seem powerful and pervasive forces fostering values counter to their own. Despite scholarly claims to the contrary, they accept a "powerful effects" model of media and try to warn others of these effects. Realizing that they cannot stop the media, they instead question them and urge greater caution and critical awareness. Many of the contributors to this volume make note of those authors like Neil Postman and William Fore, who eloquently describe what they perceive as a foundational disagreement between the mass media and the Church.

A dramatically different view takes the popular culture of the mass media as positively as they take it seriously. Because it closely touches the lives of so many, popular culture provides both an index to belief and a means for people to discover religious values. Past forms of popular culture may have addressed religious themes more overtly; if their modern relations do not, this should invite discernment rather than condemnation. Part of the beauty of Catholicism, as Andrew Greeley points out, lies in its affirmation of redeemed human nature and its manifestation in what he terms "the Catholic imagination." Some religious programming, notably the Paulist program *Insight*, also takes this perspective.

This outlook on the mass media borders on a third one suggested by a growing number of scholars, including Horace Newcomb and Paul Hirsch (1987), James Carey (1989), and Joli Jenson (1990), who loosely describe themselves as following "cultural studies." They regard the mass media not so much as products or delivery systems, to be judged positively or negatively, than as places for ritual enactment where society reconstitutes itself. In other words, mass media and their products provide a forum for society where people explore social issues, competing values, and cultural change.

In this collection Robert Wister, Henk Hoekstra, and Marjeet Verbeek all urge that the Church recognize the role it might have in this forum and make use of popular culture to understand Catholic identity and contemporary moral questions.

Fourth, *Communio et Progressio* noted that people have a right to communicate; social communication should support that right, providing both access and information. This outlines yet another approach to communication reflected in these pages: the democratization of the media. This theme finds a strong following outside the Church as well, as many scholars and activists argue that the popular culture of the media gives voice to those beyond the traditional elites. Robert White (1994), Jesús Martín-Barbero (1987/1993), and others have traced this theme, particularly in Latin America. Here, William Thorn notes how it interacts with various views of the Church and with Church governance. The right to communicate applies within the Church as well as within civil society.

Finally, some hold that the mass media provide neutral tools. Because this instrumental approach is quite common in the United States, we find it eloquently represented in Church circles as well. Whether the media act as loudspeakers or amplifiers for the Church's message indiscriminately and effectively reaching millions, or whether they provide tools for specialized targeted audiences, they cannot and should not be ignored. In the words of Paul VI, "The Church would feel herself guilty before God if she did not avail of those powerful instruments which human skill is constantly developing and perfecting" (*Evangelii Nuntiandi*, 1975/1982, #45). Angela Ann Zukowski and Frances Forde Plude suggest here some very practical uses of communication in ways that should trigger fresh thinking about how the Church might communicate.

Each of these positions presents a valid starting point for reflection on the relationship between the media and the Church in the United States. The writers representing each position draw attention to cultural and religious issues of tremendous importance. Because we do not always distinguish what we mean by "communication" or the attitudes we bring to it, we run the risk of comparing quite dissimilar things. A clearer approach to the Church and the mass media would keep people from working at cross purposes and would help the the Church to choose appropriate communication tools for its various needs.

The Culture

A focus on culture provides a different perspective on the confusion of many Catholics regarding a mass-mediated culture and the electronic mass media. These media do, of course, participate in the larger culture of the United States and, many argue, define that culture. What can a cultural perspective tell us of the Church and the media? Three themes emerge: the media as a window on the Church; the media as a window on society; and the Catholic contribution to the media culture.

The media provide the only knowledge of the Church for many people, as Phyllis Zagano carefully points out. Newspapers, radio, film, and television frequently portray the Church in their reporting and entertainment—sometimes as itself and sometimes as a shorthand device for all organized religion. This picture tends to become definitive for those, even those church members, who do not know the Church well; sometimes that picture is too narrow and even antagonistic. Such a view of the Church upsets many, particularly when they disagree with the description or feel that the media show the Church or religion in a bad light. Like it or not, the mass media are a window on the Church.

This need not be a wholly negative experience, as Wister, and Hoekstra and Verbeek illustrate. We can learn much about the Church, about important moral issues, and even about important historical issues by seeing them filtered through the lens of a media culture. If the media provide a window on the Church, then we gain self-knowledge by carefully attending to their images. Such a stance acknowledges that the Church cannot control the mass media and is one of many institutions vying for their attention.

The media do show more than the Church; for most of us, they are our main avenues to see and understand our culture. As George Gerbner and Kathleen Connolly (1978) pointed out, the media have largely replaced the Church as a source of meaning and as a universal interpreter of the world. Many writers in this volume note with dismay that loss of definition for traditional religious groups. Fewer take up the challenge to more deeply grasp how a mass-mediated culture works. Here, a careful study of the media rewards us by illuminating our own culture. If the media provide meaning, interpretation, and cultural awareness, then the Church can learn much from them to better to address its contemporaries. A mass-mediated culture has its particular styles and grammars. Walter Ong, Gregor Goethals, and Paul Soukup illustrate this by examining the Church's historical attempts to engage culture; Dennis Smolarski and Robert Waznak try to apply those lessons by studying gesture and narrative.

These essays also hint at something much more important because they highlight a significant shift for theology as it engages culture. In the past theology attempted to relate to and influence culture on one level though philosophy and on another through art and music; today philosophy continues its place as a dialogue partner for theology, though it no longer carries the cultural force it once did. Fewer in theology pursue art and music. These writers, together with Greeley, suggest that the popular arts—especially the novel, film, and television—may be the better dialogue partners for theology. To influence the culture, theology first needs to know the culture. Here the mass media provide a window both on communicative style and on key concerns.

Finally, the Catholic tradition itself has a role within the culture of the United States. Catholicism's cultural tradition has its own characteristics: its emphasis on symbolism and sacramentalism; its inculturation in popular religiosity and popular cultures; its synthetic nature; its appeal to the imagination; and so forth. Each of these places the Catholic tradition in relation to the media culture in a particular fashion—sometimes in compatible ways, but sometimes in opposition. The challenge for the Church lies in finding ways to share the riches of its culture and the riches of its message with the media culture. Andrew Greeley, Peter Mann, and Robert Leavitt, whose essays sketch out the characteristics listed above, each suggest ways in which this could happen.

They clarify the nature of culture, too. A Catholic culture treats culture primarily as the beliefs, expressions, and manner of life of a people while the mass media culture often focuses only on cultural artifacts and cultural products. When the Church is uncomfortable with a mass-mediated culture, we would do well to examine the competing claims each makes on the notion of culture itself. And so, we can extend the consideration prompted by the Catholic tradition. On the one hand, we can ask, How does the mass-mediated culture treat symbols? Can a mass-mediated culture give expression to something like sacramentalism? What shape would such a concept have in a world of "virtual reality"? On the other, we inquire, In what ways do the Church and the mass-mediated culture coincide? Both foster the imagination; both synthesize many elements to create a complex whole. The authors in this collection raise these issues for us and in doing so shed new light on what has proven a confusing situation.

The Church

How we think of the Church influences how we envision its relationship to mass media and mass culture. What Avery Dulles (1974) has described as the institutional or hierarchical Church dovetails nicely with a certain view of the mass media: a powerful central authority addressing a large undifferentiated group of people. As with most hierarchical models, the center exercises some measure of control over the message and its transmission. But Zagano, as noted earlier, points out the difficulties inherent in a competition between "centers" when the mass media present or represent the Church. The communication itself moves us beyond a unidimensional model of the Church.

William Thorn describes this shift in detail. His analysis and the earlier work of Dulles can help us to separate out—at least for examination and clarity—the ways that communication and Church vary across models. One's attitude toward communication tends to vary according to one's preferred model. An institutional model of the Church might have the Church interact with communication either as a power center or as an object. A model of Church as community supports a different kind of communication, one of wide participation and public opinion. Zukowski's and Plude's ideas for using the media fit into this model. The herald/prophet model of the Church leads to a more message-centered idea of communication. Here the central concern for communication might be the Gospel or a call to repentance. The Church's main concern lies in making its message heard, something that Leavitt, Waznak, and Smolarski all address. Finally, a servant model of the Church correlates with a concern for communication that would facilitate communication. Such a Church would build a communication infrastructure, especially for the voiceless, as it has with community radio in Latin America or with Radio Veritas in Asia. The servant Church takes on work for the communication environment, attending to issues of access, representation, and the right to communicate.

As Dulles and Thorn note, no one model of the Church can suffice. But the models do remind us that in communication as well as in ecclesiology, the Church has many expressions and plays many roles. By separating these, it is easier to learn how communication works in the current American situation and take lessons from it.

* * *

The intersection of Church, media, and American culture allows us to see more clearly how American Catholicism now responds to its present situation; this in turn allows us to ask how American Catholicism *should* respond theologically, pastorally, and administratively. That a number of authors frame their replies in terms of seminary education arises from one origin of this volume. In 1988 the National Catholic Education Association, Santa Clara University, and the Centre for the Study of Communication and Culture sponsored a week-long conference that brought seminary deans and faculty together with communication teachers and professionals in order to suggest ways to foster thinking about communication in pastoral formation. Taking the lead from some initial papers (three appear in this volume: chapters 5, 6, and 8), the group attempted to re-think curricular questions and set up a mechanism for sharing teaching ideas among seminaries. In addition the group has maintained a loose networked "think tank" to provide resources on the questions.

This volume forms a first step of making its work known and, as such, represents six years of conversations, formulations, sharing essays, and searching for others who could give cogent expression to our own questions. Some of the material here originates within the group; other material is reprinted from sources which members have found. While this volume cannot presume to be the definitive work on the topic, it can invite a broader representation of scholars, teachers, practitioners, pastoral workers, and pastoral education students into an ongoing process of reflection. The writers represent parishes, Catholic universities, and official Church offices. All write with the issue of pastoral leadership in communication in mind.

The book follows a plan that moves from theory to practice, with the essays arranged into three sections, moving from general to more specific treatments of communication in the context of pastoral work and pastoral education.

The first section gives a general orientation to the importance of communication for theology and for the Church. The essays sketch the situation of religious discourse: from the perspective of theology, from within the ambit of the Church, and from outside the Church.

Walter Ong's minor classic, "Communications Media and the State of Theology," first appeared almost 25 years ago, yet it still challenges us to think in new ways about the inescapable interplay among culture, communication, and theological reflection. Drawing on his extensive research Ong sketches the traces of an oral culture in theology. As he takes pains to point out, one finds, not causal linkages, but correlations among various aspects of a Western culture shifting from oral forms to print to electronic forms. His correlations go a long way towards explaining the contentious nature of Catholic theology well into the mid-20th century.

Andrew Greeley's sociological studies of the Church and religious belief are well known. Working from these data, he has proposed the existence of a distinct "Catholic imagination" (1990), an idea which suggests that a religious rhetoric does endure within our contemporary mass mediated culture. Such a Catholic imagination provides a glimpse at the communicative forces and tradition within the Church. In "The Catholic Imagination and the Catholic University," Greeley applies his general findings to the educational realm; briefly, he argues that a Catholic university should lead its students in reflection on the Catholic imaginative tradition. This tradition provides a strong communication of the faith and for many it constitutes their main contact with the Church. He makes a strong case "that the Catholic religious imagination is the matrix and the context for virtually all Catholic ministerial and pastoral work."

The first section concludes with a look at religious issues as presented from outside the Church. Most people today receive news of the Church and even theological information through public media. Pastoral ministers thus must accept the fact that they no longer have any strong control of their own discourse. In "MediaChurch: The Presentation of Religious Information via Media," Phyllis Zagano reviews "some of the problems attendant to the presentation of 'religious information'—not only doctrinal statements but information about the operation of church organizations—via the secular media, the growing dependence of religion upon the secular media, and the unavoidable consequences relative to the meaning of the messages of religion."

The essays of the second section situate the communication practices and devices of the Church in more specific historical and theoretical contexts. Obviously, communication is not something new to the Church. How it dealt with questions of communicating the faith in earlier eras can suggest fruitful avenues of thought for us today.

In "Visible Image and Invisible Faith," Gregor Goethals looks at the history, communication, and religious meaning of images, particularly as they come into contact with the early Christian traditions. She traces "the functions of the visual arts as purveyors of religious meaning as Christian culture assimilated two contradictory aesthetics: the aniconic tradition of Judaism and the iconic conventions of the classical world." How the Church dealt with images holds lessons for us as we ponder the ways to give contemporary theological expression to the faith or to make a religious discourse clear to a popular culture with its own traditions of expression.

Paul Soukup proposes a different kind of look at the past; instead of examining images, he calls attention to the verbal forms of theology. In "Communicative Form and Theological Style," he suggests that theologians should attend to the form of ideas (oral, written, and so on) which influence their content as well as to the content itself. Following the work of Ong, he examines some of the ways in which the mode of communication affects its content. Starting with orality-literacy theories and considering the impact of television leads him to some suggestions for re-thinking traditional courses in theology and pastoral ministry.

Robert Leavitt expands this notion in "Ministry in an Age of Communications." He reflects on the new conditions and issues facing ministry in a communication age. Starting with the ministry of the Word as a fundamental category for ministry and crossing it with the various interests of human knowing, he attempts to enlarge its range of applications to all ministry as well as to the media of communications.

Finally, William Thorn applies the categories of various models of communication to the models of the Church that Dulles (1974) first described. From this perspective he explores the structure of authority in the Church and notes how it shifts according to the communication pattern which dominates church life in any given era. Thorn argues that the structure of communication implicit in the Church reveals more about its nature than more theoretical approaches.

Section three of the book gathers together more practical essays. They range from the use of symbols to nonverbal language, from preaching to teaching church history, from teleconferencing to distance education. Each essay examines one or other direction that one could take to explore the practical expression of theology and communications. Building from concrete experience, these essay serve as springboards for local development for an awareness of communication and media in pastoral education and practice.

In "Religious Symbolism and Mass Communication," Peter Mann argues that "we have to recover the image dimension of the Gospel." Our mass culture immerses us in images which affect us in contradictory ways: On the one hand, they connect us to others, but on the other, they simultaneously isolate us. Christian proclamation should lead to community but cannot establish that community in the face of these images without returning to its own foundational image.

Liturgical communication forms the center of one kind of pastoral ministry. Dennis Smolarski examines both verbal and nonverbal communication in "Communication and the Art of Presiding" and encourages all who take a public role in worship to exert much greater care in what they do. Building on both scriptural and psychological evidence, he notes the importance of touch and significant gesture in communication, and particularly in the liturgy.

Running parallel to Smolarski's emphasis on the nonverbal, Robert Waznak, in "Preaching the Gospel in a Video Culture," stresses the importance of the word. He asks how new insights into communication might change our understanding of preaching. "Three three decades have passed since the promulgation of the first two documents of the Council [on liturgy and social communication]....We now have insights from both preaching and media scholars that were not available to those who wrote the conciliar documents." In his essay he explores those insights and their implications for preaching the Gospel.

Robert Wister provides a very different approach to integrating the fruits of the communication revolution into the pastoral education curriculum. In "The Use of Media in the Teaching of Church History" he describes his own methods of teaching, enriching the historical imagination of his students through film and video. The awareness of the importance and impact of the media can reach the students indirectly through their own teachers' uses of them. The strength of Wister's argument lies in its simplicity: He makes use of the students' knowledge of the media to invite them to a deeper reflection on historical sources.

Henk Hoekstra and Marjeet Verbeek propose a distinctive use of film and video. Building on their experiences in moral formation in The Netherlands, they describe the ways in which narratives can objectify moral experience. Their essay, "Possibilities of Audiovisual Narrative for Moral Formation," outlines a theory of moral theology and its practical application. For them, the moral application makes a much stronger learning experience than an abstract consideration of ethics or morality.

Angela Ann Zukowski widens the scope of the discussion of pastoral formation to include not just formation for pastoral ministry but also adult religious education. In "Formation of Church Leaders for Ministering in the Technological Age" she explores the possibilities of such religious education through the use of small and large media. She provides some introduction to media including computers, teleconferences, video, and so on. And then, working from case studies, she shows how pastoral communication can support that ministry of education. However, pastoral ministers still face barriers to utilizing pastoral communication: lack of knowledge, lack of skills, and lack of environmental support. Zukowski argues that pastoral ministers must learn to fully employ all these tools if they will have an effective ministry in the 21st century.

In the final essay, Frances Forde Plude provides both a technical and practical introduction to the teleconferencing which Zukowski mentions. In "Forums for Dialogue: Teleconferencing and the American Catholic Church," she explains how the Catholic Church in the United States has already made use of video teleconferencing services and satellite networks. She then invites pastoral ministers to reflect on the possibilities of community formation, in what she terms forums for dialogue.

The essays in this book, then, give an overview of the possibilities of the Church and religious discourse in our own mass media-dominated society. Rather than proposing specific answers, they invite reflection. Whether one prefers the more theoretical discussion of the initial chapters or the practical cases and suggestions of the later ones, a common issue demands our attention: How shall the Gospel take form in our day? This reflection must happen in every sector of the Church: in chancery offices, in seminaries, in parishes, in universities, and in every home. How can we become a more communicative church?

These essays offer a first reflection on how we as a Church can deal theologically, pastorally, and administratively with a mass mediated culture.

* * *

Many institutions and individuals have supported this project. First of all, we gratefully acknowledge the financial support of the Catholic Communication Campaign, the Lilly Foundation, and Santa Clara University, who underwrote the 1988 conference where many of the authors first met. The continuing support of Fr. Charles Kavanagh and his successor, Fr. Robert Wister, at the Seminary Office of the National Catholic Education Association, kept the topic alive and fostered an ongoing dialogue even after people separated. Similarly, the Centre for the Study of Communication and Culture provided international encouragement in thinking through the topics connected with culture, media, Church, and communication.

In addition, a number of other scholars, who did not participate in the conferences mentioned here, have enriched this dialogue through their research, their correspondence, and their friendship. We gratefully thank them and their publishers for the permission to reprint these essays:

Walter Ong and *Cross Currents* for "Communications Media and the State of Theology," (1969: vol. 19, pp. 462-480).

Andrew Greeley and *America* magazine for "The Catholic Imagination and the Catholic University," (March 16, 1991: vol. 164(10), pp. 285-288).

Phyllis Zagano and *The Journal of Communication and Religion* for "MediaChurch: The Presentation of Religious Information Via Media," (1990: vol. 13(2), pp. 40-44).

Gregor Goethals and Cowley Publications for portions of "Visible Image and Invisible Faith," chapter one of *The Electronic Golden Calf: Images, Religion, and the Making of Meaning* (Cambridge, MA: Cowley Publications, 1990, pp. 7-52).

Henk Hoekstra & Marjeet Verbeek and Sheed & Ward for "Possibilites of Audiovisual Narrative for Moral Formation," in Philip J. Rossi and Paul A. Soukup, (Eds.), *Mass Media and the Moral Imagination* (Kansas City, MO: Sheed & Ward, 1994, pp. 212-233).

Robert Waznak and *New Theology Review* and *America* magazine for parts of "Preaching the Gospel in a Video Culture," published as "The Church's Response to the Media: Twenty-Five Years After *Inter Mirifica*," *America* (January 21, 1989) and "Preaching the Gospel in an Age of Technology," *New Theology Review* (November, 1989).

Finally, Santa Clara University has provided ongoing help and institutional support for this project. Sheed and Ward, Inc., and its editor, Robert Heyer, have encouraged the project and brought it to completion. Series editor Robert A. White, SJ, helped with key suggestions along the way. William Thorn offered suggestions to improve this introduction. Many thanks to all.

Paul A. Soukup, SJ

I

Orientations:

Theology, Communication, Church

1

Communications Media and the State of Theology

Walter J. Ong, S.J.

I

The relationship of communications media and theology can be thought of in terms of the influence of communications media on theology, or of theology on communications media, or in terms of the responsibility of the communications media vis-à-vis theology or of theology vis-à-vis the communications media. Here, however, I propose to consider none of these matters directly, but something more profound: the interlocking of communications media and theology. We know now that in a given culture many seemingly unrelated phenomena are somehow correlatives of one another. The intellectual activity of a culture and its technological activity are correlatives; styles in art and styles in politics are correlatives, and so on, although we must not imagine correlation here as one-to-one correspondence. We can suspect that the state of theological thinking and the modes of communication in a given culture at a given time are perhaps somehow correlatives, too.

At first blush, there would seem to be no intrinsic connection between communications media and the state of theology. After theology is thought out or put together, the media simply circulate it. Media are, after all, media, things in between other things.

To get a message from me to you, I first think out the message and then put it on the conveyor. If there is air between me and you, I use this as a medium or conveyor, pronouncing words. Somehow, these sounds carry my thoughts from me to you through the intervening medium of sound (or air, or words—for the medium is often complex and breaks down into various parts or levels of manifestation).

I can also use visible signals, including not only pictures or gestures but also writing and print, as media, shipping the message from me to you

Originally published in *Cross Currents, 19,* (1969), 462-480.

over light waves. Communication can also be through other senses, though
it is less manageable here, through smell, taste, and most of all touch. The
grasp of two hands can be communication of a message. Here there is so
little in the way of medium or in-betweenness that we speak of such tactile
communication as immediate. However, even here, we can identify some
medium, for our sensory organs are media. We are divided beings, our body
is outside us as well as coextensive with us, and thus it is itself a medium.

The specific devices to which the term media now very often applies,
such as books, movies, television, and so on, are commonly felt in similar
terms. They are conveyors, moving a message from a source to a destina-
tion. Sometimes they are thought of as packaging for the message. But message is message and package is package. Any package—books, movies, television, radio—is there to deliver a previously constituted message, though
some media may deliver it more effectively than others. When it gets where
it is going, the message is presumably unpackaged and the package discarded. So what difference does it make what the packaging has been?

Theologians of course use communications media, as all scientists and
all thinkers do. One theologian works out in his own mind whatever it is he
is working out in his own mind, then puts it "across" in some medium—
sound, in a lecture, picture or print, or all these things and more—so that it
arrives somehow in the mind of another theologian. The message that is sent
through the medium is theology.

This account, I believe, gives a view of communications media that is
fairly common even today, as an assumption if not as a considered conviction. The view is sustained by our use of the very term and the concept
"medium" or its plural, "media." It is probably unavoidable, but it does not
apply with complete adequacy to what goes on in communication. Indeed,
there are a great many difficulties with it, some of them profound. We can
suggest only a few here.

First, with regard to verbal communication, the message itself even
within the mind of the "sender" processed for his own consciousness is already in a medium, that is to say, words. What we do when we think is
difficult to describe, and, I believe, in its totality impossible to describe. But
the fact is that we are never quite satisfied that we have brought our thinking to maturity within our own private consciousness unless we have it formulated in words. In composing a speech or a paper, we do not work it out
in our minds completely in wordless thought and then find words to convey
it to others. The thoughts and the words come tangled together. To think, we
have to pretend we are two persons: a speaker and a listener. Otherwise we
cannot make sense to ourselves. There is thus no way to formulate a truth
for ourselves even in our own interior without involving ourselves in a language. Now a language is essentially public, something not ours, a medium
of communication between person and person. This means that the message
cast up in our own minds is already a communication before we externalize

it in sound or writing. To put it in still another way, there is no such thing as a purely private human thought. All thought, when it is matured even for our own understanding, is thought-in-a-medium.

This suggests a second difficulty about conceiving of communication as transportation of a message from a sender to a receiver. The sender is also a receiver in the process of sending. When I speak to you I listen to my own words to see if they are making sense. This is one way I can tell whether *you* will understand. I compose my thoughts by pretending you are inside me. When you listen to me, you say the words over in your imagination because it is by pretending that you are saying them that you test whether they make sense. Communication, then, is only partially like transport or broadcasting.

A third difficulty is that connected with the primacy of one sensory field over another. It is an incontestable fact that for human communication, sound has some kind of special primacy over other sensory fields which is tied in with the special relationship between words and thought (Ong, 1967, pp. 138-161). There is a special affinity between the medium of sound and the kind of messages which thought constitutes and conveys. In view of this fact, it appears at best highly questionable to regard the medium as simply neutral. If the medium is neutral, why cannot we cast up our thoughts in touches, tastes, smells, and spectacles in exactly the same way as we cast them up in sound? Why does a word have to be a sound? Why can I not join a subject and predicate by giving off a smell or by touch? Why not work out the Constitution of the United States or *The Critique of Pure Reason* in gestures rather than sounds? The medium of sound here evidently bears some interlocked relationship with the message.

A fourth difficulty—and with this we shall move on, for the difficulties are in fact countless—has to do with the Christian message itself and consequently with specifically Christian theology. When we try to apply the construct message-moved-from-source-to-destination-through-medium to Christian revelation, we are in deep trouble.

At first we do not seem to be, for the message we are given to know is, after all, the Gospel, the Good News, which is the Word of God. Communication of news is conveyance of news, is it not? Communication of the Word of God thus would fit the model we earlier described. Perhaps it does until we learn that the Word of God is not a message separate from a person, as what I say is separate from me, but indeed is a person. This person, the Word or Son, becomes incarnate in Jesus Christ. He utters human words, as do other men, and these words convey truth. They are, moreover, indeed God's words, for Jesus is God and what He says comes ultimately from His Father, Who is also God. Nevertheless, we never know the full meaning of an utterance without a context, and Jesus' full message in any of his utterances is not merely his utterance but his own person, the Word. Whatever truth words may have is only a shadow of his person, who is truth. "I am the way, and the truth, and the life" (Jn. 14:6). Jesus Christ, God and man, is in his own person the Good News, the Revelation of the Father. *He* is what he *means*. He is also in a mediating position between the Father and the human race. In this case, it would be completely true that the medium is the message except for the fact that Jesus Christ is not a medium but the Mediator. And there are further complications. For the Word reveals not merely himself, but in himself also his Father, who is another person and not a mediator, though of the same divine nature as the Son. "Philip, he who sees me sees also the Father" (Jn. 14:9).

We must add to this a further truth, that this communication from the Father, who is both mediator and message, must be conceived of specifically by analogy with the human word, as the Scriptures make clear. "The Word was made flesh and dwelt among us" (Jn. 1:14). Conceptualizations involving other sensory analogies, as when the Nicene Creed calls the Son "light of light," are secondary to this one involving sound. "Eo Verbum quo Filius," goes the theological legion: "He is Word by the fact that he is Son." Here the primacy of the sound medium in human communication is underlined, and thus all sorts of theological questions concerning media come urgently to the fore. If the Good News is the Word, incarnate in Jesus Christ, who knew reading and writing, as the Gospels clearly report, but conveyed what he had to say not by his own writing but by preaching and personal associations, leaving behind him not a corpus of books he had written but an oral tradition in a community, what is the relationship of all this to the Bible itself, particularly the New Testament, which would be generated out of the Christian community or Church and which this Church would make so much of? Any written word is necessarily the spoken word at least once removed. The word on a piece of parchment or paper, the written word—in what sense can this be the word of God when the Incarnate Word of God is not merely something else, but Someone else, to whom all creatures are subservient in heaven and on earth, including bits of parchment or paper with writing on them?

The kinds of questions here can be spun out endlessly. Indeed, the spinning out of these questions and of answers to them, with resulting further questions, constitutes theology. Thus in these perspectives theology appears for what it is, inextricably and even dismayingly involved with problems concerning the communications media.

II

Correlations between theology and communications media are nowhere clearer than in the study of the Bible itself. Over the past few decades biblical theology as well as studies in related fields have made it increasingly clear how the Bible reflects the state of the communications media over the period during which it came into being. The Bible is made up of a diversity of literary genres, many themselves derivative from oral genres and mixtures of genres. By and large the Bible registers a culture in which verbal expression, even written verbal expression, was governed far more by habits of oral composition than is true in our day.

From the time when humanity first appeared on earth—let us say some 500,000 years ago, until around 3500 B.C., when the first known scripts appear, all verbal composition was oral. This means that for roughly 500,000 years there was no way to look up anything, and humans were constantly beset by the problems of keeping what they knew from slipping away. *Verba volant, scripta manent.* Words fly away, what is written stays in place. When knowledge was verbalized, in a culture innocent of writing, it often needed to be verbalized in ways which fostered recall. For this reason we find that verbal expression in oral cultures is often marked by heavy patterning, shown, for example, in standard themes, stock formulas and situations, type characters often equipped with fixed epithets ("wily Odysseus," "wise Nestor"), rhythmic devices, and other mnemonic aids. Poets and orators used these devices with consummate skill to produce great art forms. We know now that the *Iliad* and the *Odyssey,* for example, the products of an oral, preliterate Greek culture (why and how these epics were ever put into writing remains mysterious) consist almost entirely of stock formulas— you will recall the "wine-dark sea" and "rosy-fingered dawn," but these are only two formulas among thousands which an oral poet in Homeric Greece might command. The Greek epic poet's formulas are metrically tailored, so made up that they consist of snatches of dactylic verse which can be "stitched together" or "woven together" (the Greek term for this is *rhapsodein,* which gives us our English word "rhapsodize") in extempore fashion into thousands upon thousands of lines of dactylic hexameter.

Poets carry formulas and other patterning (rhyme, rhythm, antitheses, parallels, and so on) to an extreme. But verbal patterning is common throughout an oral culture, for it is not only artistic but operational, as Eric Havelock has shown (1963, pp. 93-94, 139). A military commander wanting to get a complicated message from Thebes to Athens in a totally illiterate culture would have to have at his command some mnemonic devices or the message would never arrive. "Thirty days have September, April, June, and November..." and so on. The Bible is filled with verbal patterning and echoes of mnemonic devices.

Because they cannot write anything down, oral cultures cannot develop sciences because they cannot develop the elaborate, abstract classifications or categories on which science depends. Imagine embarking on a study of chemistry without ever being able to write anything and doing so under the tutelage of instructors who themselves had never even heard of writing. Since there is no effective way to manage knowledge orally in elaborated scientific or categorized form, knowledge that is not caught in formulaic sayings tends to be managed through narrative. This narrative itself tends to be filled with speeches or orations, themselves full of oral patterns, and it commonly involves a struggle of one person with another, so that all knowledge set in such narrative tends to take on a polemic coloring. Thus, again as Havelock has pointed out, the demographic survey of the illiterate Grecian peoples turns up as part of a story about war, in the catalogue of ships of the *Iliad* (ii. 494-875), and a description of how to build a ship is found in the *Odyssey* (v. 225-261) when Odysseus is struggling to escape from Circe. We today would put such kinds of information respectively in a city directory and in a manual on shipbuilding, objective, nonnarrative, isolated from any polemic background. An oral culture cannot do this. It must speak what it knows for it cannot write, and it has no better place to speak of such things than in an epic narrative. Certainly a shipwright, in ancient Greece, unless he were also an epic poet, could not be expected to produce a verbalized account of how to build a ship, just as today the ordinary carpenter could not be expected to produce a manual on carpentry, although he could teach carpentry to an apprentice by demonstration.

In an oral culture then, verbalized knowledge that is not cast in rhythmic, formulaic, or otherwise patterned schemata for recall simply goes down the drain. This means that matters which do not lend themselves to mnemonic treatment are, to all intents and purposes, not thought about at all. Thus it is that patterned oral modes of expression not only determine the shape of thought but also determine actually what is thought about. Living in an oral culture affects not only how one says what he says and how he thinks what he thinks but also whether he thinks about this thing or that thing or not. Incidentally, certain habits of mind often identified by persons from technological cultures, even scholars, as "oriental" are in fact simply oral modes of operation and were probably just as evident in the West as in the East until killed off by the spread of literacy associated with growth in technology.

After some 500,000 years of talking and thinking in oral patterns, humans did not depart from these patterns quickly. Although the Bible is quite obviously a collection of writings, all these writings manifest in varying degrees oral habits of expression and of thought, as even in Western cultures writing commonly does well through the 18th century (Ong, 1965). This is true even of works in the Bible, such as the letters of St. Paul, which are obviously composed in writing and yet which are full of the formulaic patterns, the proverbs, and the echoic and mnemonic schemes—not to mention the anacolutha or fragmented sentences—which are normal in patterned expression from oral cultures. Orality is even more marked, for example, in the sayings of Jesus which are the backbone of the Gospels. These sayings are not only clothed in oral forms, they are also often quite strikingly oral-type thought. Take, for example, the Beatitudes from the Sermon on the Mount, beautifully balanced statements, each with two parts like two parts of a verse in a Hebrew Psalm. "Blessed are the poor in spirit, for theirs is the kingdom of Heaven. Blessed are the meek, for they shall possess the earth. Blessed are they who mourn, for they shall be comforted" (Matt. 5:3-5). The balanced form, which implements oral recall, also conveys the idea of correspondence between things that lie so deep in the Hebreo-Christian sense of what existence is. "What a man sows, that he will also reap." (Gal. 6:8; cf. 2 Cor. 9:6; Hos. 8:7). Events are not isolated. One thing corresponds to another. Existence has pattern. Actuality is the opposite of chaos. This basic reassurance is conveyed by the simple back-and-forth movement which both rides through and shapes the thought of the Beatitudes, and which, at another level, is doubtless connected with the bilateral symmetry of the human body. Knowledge of this sort could be arrived at in the early ages of humankind, long before the media had developed to the point where science could arise.

The orality of the Bible is many-layered. Not only do we find great masses of obviously spoken matter presented in writing as spoken ("and Jesus said...") and other matter, such as in the Pauline epistles just mentioned, which carries a heavy residue of old oral modes of expression and thought despite the fact that it was composed in writing. We also find other narrative or descriptive matter which today would normally be composed in writing, but which was not in fact so composed. Much narrative or descriptive writing in the Bible is in fact a written reduction of what was earlier orally composed and preserved. Thus, for example, in the Gospels, the narrative text on which the sayings of Jesus are threaded itself often has an oral base. Before the Gospels were written out, there were set, formalized narrations which preserved for the Christian community events from the life of Jesus and which enter into the Gospel text.

Our growing understanding of the importance of the oral, even in the case of written biblical texts, connects also with a growing understanding of the meaning of tradition in the Church's teaching that divine revelation is contained both "in written books and in unwritten traditions," as the Council of Trent has it (Denziger, Bannwart, Umberg, & Rahner, 1947, No. 783). We can only touch on this important matter here. Various studies have pointed out the tendency of Catholic theologians until recently to explicate Trent as though the "unwritten traditions" were in fact some kind of writing (Burghardt, 1951; Baumgartner, 1953), some sort of concealed second volume of the Bible which Catholics had and would not allow Protestants to look at. Before humans moved into the electronic era and thereby awoke to the limitations of writing and print, they tended to regard the inscribed word as the paradigm of all verbalization. In our newer perspectives we can find more meaning in Trent's formulation because we understand better what the nonwritten may be.

These remarks about the oral substructures of the Bible are mere hints, but perhaps they can suggest some of the richness of the oral heritage which is both novel and half-familiar. For, although we have to a large extent focused our attention away from it, the oral is still present in us, submerged beneath the structures encouraged by writing, print, and electronics. For, always and inevitably, the human word in which we still must deal is of itself an oral phenomenon. Writing, print, and computer-stored expression are all only spoken words at one or more removes. Unless someone can *say* what is in a computer, it means nothing at all.

III

Against the background sketched here very briefly, I should like to examine one development of recent years which reveals some hitherto unnoticed relationships between theology and communications media especially important in our day. This is a shift away from a basic orality in theology, an orality with profound historical roots hitherto never bared, to a multimedia theology in which the almost total communication ambitioned in electronic technologized culture interacts vigorously with the theological heritage.

This development can be brought to sharp focus by looking at the professional theology courses and the professional philosophy courses propaedeutic to theology here at Saint Louis University up to the 1960's. Some of the features in this theological course strike us today as curious. First, in the core subjects all teaching was in Latin, the textbooks were in Latin, and the examinations were in Latin. Secondly, all the examining in the core subjects was oral. The little written work was peripheral to the core subjects. Thirdly, this theology was programmatically contentious. It proceeded by stating theses and arguing them against adversaries, some very real and living but others long since dead. Frequently during the academic year minor scholastic disputations called "circles" were held, to review the matter of a course, and from time to time major public disputations covering larger amounts of material or major issues.

Because in any type of disputation both the defense and the attacks were conducted only in Latin, the audience appeal of a performance was somewhat limited. But on at least one occasion here at Saint Louis University, which I believe was historically unique, the audience included a President of the United States (*Memorial Volume*, 1904, pp. 129-131; *Woodstock Letters*, 1903; *St. Louis Post-Dispatch*, April 30, 1903). In the spring of 1903 Theodore Roosevelt was in the city to dedicate the grounds for the coming Louisiana Purchase Exposition. Wanting to know what else was going on at the Gateway to the West, on April 29 he was brought into what was then the Library auditorium on the second floor of the present Du Bourg Hall at the close of the Grand Act being performed by Father Joachim Villalonga, S.J., a Spaniard then studying at the University. The Grand Act was the most ambitious of all disputations, permitted only rarely and only to outstanding students at the very end of their theological studies. It lasted a whole day, morning and afternoon. The one who undertook it had to be prepared to repel orally and on the spot, in irrefutable and impeccable logical form and in equally impeccable Latin, without the aid of reference works or of any written notes, all attacks that the School of Divinity faculty and members of other divinity faculties across the country invited in for the occasion might bring against any or all of his announced theses, of which Father Villalonga had 212, covering the whole of theology and philosophy. In the presence of an audience of some 200 persons, which included James Cardinal Gibbons and Archbishop John Joseph Kain as well as at least one precociously ecumenical Baptist minister, the Rev. W. W. Boyd, President Roosevelt was asked whether he had any objection to urge against any of the theses. Since the question was put in Latin, T. R. looked nonplussed—this was one of the few emergencies to which he was not equal, the *St. Louis Post-Dispatch* observed.

It would be easy to write off this pattern of contentious Latin orality as simply the result of history, as indeed it was. But the juncture of Latin, orality and polemic was not the coincidence it might seem to be. In the light of history, seeming coincidences are often not very coincidental. We have become aware recently that the use of Latin and the use of contentious oral examinations were intimately connected, and that the connections are buried deep in the cultural and psychological past, where they lie entangled in the old oral world with its economy of knowledge storage, retrieval, and communication. That is to say, the juncture of Latin and oral examinations and contentious learning traces back to a mode of life before the existence of writing.

As I have attempted to show elsewhere, Latin was the great vehicle for the old classical rhetorical-dialectical tradition, which was an oral survival at the center of manuscript and later of print culture (Ong, 1967, pp. 52-87, 192-263). These later cultures preserved many of the institutions and sets of mind which belonged basically to an oral economy of thought. The position of Latin was paradoxical, for on the one hand it was a language controlled completely by writing. From the time it ceased to be a vernacular, that is, from around the sixth to the ninth century of the Christian era, Latin had been spoken by millions of persons, but by none who could not also write it. (There are still those who speak Latin: I spoke it not many weeks ago in Leningrad to communicate there with a Lithuanian priest.) For some 1100 years now spoken Latin has had no existence independent of writing. Yet, for all that, Latin has been the great reservoir for the ideals of the old oratorical and dialectical tradition. It is an old language which in its native ancient habitat shaped and was shaped by oral forms. It remained also the vehicle of medieval oralism, and when the Renaissance humanists revived classical Latin, they revived the old rhetorical or oratorical aims of ancient culture, which had been far more oral than medieval culture. The parliamentary tradition, the tradition of politics in the English-speaking world at least until very recent times, is part of this oratorical and dialectical tradition, and hence Latin was retained in schools which trained for politics and diplomacy, as did for example the British so-called public schools and their American equivalents, while it was discarded in the academies which trained for business.

I have said something about the oralism of classical antiquity already and have spelt it out in great detail elsewhere, most elaborately in *The Presence of the Word* (1967). I can here only call to mind a few of its manifestations. In the ancient world, the great ideal of classical education was to form the orator. Socrates, Plato, and to a degree Aristotle contested this ideal, and lost—they had almost no effect on the general educational pattern. The ancient Greeks and Romans knew how to write, but by our standards they did very little reading. They were principally talkers, arguers. Even Aristotle's followers were called Peripatetics, that is, Walkers—which does not exactly suggest a schoolroom text-oriented situation. Speeches in classical antiquity were not normally written before they were given (except those cases, universally denounced, where an unskilled speaker bought a speech in advance from a professional). Cicero's Catilinarian orations, for example, were written down by him almost certainly some two years after their delivery. The oral styles of thought and expression mentioned earlier in connection with the Bible are in general equally marked throughout the classical world.

By the Middle Ages writing had gained fuller possession of the sensibility of Western culture. The Middle Ages were far more textually oriented than was classical antiquity. Medieval scholars were real bookworms, indefatigable copiers and readers of manuscripts, who assembled in their florilegia vast written collections of the commonplace material which the classical world had regarded as chiefly an oral heritage.

But if they were manuscript-oriented by comparison with classical antiquity, the Middle Ages remained by other standards incredibly oral. The oral tone of medieval culture can be sensed in countless ways, none better perhaps than by attending to the teaching at the universities. Here all proof of achievement was oral. At Saint Louis University, which some years ago was given permission to microfilm all the manuscripts in the Vatican Library, visiting scholars find in the Knights of Columbus Vatican Film Library over 11,000,000 pages of manuscript on film. These are not all medieval manuscripts, but millions of pages of them are, and millions of pages have connections with the medieval universities. Yet nowhere will you find a written thesis or dissertation, a paper done as a class assignment, or a written examination. It simply had not entered the mind of medieval people that a person's knowledge should be tested by having him write something. All testing was oral, through disputations, which were simply highly formalized dialectical debates, and disputation-like oral examinations. The *inceptio* or commencement, which marked the beginning of teaching on the part of the new master of arts and which has remained in our term commencement even though most of those at a university commencement today are really not commencing as professional teachers, consisted in a lengthy—often day-long—dialectical orgy in which the individual incipient master withstood in oral disputation any and all objections to what he had to say on his subject. Oral performance governed all subjects—logic, physics or natural philosophy (which included the medieval equivalents of meteorology, astrophysics, physics, chemistry, psychology, and a good deal more), ethics and metaphysics (both of these were commonly given rather brisk treatment), law, theology, and even medicine.

Certainly those at medieval universities knew how to write—although not all the students by any means knew very well the Latin in which all the instruction had to take place (there was no way to say these things in the protean, largely unwritten vernaculars). The masters often wrote out their lectures—probably in most cases after they gave them—and students rented or borrowed or bought or otherwise acquired copies of the texts of Aristotle and others on which the masters commented orally. Notes were taken in class—in fact, too many, for many classes at the University of Paris and elsewhere consisted of nothing more than dictation. But this and virtually all other writing was at the service of the oral performance in which it all was supposed to culminate.

With gradual attenuation, this tradition persisted in the universities of Europe and at early American universities such as Harvard through the 17th century and into the 18th. It was the tradition that St. Thomas More had known and not liked too well at Oxford, that the Jesuit martyr Edmund Campion had known both at Oxford and later in exile on the Continent as well as in the formal disputations with his Protestant accusers during the imprisonment preceding his martyrdom. The same tradition is the one that Thomas Nashe boisterously and brilliantly spoofs in a Wittenberg setting in *The Unfortunate Traveller,* and that John Milton knew at Christ's College, Cambridge. It was likewise the backbone of the theological and pre-theological teaching at Saint Louis University when I was a philosophy and theology student at the University, where the steps which have gradually replaced it with other structures were effectively begun only around some 12 years ago.

The polemic associated with Latin oralism is also associated in other ways with life in the world. Partly, it reflects the real substructure of life, where truth is arrived at often, and perhaps even always, through dialectical or at least dialogic struggle. Socrates' method of teaching by attack, euphemistically called his maieutic method, was a response to the agonistic pattern of human existence. Marxist theory is a response to the same pattern, for the Marxist view of life is not merely temporarily or provisorily contentious, but essentially and permanently contentious, as is evident from Mao Tse-tung to Herbert Marcuse, who complains in *One-Dimensional Man* that something is awry when the laboring class has its needs satisfied and can no longer express itself in full negativity (1964, pp. 31-34). Nevertheless, the oralism of the Latin disputation strengthened the old polemic set in learning.

Oral culture is in basic ways more polemic or struggle-oriented than writing or print culture. Socrates was both more oral and more contentious than Plato, as Plato was more than Aristotle. First, as we have seen, an oral culture preserves its knowledge in stories, which often are agonistic in structure, accounts of struggles between person and person. These stories situate all knowledge within a generally polemic setting, giving it an agonistic flavor. Moreover, for reasons which I have attempted to explicate in *The Presence of the Word* and elsewhere and which are far too detailed to go into here, oral cultures create and sustain certain specifically polemic and anxiety structures in the psyche, which are curiously calmed or at least repressed and relocated in cultures where knowledge is stored in the quiescence of writing and print. Sound involves the present use of power. You can see, smell, taste, and touch a buffalo when the animal is dead; if you hear a buffalo, you had better watch out, for something is going on. Cultures dealing in oral-aural syntheses live in a world of happenings, tensions, and struggle.

Finally, the polemic structures in reality and in oral cultures were reinforced by the sexual polarization of Latin oralism. For some 1100 years now, Latin has been spoken, with totally negligible exceptions, only by males—girls might learn to read and write, but this meant generally the vernacular and at home, for girls did not go to school, where Latin was taught, until the 18th or even the 19th century, when they entered the classroom through breaches in the Latin wall and helped enlarge the breaches. This sex-linked character of the Latin language (paralleled in other learned languages in other cultures over approximately this same period in human existence, before print took hold) is of great importance to the oral heritage, for the oral debate, nurtured by Latin, has been a predominantly male activity, particularly before the invention of the public address system. Oral debate is in significant ways the most aggressive of all human activities, and for that reason I believe, will probably remain always masculine-dominated. The conjunction here should be noted, for it is not an evident one, though it is very real: The discarding of Latin, the minimizing of the oral in favor of writing, the suppression of programmed polemic, and the admission of women to schools and finally to theology courses, the last bastions of polemic pedagogy, are all correlatives of one another. As women came into the schools, the warlike oral Latin manner of education was driven out.

The oral disputation initiated in antiquity and promoted to high favor at European universities from the Middle Ages through the Enlightenment, at early American universities such as the University of Mexico and Harvard University, and at Saint Louis University within the memory of still young living men, was not entirely the product of purely oral culture. It depended upon the existence of a highly formalized logic, which could not come into being without writing. Early oral cultures tend, as we have seen, to fix expression in formulas and typifications, and writing serves to develop even further the oral tendencies, for, as we have also seen, a new medium often at first reinforces an earlier medium. No purely oral culture could have managed the majors and minors, the distinctions and subdistinctions, and fractional concessions combined with fractional denials, the massive logical structures and substructures and superstructures which supported the scholastic disputation and which processed thought in exactly the way in which it has to be processed to put it on one of today's computers. For, like the computer, the scholastic disputation restructured all conceivable questions in a binary series: Every statement, no matter how complex, had to be dissolved into a series of statements to which the response was either yes or no, directly or equivalently. The disputation was, in other words, basically a quantified, entirely formalized operation.

The historical roots of the Latin-based oralism which dominated Catholic theological teaching until around the time of the Second Vatican Council were very little if at all understood by either professors or students of theology; they have certainly not been understood by historians, and even less by the pseudohistorians who comment out of their impressive ignorance on theological developments past and present. Only in the last 20 years at the most have we begun to open the perspectives sketched here.

In these perspectives the combative state of post-Tridentine theology is seen to have much deeper roots than those which trace the division of Christians in the 16th and following centuries. All academic learning beyond the learning of language skills (and even here to a degree) had been purveyed in a polemic setting. From antiquity to the age of Romanticism in the late 1700's or even later, teaching had not aimed at objectively framed knowledge—although individual scholars could achieve admirable objectivity—but had proceeded by defending a stand or attacking that defended by another. The division of Christians gave this polemic intellectualism a new lease on life and seemingly preserved it longer in theology than elsewhere, as the pattern at Saint Louis University until the 1960's attests.[1] The reasons for the polemic were complex, but they trace back to oral culture, with its mnemonic and agonistic modes of knowledge storage and retrieval.

The polemic economy of oral intellectualism demands that knowledge be on the tip of the tongue and that it be sharp-edged. This is a fundamental reason for what we may call the style of earlier theology—maximized memorization and the use of formulas. The oral drive to memorization and formulary encapsulation was rendered less necessary by writing and espe-

---

[1] The complex structure of the oralism still prevalent in the theological milieu at Saint Louis University up until the 1960's has many interesting applications. Among these, some concern what has been called the McLuhan phenomenon. Marshall McLuhan was very much a part of the milieu that I have just described and which was in a state of active ferment when he was a young instructor in English at Saint Louis University from 1937 to 1944.

cially by print, which made it possible to store knowledge so that it need not be "called" to mind (note that this expression is formed from an oral base, "calling") but could rather be "looked" up (note that this expression, meaningless until there is writing, is based on considering words and knowledge itself as something essentially seen). But it took a long time for writing to eliminate entrenched oral habits of behavior, which, as we have seen, long left their mark on writing itself. In fact, because of its stable character, writing could be used and was used for a long while to fixate formulas more and more. And of course it would never eliminate them entirely, for we cannot live or think without a certain number of formulas encapsulating basic or basically operational truths.

These perspectives make it possible to see that the dogmatic formulations that Christianity has found so helpful and essential not only to its survival but also to its essential mission of proclaiming the Gospel are connected with this oral state of affairs. This is not to say that they have no other connections, but merely that an oral culture—particularly one which possesses writing but has as yet not been taken over by writing or by print—will rely greatly on formulations, for formulas are, as we have seen more requisite for its thinking processes than they are for the thinking processes of manuscript or print cultures. This does not mean that dogmatic formulations or clearly stated theses are not needed in later cultures, such as our own. Indeed, since our culture is oral now in a new way, one might argue that they are particularly needed now once more.[2] Nor are dogmatic formulations "mere formulas" in the sense of statements without true content. Probably there is no such thing as a "mere formula." If a knowledge of oral culture and of the history of the media teaches us anything, it is that formulas are far more functional in our grasp of truth than has often been supposed. Formulas can be misused, but they are fulcra on which our knowledge rests.

By contrast, what is the character of present-day Catholic theology when set off against this earlier, Latin, polemic, and at least residually oral theology? This question really opens a subject for a whole new paper, but it may also serve as a close for the present one. I shall hazard here some general statements which appear to fit with what has been said although they also call for further explication. These statements are concerned chiefly with Catholic theology. The background against which these developments have been discussed, however, is quite common to Protestant, Catholic and Jew-

---

[2] It is perhaps significant that the distinguished theologian Wolfhart Pannenberg employs the thesis form in his "Dogmatische Thesen zur Lehre von der Offenbarung" (1961). Professor Pannenberg, after first setting down a thesis, gives it an explanatory rather than a disputatious development.

ish thought, and what has happened in Catholic theology has its close analogues and often exact counterparts in Protestant and Jewish circles. By and
large, in its teaching procedures, Catholic theology remained close to the
oral world longer than did Protestant theology. This contrasts with the fact
that a theology of the word has been stressed more in Protestant circles than
in Catholic, but it accords with the fact that classical Protestant doctrine
until recently has in principle made the written text of the Bible its special
concern to the theoretical if not actual exclusion of tradition.

Present-day Catholic theology, then, is increasingly non-Latin, as it is
increasingly nonmnemonic and noncombative. Instead of being orally powered, it tends to be text-oriented and thus historically oriented, for history,
as against mythological accounts of the past, is dependent on writing. Theology in the oral tradition was, of course, in a sense text-oriented and not by
any means entirely unhistorical in that it drew avidly on the Bible, but it did
so largely to direct biblical material into the stream of oral communication.
Today even those theology students who are specialists in biblical studies
are seldom avid Bible quoters. They see the text in its place in the stream of
history and thus have gained insights impossible for earlier theology, although they are less adept at feeling it, in all its historical density and com-
plication, as speaking in its every verse to individuals. Present-day theology
tends to be print-oriented, even computer-oriented, "objective." Although
many theologians and even more amateur theologians today are quite ex-
pressly committed to commitment, urging theology must be related to real
life, one could argue that present-day theology is in a way less related to the
texture of life and thus less related to the texture of real history than the
older polemic theology because, in its irenic spirit, present-day theology
does not enter so much as the earlier oral theology does into the agonistic or
dialectical movement of history and of thought. It is fashionable to regard
the earlier polemic theology as removed from the human life world. Yet it
appears likely that a Marxist theoretician, at least, would consider its polemic economy more of a piece with existential actuality.

By the same token, present-day theology, which is inclined to down-
grade earlier scholastic theology as minimally scriptural, is in significant
ways farther removed from the biblical economy of thought than the earlier
theology was. Modern theologians and preachers generally cannot quote the
Scriptures with the *copia* of medieval theologians and preachers, as typified,
let us say, in St. Bernard of Clairvaux or St. Anthony of Padua. Technological individuals generally cannot quote anything in the organized abundance
that every educated medieval individual had to command. Present-day theology talks about the biblical world and indeed reconstitutes it with tremendous learning and finesse and deep understanding, although with a dispas-
sionate objectivity utterly removed from the biblical world. It is absolutely
necessary for us that theology do this, for we can never live directly in the
old oral world again. But earlier theology could get along rather well with-

out this reconstitution because to a significant degree it had never left the old oral world in which the Bible took form and which is so remote from us. Earlier theology did not advert to this old oral world abstractly because it was immersed in it. The last thing a fish has to be told about is water.

Present-day theology is nonformulaic. Our immersion in typography has disposed us to think of fixity of expression as enforced by print. We must therefore remind ourselves that quite the opposite is true. Fixity of expression—and hence formulaic expression—is encouraged by an oral noetic economy rather than by print. Print fixes an individual utterance or series of utterances (a book) so that countless mechanical copies of it can be made. But it does not fix utterance so that other books set out to repeat those that went before. Quite to the contrary: Since what is in a given book is indefinitely multipliable without anyone's ever saying or composing it again at all, print encourages the writer of the next book to be as different as possible. Print fosters originality. Oral culture discourages originality. It tends to make each new utterance an echo—and even in places a sheer formulaic repetition—of what has been said before and, as it was being said, has necessarily vanished. The relatively nonformulaic character of present-day theology thus registers a print economy of thought.

This nonformulaic print economy marks even the new oral electronic media and thus identifies the new oralism to this extent as different from the primary oralism of early cultures. We use slogans, it is true, but slogans are not formulas. Slogans are action-oriented, rhetorical, topical, evanescent. Formulas are basically descriptive, interpretive, enduring. They are filters through which actuality is drawn into the consciousness and are much more basic and profound than slogans. Slogans tend to be programmatic and are discarded when they have served their purpose. The graffiti in the University quarter at Paris and in other riot centers are slogans, not formulas. As slogans, they are more original than formulas and less enduring.

The nonformulaic economy of present-day Catholic theology, its abandonment of the older formulary, deliberately polemic mode, aligns it with the print economy and, insofar as this economy structures the new oralism, with this new oralism as well. In a more direct way, too, the new oralism is asserting itself in Catholic theology as in many other branches of knowledge. The new oral electronic media—most notably radio and television—tend to promote spontaneity, the unrehearsed reaction of interviewee and audience (for whom of course the interviewer is the surrogate). Quiz sessions and unrehearsed interviews are regular media fare, and the greatest television scandal thus far occurred when it was discovered that purportedly impromptu programs were in fact rehearsed. In fostering on-the-spot production with the existential focus on the present that comes naturally to the sound media, the new orality approximates the older primary orality, uncontrolled by written or printed references. Despite his formulas, the oral poet or story-teller did not have his narrative memorized word for word and

hence absolutely set but instead used his fixed formulas to vary his performance, amplifying or curtailing a given story in accordance with here-and-
now audience response. The oral-culture openness to spontaneity in a context of performer-audience interaction no doubt helps create the demand for
greater classroom discussion which is felt in theology today as in other disciplines. Outside the classroom, the discursive catechesis of today similarly
contrasts strongly with the previous use of catechisms, which are question-
and-answer media closely tied to the textual fixation effected by print, for
catechisms, while occasionally produced in medieval manuscript culture, really came into their own quite suddenly immediately after the invention of
alphabetic type. At a still more popular level today, radio and, more particularly, television demand a discursive and even conversational casualness
where they have occasion to present theology, or any other academic subject. Formal debate and formal reading of lecture notes are either ruled out
or disguised. The conversational casualness is a mark of orality, but orality
of a new kind, unlike the old primary orality, which trafficked in the formality and the formulas discouraged by electronic oralism.

The relationship of demythologizing programs to the stages in the media would be matter for an entire supplementary paper. The relationship can
only he touched on here. With the figure of the hero which accompanies it,
myth belongs in a certain way primarily, although by no means exclusively,
to the oral state of communication, where, in its grossest sense as narration
regarding more-than-human beings, it is elaborated as a means of assimilating, organizing, storing, and retrieving knowledge. Havelock has shown this
in great detail for Greek culture (1963). That is to say, although myth does a
good many other things, too, in the noetic economy with which we have
here been concerned, it structures for oral memory. It also connects with the
iconographic mode of thinking encouraged by memory systems, as Frances
Yates has profusely documented (1966, pp. 105-172) and in this also relates
to oral noetics, for memory systems are chirographic and typographic devices serving residually oral needs. With the advent of the electronic media,
the same forces which tend to replace the hero with the antihero inevitably
affect the currency and serviceability of myth, although they also mature a
greater understanding of myth than before. However, in the perspectives
suggested here, frontal attacks on myth in programs of demythologization
appear in general related to older chirographic and typographic frames of
thought rather than to the newer electronics. They place heavy reliance on
rationalism, which, again as Havelock has brought out, has its roots in writing. (It has still stronger roots in print.)

In their rationalism, demythologizing programs are matched by the dehellenization programs which seem otherwise to oppose them. Both programs are highly abstract and rationalist. "Dehellenization" is, ironically, a
thoroughly hellenic concept (identify error and dissect it out cleanly). As
such, it is an echo out of the chirographic and, more particularly, the typo-

graphic era rather than a response to the electronic. Real adjustments are generally both less programmatic and less negative than either of these. We have as yet no name, so far as I know, for what theology is doing positively to adjust to our electronic culture as such, and we have only skimpy descriptions, such as that here. ("Demythologize" and "dehellenize," incidentally, appear to be not formulas but slogans, in the senses of these terms earlier explained.)

Finally, a significant character of present-day theology is that, like other fields of knowledge today, it is rapidly expanding and indeed exploding, and at the same time interlocking with other disciplines, such as anthropology, psychology, biology, sociology, history, and literary criticism, and with accelerating speed. Earlier theology was dominated by a world view in which knowledge was in short supply and great effort was called for to keep it from slipping away. Today we have almost innumerable devices for storing knowledge and multiplying access to it in its stored form: photocopying, electronic tapes, computers, and other electronic devices, not to mention rapid transportation, which serves the things of the mind perhaps even more than those of the body. We live in an economy of noetic abundance, whereas earlier humans lived in one of scarcity. We live also in an intellectual world equipped to reflect on its own history as never before. Since Christian theology is more deeply embedded in history than any other theology and since it places a high value on history, in which the Son of God became flesh, the possibilities here are bright for the future.

2

The Catholic Imagination and the Catholic University

Andrew M. Greeley

One of the prime functions of a Catholic university or undergraduate college ought to be to reflect on the Catholic imaginative tradition. This is a very modest suggestion. I do not say that this is the only role of the Catholic university or its most important role or a role that is unique to it. All that I am saying is that, when one wanders onto a Catholic campus, one would expect to find among other things a propensity to reflect with appropriately intellectual rigor (depending on the specific activity involved) on the Catholic heritage. Or if one comes upon a campus that has enough Catholics on its faculty to please the Vatican and there is no reflection on the Catholic imaginative heritage, then one might well wonder whether this campus has any right to be called Catholic.

To reflect on the imaginative heritage is to reflect on what is in the raw and primordial sense, the essence of Catholicism. Catholic poetry antedates and exceeds Catholic prose.

It would consume far too much space to attempt to prove my theory of the Catholic imagination. I have essayed this in journal articles and a somewhat less technical level in my book *The Catholic Myth* (1990). The reader might also consult David Tracy's magisterial *The Analogical Imagination* (1981), the book from which I derived the sociological hypotheses that serve as the basis for my theory of the Catholic imagination.

My theory of the Catholic imagination can be stated in the following premises: Religion begins in (1) experiences that renew hope. These experiences are in turn encoded in (2) images or symbols that become templates for action and are shared with others through (3) stories that are told in (4) communities and celebrated in (5) rituals. This model is circular, not a straight line, and hence the stories, communities, and rituals in their turn influence experiences of renewed hope.

Originally published in *America, 164*(10) (March 16, 1991), 285-288.

Because we are reflective creatures we must reflect on our imaginative religion. Because we are creatures who belong to communities with heritages, we must be critical of our imaginative religion to make sure that it stays within what the community has traditionally taken to be its boundaries. Creeds, catechisms, theological systems, even teaching authorities are an inevitable and essential result of reflection on and critique of experiential religion. I do not want to deny the importance of intellectual religion. I am merely saying that religion takes its origins and its raw power from experiences, images, stories, community, and ritual, and that most religious socialization (transmission) takes place through narrative before it takes place in conceptual, analytic form. Religion must be intellectual but it is experiential before it is intellectual.

Jesus was a storyteller; the parables are the essential Jesus; they share with us Jesus's experience of the generous, hope-renewing love of the Father in heaven—who, be it noted, in the stories of Jesus loves with a mother's forgiving tenderness as much as he loves with a father's vigorous protection.

The Jewish tradition is passed on especially in the stories of the Holydays and the Passover. The Catholic tradition is passed on especially in the stories of Christmas and the Easter Passover. Maybe half our heritage is transmitted to children around the crib at Christmastime—and especially in the wonderfully mysterious explanation of the Incarnation to children, that Mary is God's mother.

The analogical or Catholic imagination, to summarize and simplify David Tracy, emphasizes the presence of God in the world. It perceives the world and its creatures and relationships and social structures as metaphors, sacraments of God, hints of what God is like. I often illustrate the theory by noting that Catholics have angels and saints and souls in purgatory and statues and stained glass windows and holy water and an institutional church that itself is thought to be a sacrament. Protestant denominations, on the other hand, either do not have this imagery or do not put so much emphasis on it. The Catholic imagination is defined by the practice of devotion to Mary the Mother of Jesus. To fall back on the mother tongue, *ubi est Maria, ibi est ecclesia catholica* ("where Mary is, there is the Catholic Church").

One side, the Catholic analogical imagination, leans in the direction of immanence; the other, the Protestant dialectical imagination, leans in the direction of transcendence. Which is better? Neither. Which is necessary? Both.

The analogical and the dialectical imaginations are not mutually exclusive. No individual is completely possessed by one or the other, nor does any denomination or group have a monopoly on one or the other. The two imaginations represent propensities, tendencies, emphases.

My sociological research confirms the theory of the analogical imagination. In 12 countries Catholics and Protestants do have different images of reality encoded in different images of God. Catholics do indeed tend to picture creation and human society as metaphors for God. The Catholic religious experience does tend to be sacramental (or incarnational). Catholic symbols are indeed analogical or metaphorical. Catholic stories tend to be comedy. The Catholic community tends to be structured and organic (in Emile Durkheim's sense of the word), and Catholic rituals tend to be celebratory.

Thus a young Catholic growing up absorbs cues about his or her religious tradition from many different sources and in many different forms. Formal religious instruction, the writing of theologians and the pronouncements of the Vatican are among the voices he or she hears, but these largely propositional voices are heard long after the more imaginative and poetic voices of parents, family, neighbors, parish clergy, and local community. The Catholic imaginative heritage is usually transmitted to a young person in great part before the person encounters any formal religious education—and cannot be undone by such religious education.

This is not a particularly revolutionary notion. If you leave aside for a moment the religion classes in which you learned or which you have taught and reflect on your own absorption of Catholicism, you will, I think, acknowledge that it was a process something like the one I have described: You heard the poetry before you learned the prose. You had listened to the stories before you encountered the institution (for which you may want to add "Thank God!").

Like all symbol and narrative systems, the Catholic imaginative tradition is dense, polyvalent, multilayered. Its logic is poetic rather than deductive. One can find different and even contrasting cues in it depending, for example, on the experiences of family life with which one approaches it or the different ideological biases one seeks to confirm. (Consider the many different uses to which the symbol and the story of Mary the Mother of Jesus have been put.) In general, however, the Catholic imaginative heritage has enormous appeal ("once a Catholic, always a Catholic") because at its best moments it tends to be warm, supportive, filled with wonder and affection, and grateful for the goodness of nature and human relationships (their "sacramentality"). "Wherever the Catholic sun does shine / there is music, laughter, and good red wine. / At least I've always found it so / Benedicamus Domino."

Most Catholics like being Catholic. They do not want to give up their Catholicism—the experiences, the images, the stories, the communities, and the rituals of their precognitive heritage—and, in fact, most of them don't give it up come what may. The defection rate of those who were born Catholic and who no longer define themselves as Catholic is today 15% in this country, precisely what it was 30 years ago.

This fact brings me to my final premise: In any conflict between propositional Catholicism, whether imposed by theologians, liturgists, and religious educators on the one hand or the teaching authority on the other, and imaginative Catholicism, the latter will win going away. Mind you, propositional religion is essential because we are reflective beings. Hence theology, liturgical theory, and religious education as well as the corrective judgments of the teaching authority are necessary (as they would be in any community shaped by a heritage) to criticize and reflect upon experiential and imaginative religion. Nonetheless, these necessary reflective behaviors, if they are to serve any useful purpose, must be carried on with an awareness that the origins and raw power of religion are to be found in the poetic rather than the prosaic dimension of the self.

It would be well if all the propositional teachers on both the left and the right would understand the depth, the antiquity, the tenacity, and the appeal of the heritage with which they often try to mess.

Obviously, the imaginative tradition requires tools of reflection in this era different from in the past. Just as obviously, it must be reexamined so that it can grow and expand. But both reflection and reexamination must take place in a context, first, of awareness of the tradition and, second, of respect for it. Catholicism was not born in 1965.

To summarize this model: A distinctive Catholic religious culture extends beyond the boundaries of institutional religious propositions, a Catholic poetry that is wider, richer, and deeper than Catholic prose, a powerful and pervasive symbol system that purports to offer ultimate explanations in narrative form for creation and for human life and death. This culture or, if you wish, subculture may be pictured as a repertory of images that give names to the phenomena of human life. It exists only partially in most individuals and communities and perhaps perfectly in few or none. It is not absolutely unique and coexists with strains of other religious subcultures, many of which it subsumes. Yet it is different. Catholics name reality differently, though not totally differently, from the way others do.

Finally, one can suggest with considerable persuasiveness that the Catholic religious imagination is the matrix and the context for virtually all Catholic ministerial and pastoral work.

Question: How, then, might one reflect on this heritage in a Catholic college or university? I have five suggestions.

(1) The most obvious kind of reflection is that which once seemed to exist in superabundance on the Catholic campus, research about and courses on the high-culture component of the Catholic imaginative heritage—History of Catholic Art, 19th-Century Catholic Poets, Recent Catholic Fiction, French and English Catholic Novelists of the First Half of the 20th Century, Current Catholic Film Makers (I think of Lee Lourdeaux's wonderful book (1990) on the Catholic ethnic influence on Capra, Ford, Coppola and Scorsese).

Could a young person really claim to have had a Catholic education if he or she has not read, reflected on and perhaps even committed to memory Hopkins's *May Magnificat*?

(2) Hence, the second reflection I would suggest as a possibility would be on Mary and the saints. The Mary story is, if not *the* privileged symbol (in Paul Ricoeur's sense of the term) of the poetic logic of Catholicism at

least *a* privileged symbol, a key to understanding the whole system. Those elites on the right who concentrate on the propositional and institutional elements of the Catholic tradition have turned the Mary story to dry dogma or sweet saccharin, and on the left have ignored the Mary story altogether. Both responses to the Mother of Jesus, I would suggest, are perilous—not to the Madonna who is alive and well but to the elites. If one does not understand the most powerful religious narrative in 15 centuries of Christian history, one understands nothing at all about Catholicism.

Similarly, the saints, whose lives, as Kenneth Woodward has recently pointed out in his *Making Saints* (1990), are stories of God's love, provide marvelous material for both classroom instruction and scholarly research. I note that the leading publisher of lives of the saints today is the University of Chicago Press and that the first book that attempted computer analysis of medieval saints (and with considerable success) was written, not by a faculty member of a Catholic university, but by my colleague Donald Weinstein of the University of Arizona.

(3) I would also propose for reflection the traditional Catholic social theory, outlined by Aquinas, developed in the last century by Jesuit scholars and in this century by another Jesuit, Oswald von Nell-Breuning and expounded by Popes Leo XIII and Pius XI. This theory, with its emphasis on society as an ordered and cooperative system, like Dante's *Commèdia,* is more the result of an underlying Catholic imagination than the cause of it. Poetry again shapes prose much more than the reverse. The Catholic imagination sees human society as a sacrament of God's love and therefore seeks a third way between Hobbesian individualism and Marxist collectivism. The core of this Catholic theory is the principle of subsidiarity—nothing should be done by a higher or larger organization that cannot be done as well by a lower or smaller one.

Now that the gods of Marxism have collapsed with the falling Berlin wall, it might be appropriate to begin again to reflect on a communitarian social theory that advocates decentralization instead of centralization. The politician who believes that political power ultimately grows, not out of a barrel of a gun, but out of voting decisions in the precincts, has an organic image of society even if he does not know the word. The good precinct captain and the good parish priest have the same image of social action—one must be out on the street listening more than talking, out with the people in the smallest units of society in those places where men and women live, love, raise their children, reconcile, worship, and die.

(4) This observation points to another possible area for reflection—the unique American Catholic experience of immigration into the neighborhood parish, surely one of the most extraordinary forms of community that human ingenuity has ever discovered; within the neighborhood parish the parochial school is one of the most effective techniques for generating and supporting local community that humankind has ever used. American Catholic elites for

the last five decades have reflected on everyone else's experience but their own—French, German, Dutch, Latin American. It would be useful also to be interested in our own.

(5) If religion is image and story before it is anything else and if Catholicism has the richest imaginative tradition of any of the religions of the Holy One, then we might expect to find artists, poets, and writers in residence on Catholic campuses, men and women who would manifest concretely how the religious imagination works.

My illustrative examples are from the social sciences and the humanities, the areas I know best. But it would seem to me that both the cosmological issues with which my Jesuit colleagues at the University of Arizona wrestle, and the leading-edge biological issues about the organism directing its own evolution, also provide interesting possibilities for Catholic instruction and scholarship.

My suggestions for a role (not the role) of Catholic colleges and universities are, as I said at the outset, modest, not grandiose. While modest, however, my suggestions may have the merit of being feasible.

Am I daring to suggest that the sociologist is more important than the theologian, the college professor, and, heaven save us, the bishop? Not at all. I am saying that all are equally unimportant (though still equally necessary) when compared with the poet, the artist, the storyteller, the mystic, the saint.

Those of us who work in whatever form with the institution and the proposition must finally realize that while our slice of the pie is critical, it is not comprehensive and that we can no longer afford to ignore the rest of the pie. The prose writer must listen to the poet. The institutional leader and the theologian must listen to the storyteller.

3

MediaChurch: The Presentation of Religious Information via Media

Phyllis Zagano

The intent of this chapter is to review some of the problems attendant to the presentation of what I call "religious information"—not only doctrinal statements but information about the operation of church organizations—via the secular media, the growing dependence of religion upon the secular media, and the unavoidable consequences relative to the meaning of the messages of religion. I do not address the American phenomenon of nondenominational religious broadcasting here, but rather focus on the practical and theoretical implications of secular media upon denominational structures and their adherents within the United States.

Religious Information in a Secular Age

While there appears to be an advance in the amount of space and time devoted by media to religious discussion and church operations (Hynds, 1987) it is becoming increasingly apparent that the quality of the coverage serves neither specific denominations nor their intent (Mechling, 1988; Zagano, 1987). One could argue in fact, that denominations are in trouble because they no longer have unbreachable channels of communication for their messages and depend either willingly or unwillingly on the secular media. That is, where once the primary dispenser of information about religion stood in the denominationally-approved pulpit and spoke denominationally-approved words, secular media transmit more information faster and to a larger number of people than any evangelist could have ever imagined.

With or without their cooperation, the internal discussions and doctrinal messages of American denominations are available to the public at

A version of this chapter was originally published in *The Journal of Communication and Religion, 13*(2), (1990), 40-44.

large through the secular media. In fact, people learn of the very inner workings of their religious structures from a secular source. It would appear that
a part of the difficulty in the presentation of religious information via the
filter of secular media is the seemingly necessary subjectivity[1] with which
the American media presently approach all discussion, and the concomitant
subjectivity with which the American public receives that discussion. In
fact, the general subjectivism in American public discussion as it is conducted both by and in the media reduces the ability of any person or entity
to argue on behalf of the very existence of objective truth, upon which denominational discussion depends. Beyond, with a reduced acceptance of the
possibility of objective truth comes a reduced probability of any ability to
transmit objective truth from one person to another. This is an old problem
with an electronic twist, something Sigmund Freud, Albert Einstein, or Karl
Marx would not have imagined.

Even so, this is not to be construed as methodological incursion of decon-
structionism into the manner by which Americans receive televised messages or
messages via any other journalistic medium. Clearly, the majority of the TV
generation have never heard of Heidegger or Derrida or Foucault or Barthes.
But the method by which deconstructionists receive the text of artistic creation
is identical to the method by which most people understand television and other
journalistic media. As Alan Bloom has summarized it,

> The interpreter's creative activity is more important than the text; there
> is no text, only interpretation. Thus the one thing most necessary for us,
> the knowledge of what these texts have to tell us, is turned over to the
> subjective, creative selves of these interpreters, who say there is no text
> and no reality to which the texts refer. (1987, p. 379)

Without arguing for or against the deconstructionist view of the interpretation of art—art being what deconstruction can better deal with—we can
understand the application of the theory of deconstruction to the question of
simple sending and receiving of information relative to religion and religious belief.

Standard communications theory speaks of the steps by which a message gets from one person to another. A sender first determines the message
and then encodes it in words or in pictures or in both. Presently, for the sake
of clarity, let us restrict ourselves to the encoding of the message in words.
The sender encodes the message in words and transmits this encoded mes-

---

[1] Most information is treated as if it is an expression of opinion, and repeated
attempts are made to "balance" that opinion. When religion says, for example,
abortion is wrong, media presents the "opposing viewpoint." Religious discussion
thereby takes on a more public character, and often unprepared denominational
authorities are left to do public relations battle with media professionals.

sage, that is, writes down what he or she has to say. The sender then sends the message (perhaps through some news medium) and it arrives within the purview of the receiver who must then go about the task of decoding the message. Only when the receiver has been able to decode the message, that is, only when the receiver has been able to read or hear the message, is he or she able to set about the task of first understanding it and then judging whether it is true or false. The receiver's judgment depends upon many things: his or her own understanding of the message, respect for the sender, and trust in the medium which has transmitted the message.

Indeed, there are a number of variables which govern the abilities of a sender as encoder and a receiver as decoder. Language, culture and educational levels interact to make the message more of a moving target. Physiological problems—ranging from differing abilities of the senses to actual internal information processing problems—often create barriers which cause confusion on the part of sender or receiver. These differences affect not only the persons involved, but the mechanical means of information transmission as well. Dyslexia, for example, is a learning disability which does not imply below-normal intelligence but which is manifested by difficulties in encoding language, in decoding it, or in both. It is the analog of technical transmission problems which color the sending or receiving of information electronically.

Keeping in mind the myriad problems attendant to sending and receiving messages, one can now address the obstinate problems of the apparent equation between fact and opinion. This is most certainly not a new problem, but it renders powerless even the most advanced methods of encoding-sending-receiving-decoding information. In addition to the conditions the deconstructionists remind us of and which genuinely can color the receipt of all information (artistic or not), religion and religious truth are faced with a popular form of subjectivism, epistemological relativism. Epistemological relativism, which can be reduced in common parlance to "that's true for you but not for me," changes all fact to opinion. What is fact for one individual becomes opinion for another. Since no central referent is agreed upon, the focus of discussion is in constant flux depending upon the points of view of the speakers.

Yet a central referent is necessary if the speakers are to understand each other. In fact, if communication is to be engaged in at all, the existence of a central referent is crucial. Without it, there is no communication among or between persons. In Wallace Stevens' poem "Anecdote of the Jar" it is the simple jar which establishes the reality of the hill and sets the rest of the "slovenly wilderness" in relation to it:

> I placed a jar in Tennessee,
> And round it was, upon a hill.
> It made the slovenly wilderness
> Surround that hill. (1923/1954, p. 76)

Stevens is making the same argument as I do here: There must be a single reference point in order for coherent discussion to evolve. Yet in a subjective society, the discussion of religion becomes a near impossibility, solely because religion and religious belief depend upon communal agreement on a central referent, or at least upon agreement of the factual existence of such a central referent. That central referent, however, is an unnameable reality which may be perceived differently but which is in fact (that is, in a fact agreed to by the discussants) immutable in its essence.

Religion's Dependence Upon the Secular Media

It is not difficult to understand why religion and religious belief are so little understood by the secular public when we realize that the larger portion of individuals receive personal religious information from the secular media. Even if they attend their own denominational worship services and read the religious media of their own denominations, they still receive the news of other denominations through secular media. In general, such coverage is "by outsiders for outsiders." This is put in even starker relief when considering the new religious movements (Van Driel & Richardson, 1988, p. 37). The coverage of "mainline" denominations, however, is increasingly similarly misinformed and hostile.

If denominational adherents receive their information via secular media, it is important for denominations to know whether the discussion evoked is legitimate according to its own determinants. The question naturally arises: Is it at all possible for religions to coherently discuss the varied problems attendant to moral, ethical or theological issues regarding denominational teachings via the media? Because the secular media have so far outstripped the religious media, denominations must now depend upon, or at least consider the use of and possible adverse effects of, the secular media. As I have argued elsewhere, even "the Vatican must depend now not upon its own controlled information systems, but rather on the uncontrolled information systems in place within the world media" (1987, p. 29).

What has evolved, in part because of an acceptance of subjectivism, is a situation whereby the religious discussant on the world scene is just another opinion maker, and the pronouncements of even the head of a denomination relative to the truths of his religious faith are often "balanced" by an "opposing viewpoint." This is complicated by the fact that often the pronouncements of a religious denomination are encoded in such a fashion that they may only be decoded by clergy educated to that denomination. In fact, the very means by which a denomination might seek to guard the purity of its message becomes the reason that message is not available to the ordinary adherent and, consequently, very available to interpretation by the media.

The Question of Meaning

The application of deconstructionist methods to religious Scripture is, if not caused by, at least related to the development of "receptive hermeneutics." The argument of deconstruction as applied to art—that it need only excite within me a personal response relative to my personal history—can be fairly argued for the experience of Scripture in hermeneutics, but need not be extended to the point that such personal reflection either validates or invalidates what the text says. The extreme understanding of the deconstructionist or receptive hermeneuticist is that the text is only valid if the receiver says it is. Needless to say, this endangers religious systems which argue that there indeed exists objective truth, and it is represented in greater or smaller part within the religious system's Scripture.

The result of this questioning of meaning on the part of the receiver of information is that not only Scripture, but pronouncements about religion and religious belief of a denomination, can be dismissed as mere propaganda to be accepted or rejected at will. The question of interpretation, and the consequent development of receptive hermeneutics[2] presents a situation whereby the text of Scripture is meaningful only as it exists within my own culture and, to the extreme, within my own history. As we have seen, while there is some argument on behalf of this, there is the danger of rejecting all information about religion and religious belief unless it fits in with private vision and personal history. In such a schema, not only does the text mean (or have meaning) only as I read it in my own life and in my own culture, the text actually *is* as I read it, and only as I read it, within this personal and societal context.

The text can comprise anything. Let us take for example a particular line of Scripture as it exists translated in a denominationally-approved bible. If the authority of this Scripture passage depends upon its ability to have "meaning" in the present culture, then there is every evidence that a great deal of Scripture—this passage included—will have no meaning at all in a great many cultures. In fact, if the authority of denominational teachings based on this passage depends upon the passage's ability to have "meaning" in the present culture, there is every evidence that the denominational teachings will have no meaning at all in many cultures. Just as the presentation of what is denominationally perceived as religious truth in a fashion whose decoding is limited to those educated into the theology of the denomination eventually limits the public knowledge of the truth (because, as noted above, people receive their information from media rather than from denomina-

---

[2] For our purposes, as defined and developed by Friedrich D. E. Schleiermacher, Edmund Husserl, Martin Heidegger and Hans-Georg Gadamer. See, for example, Mueller-Vollmer, 1988.

tional spokesmen or clergy) so the dependence of a denominational teaching on a particular cultural adaptation of a particular Scripture passage will eventuate a generally "meaningless" message in the larger number of cultures. In short, it becomes nearly impossible for those outside the national media loop to "receive" and "decode" the "message," let alone find any authority in it, given its alienation from the facts of their culture.

In less extreme ways, denominational teachings are received differently within different segments of American society. Even those faithful who have been able to receive a denominational teaching without a biased lens, or through subjectivism, or through the outlook of epistemological relativism, still face the problematic differentiations of inculturation. Those who have not been inculturated into the society which has generated a specific teaching have little means of understanding it (or "appropriating" it, in the language of hermeneutics). This is in part a problem of class distinction, and in part a problem of technological advance. When a denomination makes a moral theological statement about a specific technology (i.e. nuclear deterrence, *in vitro* fertilization, or genetic manipulation) the denomination ofttimes speaks to and with a certain level of sophistication. For those who have specific knowledge of the technology under discussion, the denominational statement can be dismissed as simplistic; for those who have no knowledge of the technology, the statement can go unheard except in political or economic terms.

The problem of understanding is obvious outside the United States specifically because of its inherent causes, the media. For example, consider whether ordinary individuals in a non-technological society can find meaning in religious discussion about genetic engineering. Theirs is not a technological culture. The very context of the discussion is beyond the current development of their society. How can they "receive" and "decode" the "message," let alone find authority or even meaning in it, given its essential alienation from the facts of their culture?[3] Their problem, or any problem of understanding, of "appropriating" the discussion, is not a moral or educational fault but simply a fact of life.

Conclusions

That secular media transmit denominational discussion faster and often more completely than denominational vehicles is a given. The ancient conjoining of information and authority is, if not now broken, at least hanging

---

[3] The paradox of course is that individuals from a non-technological society would probably have fewer problems evaluating the technology in moral terms.

by a rusted hinge. The media have leveled the wall between the person with authority and the person without; both the pronouncer and the "opposing viewpoint" are vested with the equalizing mantle of media (Meyrowitz, 1985, chap. 10), and television has become the cathedral of the 20th century.

Yet the furthest extreme of privatized religion is no religion, for the concept of "church" depends upon a group of cooperating individuals. Clearly, denominations must deal with an increasing literacy relative to their denominational discussion which is not borne of their own efforts. The fact of religious information in a secular age will not disappear, nor should it. Denominations would well serve themselves if they developed a systematic and professional method by which they routinely dealt with the secular media without belying their structural integrity. In an ordinary business operation, this involves establishing designated "spokesmen." Yet the nature of religious organizations is such that the chief spokesman is the chief cleric. It would seem, then, that denominational leaders and adherents who have the substantive knowledge of their denominational beliefs would benefit from the kind of advanced homiletics training which recognizes the power of media without ignoring the power of the pulpit. This is necessary in large measure because denominations are increasingly dependent upon secular media; whether or not they approve of the denominational message transmitted beyond their control to their followers is irrelevant. The message is there. The task of the denomination is to address the question of meaning, in light of its traditional methods of transmitting information and in light of the secular media. Such is central to the fact of the growing MediaChurch, which is growing through the presentation of religious information via the media.

II

Contexts:

History, Philosophy, Theory

4

Visible Image and Invisible Faith

Gregor Goethals

When the apostle Paul preached in Ephesus, he so angered the silversmiths of that city that he nearly lost his life. This incident recorded in the Acts of the Apostles is marvelously compact in describing Paul's encounter with rioting artisans whose livelihood was endangered by the apostle's preaching. The essence of Paul's message was that faith in Christ and the worship of God do not depend upon images made by human hands. Witnessing to the experience of the early Christians, and in light of his own Jewish background, Paul directly challenged a religious tradition in which images were indeed a necessary part of religious rites and a basic language for public communication....

This confrontation between Paul and the silversmiths is more than a record of one of the perilous events in his ministry, because it also illustrates radically different views about religion and its relationship to the visual arts....

Since the purpose of this chapter is to explore the role of images in the communication of religious meanings, it would be a useful beginning to look at the conflict at Ephesus in greater detail. That is, first we will consider briefly the tradition threatened by Paul's preaching. But this is not simply an academic exercise in looking backward;...many of the technological images in our own contemporary world function like images in the classical world. Statues and relief sculpture on ancient monuments communicated stories that identified Greeks and Romans, providing symbols of political and mythic authority. Similarly the popular arts today permeate public space, reinforcing the mythologies of a democratic society....

The visual arts were intimately related to all early religions. Images and objects were necessary to both public and private acts of piety, while an

---

This chapter is excerpted from material originally published as Chapter 1 of *The Electronic Golden Calf: Images, Religioni, and the Making of Meaning* (Cambridge, MA: Cowley Publications, 1990), pp. 7-52.

autonomous, disconnected realm of art such as we have today simply did not exist. Instead of artists, there were painters, sculptors, potters, stone masons, and silversmiths—all of whom pursued their crafts in a society where religious, political, and aesthetic elements were fused. To illustrate this situation, let us consider some of the images and the roles they played in the classical tradition. I have chosen examples from this tradition in part because of Paul's missionary activity among the Gentiles, but we will see later that the visual codes for the shaping of images in this culture were to make a profound impact on the mainstream of Christian art in the west.

In the classical Greek tradition, religious art and buildings–temples, treasuries, theaters and free-standing statuary–were clustered together in sacred precincts....At these sites images functioned in three ways. First, they had a sacral role. The temple was considered to be the dwelling place of the deity, and a statue of a god or goddess was placed in the cella or main room....While some saw these images as embodiments of the deity, the more educated and sophisticated viewers regarded them as symbols (Bevan, 1940, pp. 21-30). Other kinds of images and objects served as votive offerings to gods and goddesses in gratitude for favors or as petitions. Second, these images also commemorated special persons, both living and dead, who distinguished themselves in battle, games, or political life. Finally, the painted and carved images that adorned the architecture at sacred sites performed a narrative, pedagogical function. The sculpture of temple pediments and friezes represented fundamental social myths that uneducated persons who could not read or write could still absorb visually. Through vase painting and relief sculpture, the Homeric accounts of the Hellenes and the action of gods and goddesses in human affairs reached the people.

Such arts rendered visible the events, myths, and deities that were particularly significant for the populace. These storytelling, figurative works brought to common people concrete embodiments of myth and a world view. More than merely descriptive, they also served a normative purpose in reminding ordinary people of values to emulate. There, before their eyes, were heroes, gods, and goddesses with whom they could identify. Judging by the expenditures of political leaders from Pericles to the Hellenistic monarchs, we can surmise that these rulers had some sense of the value of visual models to reinforce loyalty and strengthen ties to the body politic.

From the classical sculpture and the painting that has survived on Greek vases we can deduce what can be called a classical aesthetic, that is, a particular set of conventions or codes for transforming legends and myths into visual images. These formulae enable us to understand the process of communication that took place through the use of concrete, representational forms. The human figure was essential for visual narratives. While captions were often used, the viewer who was familiar with popular mythology could grasp the meaning visually through characteristic gestures, human actions, and symbols associated with heroes, gods, and goddesses....

Next, the classical representation of the human figure depended on both careful observation and the process of abstracting or generalizing. There is ample evidence that the artists studied and analyzed the human figure with care and skill, yet classical Greek sculptors and painters, unlike the later Romans, stopped short of what we might call "realism." Their observations were balanced by a concern for a canon or an ideal. Finally, the classical artisans sought to create the illusion of space; they were interested in the interaction of figures and background. While scientific perspective was not worked out until the Renaissance, these earlier artists understood that overlapping shapes and diminishing scale could give the illusion of volume and three-dimensionality. Although the classical code was modified and transformed throughout the centuries, these fundamental principles of visual narrative have persisted throughout western culture.

Early Christian Rejection of Images

Wherever the apostles traveled in the Greco-Roman world they confronted cultures in which images were basic forms of public communication. To the Gentile, the second commandment was an absurdity; but to the apostles, as to their Jewish ancestors, the images of gods and heroes, votive sculptures, and mythologies in stone were idolatrous as well as irrelevant in a world governed by God. Moreover Paul's preaching and missionary activity among the Gentiles came at a time when early Christians looked toward an imminent return of the Messiah and a radical transformation of the whole order of society. Paul's eschatological view of the world, as well as his emphasis upon faith alone, contributed to his devaluation of classical culture.

Even when messianic hopes dwindled, later church leaders had to cope with a hostile pagan environment in which images played a major role in communicating and perpetuating religious and political authority....The early church fathers were opposed both to the meanings expressed in the classical images and to the aesthetic forms themselves. Tertullian, for example, insisted that not only was the worship of an idol forbidden, but also the making of an idol by a Christian worker. In the early church, painters of idolatrous pictures were compared to harlots, drunkards, brothel keepers, and actors. Tertullian's views about images are very close to rabbinical attitudes, which forbade the making of a likeness of any kind. This stalwart iconoclast did not approve of the depiction of anything—sacred or secular; he believed that "for the servants of God the whole expanse of the universe is thus excluded for the purposes of such an art" (Bevan, 1940, p. 86).

The Alexandrine patristic theologians, Clement and Origen, also argued against the making of images. While these men assimilated the classical learning of Greece and transformed much of its philosophy for Christian theology, they rejected Greek culture's visual aesthetic. Clement refers to Moses, who "made an express and public law against the making of any carved or molten or molded or painted image and representation, in order that we might not direct our attention to sensible objects, but might proceed to the intelligential." For Origen, pagan image worship drags the soul down instead of directing the mind to a divine invisible reality. Clement, echoing the Platonic view, also maintains that images are not "true." Human beings are images of God—but an image of the image, the statues made in the likeness of human beings and far removed from the truth, appear only as a "fleeting impression." He considered preoccupation with images as "madness in a life" (Bevan, 1940, pp. 107, 87).

Yet in spite of these denunciations, paintings began to appear in the ritual spaces of early Christianity. Scholars have speculated about the reason for the gap between the strictures against images and their growing importance in the church. While educated theologians assimilated and transformed the philosophical traditions of the classical world, the common people they sought to convert and instruct were accustomed to images, to *seeing* sacred stories.

Missionaries and apologists preaching and teaching the Christian gospel in the Mediterranean world came face to face with country and urban people who had learned their religious, social, and political views primarily from narrative images and objects. If the church wanted to appeal to these groups and communicate to them, it had to speak, at least in part, that common visual language. Some church leaders understood this. Paulinus, Bishop of Nola, recognized that in order to attract people to Christianity from pagan religions, images were important. He was one of the first leaders to justify such pictures as a means of instructing the unlearned in sacred stories. The crowds who came to St. Felix were, in his words, peasant people "not devoid of religion but not able to read"; they were converted to Christian faith through gazing at images of the works of the saints (Godschmidt, 1940, p. 63; Bevan, 1940, pp. 124-125). In contrast to Tertullian's earlier world-rejecting attitudes, Paulinus expressed a positive view of images and their uses in conversion and instruction.

Yet even before this, some Christians had begun to appropriate visual language in some ceremonial spaces, and in the environment of classical culture a Christian iconic aesthetic slowly emerged. By medieval times churches had over the centuries found a narrative role for the visual arts similar to that of the classical world. On their facades were carved the figures and stories of sacred history; inside there were images and objects—representations in glass, paint, wood, metal, and stone—which served as aids to devotion. Yet always present, ever ready to erupt, was a persistent aniconic attitude which resisted and often sought to reform such use of the image. Bernard of Clairvaux expressed this in the 12th century, while iconoclastic movements surfaced dramatically during the Protestant Reformation. I want to highlight certain moments of the past which illustrate how religious concerns may evoke both an iconic and aniconic aesthetic.

Toward an Iconic Aesthetic

In the Roman catacombs and in the Christian baptistry at Dura-Europos, a garrison city on the Euphrates at the border of the ancient Roman empire, important instances of pre-Constantinian painting in ritual settings have been found. In the catacombs frescoes of the late second and third centuries embody the basic conventions of Roman painting, while at the same time significantly modifying its forms, functions and symbols. The paintings are located in areas that had special meaning to the individual and community. Christian burial was accompanied by the expectation of resurrection and Christ's return, and at these burial sites the images celebrated victory over death and anticipated the world to come.

Clearly the primary concern of the Christian community was not technical proficiency in representation, but the expressive significance of the image. For example, there is no comparison between the beautifully crafted images in the Pompeiian Villa of Mysteries and the small, sketchy ones that appear in Roman catacombs. In this respect Christian paintings resemble those found in pagan and Jewish catacombs of the time. Art historian Ernst Kitzinger has called attention to the aesthetic revolution that occurred during the third century in which "classical art transformed itself." Christianity did not, he says, "spearhead" these new forms; but since it grew rapidly during this period, it appropriated the aesthetic (Kitzinger, 1980, pp. 19-20; Weitzmann, 1980; L'Orange, 1965).

From the reservoir of this late classical style Christian artisans drew the fundamental language of the human figure, its gestures, expressions, and actions in space. However crude the drawing or painting, Christian faith and hope could be "told" through figural representations. Moreover, the apparent lack of technical skill or concern for style contributed to the animated, expressionistic rendering of the human figure that suggested soul or spirit. This was a symbolic asset for Christians primarily concerned with the non-material and transcendent dimensions of human experience.

Some paintings in the catacombs seem to be portraits of the deceased, while others illustrate biblical motifs. Popular subjects included the Three Hebrews in the Fiery Furnace, the Sacrifice of Abraham, and the Good Shepherd. Most scholars agree that deliverance through God's action is a major theme expressed in both Old and New Testament symbols....Some of the portrayals are cryptic—the Eucharist, for example, was frequently symbolized in a small vignette of loaves and fish—while other signs were conventional. The fish became a popular one, deriving its significance from an acrostic based on the initial Greek letters of the words "Jesus Christ, Son of God, Savior."

Since the catacombs were not places of public worship, their images suggest an unusual attempt to express faith. Art historians have contrasted the sepulchral representations of the catacombs to traditional didactic religious art, interpreting images of exhortation and encouragement. They can also be viewed as a confessional art. Against the background of Christian hope for deliverance and confidence in resurrection, the images are like prayers, which have both a private and a public dimension. This experimental aspect, particularly prominent in the extreme situation of persecution, appropriates the late classical aesthetic to communicate an intensity and pathos which later disappears. With the conversion of Constantine the relationship between faith and image changed, and after the early fifth century, the catacombs were only infrequently used for burial.

A different kind of religious painting was discovered early in the 20th century. At Dura-Europos excavations uncovered the remains of many kinds of religious sanctuaries, including a Jewish synagogue and a Christian baptistry. A garrison city at the outer edges of the Roman empire, Dura-Europos was a multi-cultural crossroads and caravan city inhabited by people of diverse religious traditions. After it was attacked and destroyed about the middle of the third century C.E., desert sand covered the ruins of the city until its accidental discovery.

Paintings from both the Jewish synagogue and the Christian baptistry at Dura-Europos have provided extraordinary material for scholars who previously had only fragments to work with....

In his study of the baptistry, Karl Kraeling, one of the Yale scholars associated with the Dura excavations, has proposed three principles to help our understanding of its images. First, interpretation should be in keeping with the general historical and cultural context to which the decorations belong. This context should be understood to include the pictorial decorations and pagan temples and the Jewish synagogue at Dura. Second, any interpretation should keep in mind the purpose which the baptistry served, that of solemnizing the baptismal rite. Third, it should develop as far as possible out of those Christian sources that are most clearly related to the region from which the decorations come and to the purpose which they serve (Kraeling, 1967, pp. 178, 179; Rostovtzeff, 1938). Kraeling has also emphasized the close relations between the paintings and contemporary liturgy, analyzing the images of the baptistry in light of the liturgical and literary sources that were available to the small Christian community in the mid-third century. He has found the selection of images and their organization on the walls are particularly suited to the rite of baptism which took place there.

First and most important is the baptismal font on the west wall. Within an arched niche of the baptistry is a curved shape with a painted image of the Good Shepherd watching over his sheep and carrying a large one on his shoulders. In the lower left-hand part of this area is a crude sketch, almost graffiti-like, representing Adam and Eve with a tree and a serpent. Although the room is small, on the other walls are several painted vignettes. These include Christ's healing of the paralytic, who literally takes up his bed and walks; Christ walking on the water, reaching out to a sinking Peter as other disciples watch from a boat; the woman at the well; and David and Goliath.

A large, fragmented set of paintings related to the resurrection story covers the east and north walls. Taken together, all of these images emphasize the theme of salvation through the work and person of the savior, Jesus Christ. To these early Christians victory over sin and death was associated with the rite of baptism. Like the images found in the synagogue, these were related to the liturgy and derived from the baptismal practices and doctrines familiar to the local congregation.

Thus, in spite of the rejection of images by early church fathers, Christians did use them in their ritual spaces. However, the catacombs and the baptistry at Dura-Europos reveal only a very modest appropriation by Christians of the rich formal language of classical art. It was not until the Constantinian era that the visual arts began a dramatic development. Under the political leaders of the Holy Roman Empire, church building and decoration accelerated. The church of San Apollinare Nuovo in Ravenna was built between 494 and 526 during the reign of the Arian ruler, Theodoric. When the city later came under the domination of the Emperor Justinian, some changes in the church's interior were made, and the building was reconsecrated by orthodox Catholics.

The interior wall surfaces above the columns of the nave are covered with three levels of shimmering mosaics. On the left wall, at the lowest level, are figures of female martyrs processing toward Mary, who is seated on a throne and holding the Christ child. To the right, on the south wall, is a parallel procession of male martyrs moving toward Christ. These processional figures replaced earlier mosaics which depicted King Theodoric and members of his court. On a second, higher level are single, majestic figures of Old and New Testament heroes which fill the space between the clerestory windows; above these are panels depicting sacred stories from the gospels. Mosaics on the north side describe episodes from the teaching and ministry of Christ, such as the raising of Lazarus and the healing of the paralytic and the man possessed by demons. Opposite, on the uppermost level of the south wall of the nave, a symbolic sequence moving from the altar toward the western entrance tells the story of Christ's passion, his death, and resurrection.

Such scenes are to be understood not only as visual narratives, but as representations of the liturgical drama: "The Savior's life, death, and resurrection did not happen once in the dim past but take place mystically within the faithful themselves as they are enacted in the liturgy" (von Simson, 1948, p. 79). The biblical subjects at San Apollinare Nuovo, like those of the Dura Baptistry, appear to be selected and arranged to reinforce the liturgical rites that occur in the sacred space. At the same time, it needs to be noted, as Kitzinger has done, that originally the prime space, the lowest level, was filled with mosaic images of the Ostrogoth king and his retinue which ended up before the representations of Christ and the Virgin (1980, pp. 62-64).

By the late sixth century, images were found in churches throughout Christendom, but certain dangers accompanied their widespread acceptance. Gregory the Great sanctioned the narrative role of images, yet made a fundamental distinction between worshiping an image and learning from it. Responding to a bishop from Marseilles, who had broken up pictures in his church to prevent his congregation from offering homage to them, Gregory concluded that the bishop was right to forbid the worship of images but wrong to destroy them:

> It is one thing to offer homage to *(adorare)* a picture and quite another thing to learn, by way of a story told in a picture, to what homage ought to be offered....If anyone desires to make images, do not forbid him; only prohibit by all the means in your power the worshipping of images. (Bevan, 1940, p. 126; on the Orthodox use of images, see Benz, 1963, and Ouspensky & Lossky, 1983)

Gregory's distinction between learning from images and paying homage to them restored and institutionalized one of the principal functions of classical visual images—the story-telling or narrative role. At the same time, he was clear about their misuse. His attitude reflected and shaped the subsequent use of images in western Christendom. Throughout Europe, Christian motifs and symbols appeared in churches, baptistries, and sepulchres. Liturgical objects, reliquaries, and sarcophagi were embellished with images, and manuscripts were handsomely illuminated with pictures illustrating the sacred stories of Scripture.

The examples used thus far reflect ways in which image usage by Christians drew upon the transformations of Greco-Roman forms set in motion during the third century. Over time these changing pictorial conventions were used to communicate Christian symbols and enliven liturgical spaces. The use of elaborate media, such as mosaics, depended upon the patronage and support of powerful political and religious leaders. Yet those who supported the uses of images in Christian devotion, both public and private, were not preoccupied with what we think of today as art. When paintings and sculptures appeared in churches, they complemented the liturgy and were seen as aids to devotion or acts of piety. Even so, some theologians continued to be uneasy about images in worship spaces.

Medieval Developments

In the 12th century appeared two Christian thinkers who responded to the visual arts in opposite ways. Suger, the Abbot of St. Denis, was a spokesman for the importance of the arts in the expression and evocation of faith. His work and writing affirmed the visual arts in worship. Suger's contemporary, Bernard of Clairvaux, on the other hand, is known for his criticism of images and his reforming vigor in bringing aesthetic simplicity to the buildings of the Cistercian order. Nevertheless, in Cistercian architecture there are important visual elements, and even in the total absence of images the buildings present an aesthetic of their own.

Both Suger and Bernard were symbolists, yet their activities and attitudes resulted in contradictory kinds of Christian aesthetics. They differ most notably on the use of figural art in the embellishment of liturgical space. Suger's aesthetic illuminates the philosophy of the *via affirmativa*. Material objects, whether natural or made by human hands, can inspire devotion, enhance meditation, and lead the soul to the experience of transcendence. Bernard's emphasis upon asceticism and his concern for the primacy of the word in religious communication, however, led to a renunciation of visual images, particularly for monastics. Bernard's thought provides the basis for a *via negativa* in the visual arts, a rejection of images in pursuit of spirituality. This attitude, detected in some ancient and medieval thinkers, would surface again in 20th-century artists in search of transcendent reality.

Suger was influential as a medieval advocate for the use of the arts in communicating and celebrating the gospel....Panofsky attributes Suger's religious aesthetic to his interest in the ideas of Pseudo-Dionysius the Areopagite. A mixture of neo-Platonic and Christian doctrines, these ideas described the fluid, vital connections between the highest spiritual sphere and the material world. Since all visible things are "material lights" that mirror the ultimate Light, the contemplation of objects can lead to the source of all goodness and being. In appropriating the mysticism of the *via affirmativa*, one could apply it to all natural objects and artifacts.

> This stone or that piece of wood is a light to me....As I perceive such
> and similar things...they enlighten me and soon, under the guidance of
> reason I am led through all things to that cause of all things which
> endows them with place and order, with number, species and kind, with
> goodness and beauty and essence, and with all other grants and gifts.
> (Panofsky, 1979, p. 20) ...

Recent interpreters of Suger argue that...he found the arts conducive to religious contemplation, grounded in the physical beauty of the building. "Religious architecture was here performing what sensitive and imaginative souls might consider to be its proper function, namely offering a foretaste of paradise through the senses...it brings heaven down to earth" (Kidson, 1987, p. 7). Suger himself noted in a later passage that the liturgical images and objects are not in themselves salvific. It is the Eucharist that is essential, and he agreed with his more ascetic critics that "a saintly mind, a pure heart, a faithful intention" are central to religious devotion. But he insisted that devotion expressed through beautifully crafted objects was appropriate.

While the abbot's efforts focused on the redecoration of St. Denis near Paris, other 12th-century churches exemplify the increasing presence of images for instruction and contemplation. St. Mary Madeleine in Vézelay, central France, is one of the best preserved of the Romanesque pilgrimage churches. Although it was damaged by fire as well as by iconoclasts of the French Enlightenment, one can still find there rich and beautiful examples of Romanesque architecture. It allowed for the circulation of the pilgrims throughout the sanctuary, in the aisles, around the ambulatory and down steps into the crypt beneath the altar, which once housed relics associated with the patron saint. A modern pilgrim can still move in and out of its spaces, following the narratives that 12th-century stone carvers created out of biblical stories, moral allegories, and the virtues and vices.

At the entry to the sanctuary are three portals whose...general theological symbolism is clear: These portals through which worshipers pass into the ritual space of the sanctuary dramatize the Incarnation. Over the south portal the tympanum depicts the birth of Christ, the moment when "the Word became flesh and dwelt among us," the human beginning of the mystery of the Incarnation. Above the north portal the sculpture on the tympanum portrays the appearance of Christ to his disciples on the road to Emmaus and his ascension into heaven. The large central portal is generally assumed to represent Pentecost: the manifestation of the Holy Spirit to the followers of Jesus and the beginnings of the church.

While interpretations of some details of these portals may differ, it seems clear that these gateways to the liturgy and sacraments depict the essential message of Christian faith. God assumed the form of a human being and dwelt among us; after Christ's resurrection he appeared to his disciples and commissioned them to go throughout the world to teach and preach; and the Holy Spirit came to them to manifest his living and continuing presence. Missing in these portals is the story of the crucifixion, death, and resurrection, for that part of the Christian drama takes place within the sanctuary, in the liturgy itself....

To some religious leaders the images at Vézelay and other churches were tolerated primarily as a means to instruct the illiterate. For persons deeply committed to the religious life no such aids to devotion were necessary. Indeed for those called to the monastic life, images were considered a distraction and, worse, a shameful extravagance.

Bernard of Clairvaux: The Aniconic Aesthetic

The opinions of Suger's contemporary, Bernard of Clairvaux, who objected to the use of images and objects in the church and sought to eliminate them, were expressed in a famous letter to William, Abbot of St. Thierry. He writes critically of the "usual" custom of images in churches, describing them as "curious carvings and paintings which attract the worshiper's gaze and hinder his attention" (Holt, 1957, p. 19). But, he adds, let this comment pass if bishops, responsible for both the "wise and unwise," are unable to arouse the devotion of worldly people by spiritual things and try then to do so by material adornment. While Bernard is willing to tolerate images under certain circumstances, he completely opposes them in monastic churches. Bishops may have an excuse for permitting images as a means to devotion; monks do not.

> But we who have now come forth from the people; we who have left all the precious and beautiful things of the world for Christ's sake....Whose devotion, pray, do we monks intend to excite by things? (Holt, 1957, p. 20)

In the course of his letter, Bernard develops a number of objections. One passage shows very clearly his preference for "the word" as he offers what has become a recurring argument:

> In short, so many and so marvelous are the varieties of divers shapes on every hand, that we are more tempted to read in the marble than in our books, and to spend the whole day wondering at these things rather than in meditating on the law of God. (Holt, 1957, p. 21)

For Bernard, worship and contemplation were centered on the word of God. He would have had little sympathy for Suger's position that images can initiate and inspire reflections on God's glory in ways that words cannot. At most, he would have admitted validity of the image only for the uneducated.

Bernard reinforced his position by pointing to the exploitation and abuse of images. In the same letter to William he observes that in the presence of material splendor, persons are more "kindled to offer gifts than to pray."

> Their eyes are feasted with relics cased in gold, and their purse-strings are loosed. They are shown a most comely image of some saint, whom they think all the more saintly that he is the more gaudily painted. Men run to kiss him, and are invited to give; there is more admiration for his comeliness than veneration for his sanctity. (Holt, 1957, p. 20)

Elsewhere, Bernard showed an appreciation of images and a sensitivity to a different kind of offense: their desecration and defilement. He notes that where pictures of saints are inlaid on floors, insensitive persons spit on an angel's face and the "countenance of some saint is ground under the heel of a passerby" (Holt, 1957, pp. 20-21; Schapiro, 1977, pp. 6-10).

Finally, Bernard's arguments gather ethical force and intensity in a condemnation that reminds one of the wrath of the prophet Amos when he lashed out at those who sold the righteous for silver. "The church," Bernard writes, "is resplendent in her walls, beggarly in her poor." Churches adorned with glistening, wonderfully fashioned precious objects feed the eye of the rich at the expense of the indigent. Stones are clothed in gold while human beings go naked. And while some people find delight in images, the needy find no relief. Bernard concludes with indignation, raising the question of the church's priorities and responsibilities: "For God's sake, if men are not ashamed of these follies, why at least do they not shrink from the expense?"

He was convinced that the arts were an unnecessary luxury and that Christians ought first of all to be concerned for the poor (Holt, 1957, pp. 20-21).

While Bernard was critical of the visual arts, he assiduously cultivated the arts of writing and preaching. For him the word was paramount in religious communication. Etienne Gilson has written that the Cistercian leader, schooled in the tradition of Cicero and Augustine, took great pains with writing. Bernard's walls were bare, but his literary style was not. "In spite of all his formidable asceticism St. Bernard was no puritan when it came to literature" (Gilson, 1940, p. 63)....

Bernard was one of the most powerful and influential churchmen in 12th-century Europe;...[his] emphasis upon the nourishment of faith by preaching and Scripture has a profound effect upon church building, where his influence led to the development of a different kind of aesthetic—a religious symbolism that was aniconic, that is, devoid of representational imagery....

Like other monastic groups, the Cistercians [Bernard's community] constructed their monasteries as complex, self-sufficient functional units. In view of Bernard's position on the use of painting, sculpture, and ornament, one might conclude that the power of visual forms would be negligible in churches built under his influence. But a particular type of beauty resulted from this rejection of images and the creation of fitting places for liturgy and contemplation. Out of their concern to develop simple, imageless spaces came certain visual elements and principles which constitute a distinctive aniconic aesthetic....

Cistercian scholar Conrad Rudolph points out that the elimination of paintings and sculpture is designated as a restriction to the monk alone. Gregory the Great had already presented the authoritative position on imagery in the western church, justifying it as a means of instructing those unable to read for themselves. Thus the Cistercian strictures were addressed to "literati," the monastic communities....

Elements of an Aniconic Aesthetic

As they clarified liturgical space in their sanctuaries, Cistercian builders fused abstract shapes and functional forms into a new symbolic and ornamental order. In contrast to the sculptured images at Vézelay, they developed aniconic, or imageless, metaphors and symbols....

A primary visual element in these churches—light—has its own symbolic associations with divine reality....Light reveals itself at the same time that it reveals other things. Moreover, a luminous body—the sun, for example, which sends forth light continuously—seems to suffer no loss of substance. Bevan points out further the traditional association of light with truth, joy, awe, and glory (1957, pp. 125-150)....

Both aesthetically and symbolically, the dominant feature of Cistercian light is its revelatory quality. On the one hand, bright clear light reveals human and inanimate forms in all their starkness, neither embellished nor clothed by color. This disclosure is congenial to the Cistercian emphasis upon humility and purity and their quest for simplicity. But light itself becomes a symbol of divine, ineffable reality—the source of being as well as of seeing. Its clarity and brilliance may easily become a visual affirmation of the mystical poetry expressed by the psalmist: "In thy light do we see light."

A second formal and symbolic element in the Cistercian aniconic aesthetic is the use of abstract shapes—circles, halfcircles, squares, and ellipses—which orchestrate a variety of spaces....In contrast to the narrative sculpture at St. Mary Madeleine, no stories are being told. Yet the simplicity and purity of the primary geometric shapes generate symbolic overtones. One may deduce a kind of "meaning" from the deliberate elimination of representational imagery and from the resolve to use only pure forms as ornament. These decisions can be linked to a larger, more ancient mystical tradition in which numbers, abstract forms and relationships symbolize religious knowledge and experience; knowingly or not, Cistercian builders were constructing a similar aniconic aesthetic in which visual experience itself undergoes a purification. Materials are purged of concrete references to familiar human experience. Through the intensification and amplification of pure geometric forms one is drawn into an environment that empties the mind of all images and prepares it for ritual.

A third element in the Cistercian aesthetic is the concern for order and proportionality. Peter Berger in *A Rumor of Angels* refers to "signals of transcendence," experiences that point beyond natural or human reality. The first of these signals is the human propensity for order.

> Throughout most of human history human beings have believed that the created order of society, in one way or another, corresponds to an underlying order of the universe, a divine order that supports and justifies all human attempts at ordering. (1970, p. 53)

This desire for order, he says, is grounded in faith or trust in the ultimate order of the universe. The search for order is metaphysical, rather than ethical, and gives cosmic scope to the human need for meaning. What we may regard as a "signal of transcendence" in our contemporary secular world was, in the medieval world, a profound certainty....

Cistercian concern for order is distinguished by its clarity and transparency. The unadorned structures emphatically display the principles of balance, rhythm, repetition, and the proportionality of related shapes and spaces. Like the simple shapes, the principle of order has symbolic power as well as functional effectiveness....

While light is a symbol common to both the iconic and the aniconic aesthetic, so also are order and unity in complexity. Architectural elements, however, devoid of images, can express these abstract symbols in a powerful way. Moreover, an austere clarity and simplification were at times requisites for mystical contemplation, as Dionysius pointed out:

Now when the mind, through the things of sense, feels an eager stirring to mount toward spiritual contemplations, it values most of all those aids from its perceptions which have the plainest form, the clearest words, the things most distinctly seen, because, when the objects of sense are in confusion, the senses themselves cannot present their message truly to the mind. (1972, p. 103)

This passage is especially instructive, suggesting that unadorned, distinct forms have particular value for contemplation.

A deeper dimension of the visual language of the imageless aesthetic is suggested when, in *The Mystical Theology*, we read of the renunciation of the self and of all things so that in purity the self is led upwards to the "ray of that divine Darkness which exceedeth all existence." Through stripping away, through the purification of the tangible, one ascends to unity with God. Emptiness, silence, even bewilderment—in Dionysius' words, the "darkness of unknowing"—characterize the journey by which the medieval mystic was united with the One who is wholly unknowable. In their passion for simplicity the Cistercian builders developed an architectural expression of the awesome beauty and emptiness of the *via negativa*. The stark forms are a fitting context for the "true initiate into the darkness of unknowing" who, renouncing understanding, "is enwrapped with that which is wholly intangible and invisible...beyond all things" (p. 194)....

It is important also to remember that the spare, mathematical beauty of these Cistercian churches was enlivened by liturgy and humanized by the literary forms. A rich verbal symbolism—stories, allegories, sermons, the reading and interpretation of Scripture—replaced the visual narratives of Vézelay....

Although their attitudes toward images indicate different assumptions and interests, the aims of Suger and Bernard were similar. In neither of these medieval thinkers was there any sign of a gnostic tendency to locate evil in material substance. Each in his own way transformed cultural forms to express and shape religious communication. Since their aesthetic gifts, sensibilities and communities differed, they chose contrasting media to witness to and awaken the life of the spirit. As we have seen, Suger selected the most precious objects and images to enhance the liturgical setting. Committed to poverty and simplicity, Bernard and his followers ruled out such adornment. Still, both 12th-century men were leaders for whom Christ became a transformer of culture. The ascetic Bernard has indeed been described as "a poet, a creator." To put the artist Bernard in perspective, Leclercq has written that the "extreme frontiers of literature...open into the whole realm of the ineffable." But even for Bernard the word of God yielded to the inexpressible. Leclercq quotes Bernard as saying, "What takes place between God and me, I can feel, but not express. When with you, on the contrary, I try to speak in a way that you will understand." Yet in the same passage Bernard cautions, "Prepare not your ear but your soul; for it is grace that teaches it and not language" (Leclercq, 1961, pp. 328-329). Suger's concerns may be understood in similar ways. The visual arts are used as a means to communicate on a human plane, to lead persons toward the vision of God, but they are not the vision itself. The bond between Suger and Bernard was their common concern for liturgy. While differing in their attitudes toward particular arts, they were equally passionate in appropriating cultural forms for use in public prayer and worship. Suger's ultimate defense of the arts was that they serve the mystery of the Eucharist. Bernard's monks, in their worship, contributed poems, hymns, reflections, and sermons. It was indeed through liturgy, Leclercq notes, that all human resources attained their final potential and were offered to God in homage and in recognition of the source. "In the liturgy," he writes, "love of learning and the desire of God find perfect reconciliation" (p. 308).

Triumph of the Image

In the Middle Ages the use of images became widespread throughout Christendom. While Cistercian functional forms contributed to the development of Gothic architecture, Bernard's strictures ultimately had little impact outside the order....By the 13th century the iconic aesthetic reigned supreme....

In their theological statements medieval churchmen reinforced and extended earlier positions which justified the use of images for particular purposes. Their arguments generally followed the line of reasoning established by Gregory the Great: Images provided a narrative of biblical history and religious instruction for the unlearned, just as reading the Old and New Testaments enabled the educated to learn about their faith from the Scriptures. In addition, these images were considered a tangible, visible aid to devotion and contemplation. In this connection Thomas Aquinas spoke of the "double character" of the movement of the soul toward the image. The soul, he said, moves toward the image insofar as it is an inanimate carved or painted object. At the same time, the soul is attracted to the image because it represents a reality other than itself. But, like Pope Gregory, Aquinas emphasized that *no veneration at all* is offered to the image itself—the carving or painted surface. Through the image or object the devout person may express devotion, not to the object, but to that to which the symbol refers. When the representation points beyond itself to Christ, it is Christ who is venerated (Bevan, 1940, pp. 150-151). As aids to instruction and devotion, visual symbols became an integral part of medieval culture....

In developing arguments for the use of images Paulinus of Nola, Gregory the Great, Thomas Aquinas, and others were recognizing the persistent human need for aids in approaching and symbolizing transcendent reality. While their historical perspectives differed, all were attempting to clarify the role of visible and concrete symbols in Christian pedagogy and devotion and to make important distinctions between the material representation and the divine reality it symbolized. Yet such distinctions often became blurred, particularly in the popular piety of the uneducated and unsophisticated.

The Protestant Challenge

The extravagance of medieval Catholic culture became a common concern of 16th-century reformers. Their reforms were more radical and pervasive than those of Bernard and the Cistercians, whose objections to images had long been overshadowed by the grandeur of late Gothic art and architecture. The Protestant Reformation came with such force that the iconic aesthetic itself was shattered along with cathedral images.

For Martin Luther the arts were important for instruction and as aids to devotion, and in this respect he stood apart from other reformers. The disagreements can be seen clearly in the conflict with his colleague Andreas Carlstadt, who rejected both church music and religious images as distractions, and, most important of all, interpreted the sacraments of the Eucharist as purely spiritual. The key issue in this dispute, underscored by historian Roland Bainton, was Carlstadt's disparagement of all material objects as aids to devotion. Bainton singles out the essential clue to Luther's attitude toward the arts; for Luther, the spirit and flesh were never disjoined. In his devotions, he was "aided by the sight of the crucifix, the sound of the anthems, and the partaking of the body of Christ upon the altar" (1966, Vol. 2, p. 25). Thus Luther maintained a sacramental view of the unity of flesh and spirit, acknowledging the mystery of the relationship between the visible and the invisible. And as Luther's reformation proceeded in Germany, his followers did not deface or destroy the art and architecture they took over. Moreover, for Luther the liturgy offered new dimensions in musical expression.

The most far-reaching aesthetic transformations arose through the influence of John Calvin and Ulrich Zwingli, whose reforms went beyond Luther's. Calvin rejected all images as aids to devotion—even the crucifix—and permitted only a simple cross. Although he allowed the congregation to sing psalms, Scripture was the primary guide and aid to devotion. Zwingli, for his part, rejected both music and images. Although he himself was a talented musician, who from an early age had shown great interest in music, he ultimately eliminated it from liturgy.

Zwingli formulated his most complete arguments against images late in 1524 or early in 1525 in a document entitled, "An Answer to Valentine Compar." He builds his case against his critic Compar on the distinction he makes between true and false Christian belief. The true believer, said Zwingli, is one who trusts God alone as an absolute and unconditional good. Since the true believer knows that help, protection, grace, death, and life rest solely in God's hands, there is no need to erect another "father, helper, solacer, or protector." Anything or any person placed between God and self encourages idolatry. Zwingli consistently used the term "strange god" in describing the psychic process that occurs in one's interior life when something or someone displaces God at the center of existence (Garside, 1966, pp. 163-166).

Such "strange gods" included not only images but also wealth, power, prestige, possessions—anything that directs one away from God....All idolatry originates in the human tendency to place ultimate confidence and loyalty in material objects or some cause other than God. An important additional factor, however, is Zwingli's sympathy toward a kind of Platonic dualism which tended to devalue the material world. Thus, unlike Luther, he rejected the cultural homage that medievalists brought to the eucharistic mystery and so desacralized all material elements as aids to devotion. (In this respect historians have emphasized the profound effects of Erasmus' thought on Zwingli's views. Although he never broke with the Catholic church, Erasmus had a tendency to dematerialize and rationalize worship; in Zwingli's thought, a similar pattern developed.) Zurich's churches became highly rationalized, functional spaces in which liturgy consisted essentially of the preaching and hearing of the word of God. "Faith," writes Zwingli, "is from the invisible God, and is something completely apart from all that is sensible. Anything that is body, anything that is of the sense cannot be an object of faith." After all the images were removed and the churches whitewashed, he found them to be positively luminous: "The walls are beautifully white" (Garside, 1966, p. 160). Thus all of the arts that had for centuries witnessed to Christian faith were unequivocally rejected....

The radical reshaping of liturgy by Zwingli, however, denied any sacramental relationship; materiality and faith were separated. The believer was oriented to God solely by faith and Scripture. Christian worship centered not on the Eucharist but on the reading, hearing, and interpretation of the Bible. Emptied of visual images, liturgical space became a place in which preaching and the reading of Scripture were paramount.

In his efforts to root out what he considered idolatry, Zwingli developed an anti-sacramental theology which demystified the unity of flesh and spirit. The separation of the expression of faith from material substance was complete, and even the starting point of the *via negativa* was lost. Moreover, this severely rational, imageless liturgy was imposed on the whole community of believers, lay and ordained. Eventually, music was reintroduced into Zurich's churches, but the theology and liturgy of the Swiss reformer dramatically changed the relationship between Protestant artists and religious institutions....

We have briefly traced the functions of the visual arts as purveyors of religious meaning as Christian culture assimilated two contradictory aesthetics: the aniconic tradition of Judaism and the iconic conventions of the classical world. Over time the figural, visual language observed on ancient monuments—friezes and statuary, for example—was continually transformed by Christian artisans and served a number of functions. Like ancient visual narratives, the carved images at Vézelay and Chartres helped to define the status quo and to legitimate the prevailing social order, reminding believers of what values they should emulate. In the Middle Ages visual images instructed the unlettered in both Scripture and doctrine; in the liturgy they served as aids to devotion and the nurture of faith.

The asceticism of the radical reformers had a marked influence on the role of the visual arts in church and culture, and this influence extended to the New World, particularly in New England, where Protestant settlers laid a foundation for a new relationship between invisible faith and visible forms.

5

Communicative Form and Theological Style

Paul A. Soukup, S.J.

In March of 1519 Froben's press in Basel issued the second edition of Erasmus' New Testament, the first having been published three years earlier. While scholars criticized the first edition for errors introduced when Erasmus rushed it through the presses, preachers and mobs stirred against the second edition because Erasmus dared to change one word in the translation. Where the Vulgate had *verbum* in John 1:1, Erasmus substituted *sermo*: "In the beginning was the Word" became "In the beginning was the speech" (Boyle, 1977, pp. 3-6).

First defending his decision on philological grounds and on usage by the Fathers (hardly anyone before Jerome had used *verbum* to translate *logos*), Erasmus soon switched his defense to one based on theological method. Since theology imitates the divine Logos, a misunderstanding of that Logos will inevitably lead to bad theology.

> Erasmus believed passionately that only the appropriately correct word could flower into true theology; semantic error must necessarily generate theological error. Thus while he refrained from pronouncing *verbum* unorthodox, Erasmus was nevertheless convinced that this translation of *logos* eclipsed the ancient faith in a Christ who is the Father's eloquent discourse to men, leaving only a corona of truth visible to the trained eye. *Verbum* or *sermo*? The implications for theological method are substantial, for Erasmus held the *Logos* as the paradigm of human language, whose most eloquent expression was true theological discourse. (Boyle, 1977, p. 30)

The implications for any consideration of communication and theology are substantial for this argument claims, in short, that the form of theology influences the subject matter of theology.

In association with her study of Erasmus, Marjorie Boyle speculates that Latin theology's use of *Verbum* leads to a confusion between revelation and the doctrine of the only-begotten Son. Both are *Logos*, a fact that the Fathers used to show the continuity of creation and redemption, and the contiguity of God's Word and the human word. Augustine's psychological theory of the trinity in the *De Trinitate* makes brilliant use of each of these associations. At the same time, he clearly relates the one Son of God with the one Word, something that would have become more problematic had he used speech (*sermo*) or discourse (*oratio*) rather than word (*verbum*). *Verbum* suited Augustine's purposes well since, as a wordsmith, he considered the activity of the word one of the central activities of human life.

Other instances in the history of theology demonstrate a similar link between the form of theological language or discourse and its content. When the interpretation of Scripture rests in an oral context (in liturgy or in preaching), its corresponding theology consists of stories. Such stories usually move to moral interpretations, providing guides to life and activity. Both the Jewish tradition of midrash and the patristic accounts of the desert fathers provide examples of this trend. When the interpretation of the Scriptures becomes textual interpretation, scholars replace orators and pay greater attention to definitions, to the logic of the text, and to the systematic development of ideas. Unsurprisingly, their texts take on lives of their own and the Church begins not only to proclaim the Gospel but also to adjudicate competing theological claims. The content of theology becomes increasingly more speculative and technical. The scholastic period with its emphasis on definitions and systems and its explorations of the nature of God and creation illustrates this trend (see, for example, Stock, 1983, pp. 526-527).

This essay explores the ways in which the form of communication affects the content of communication—how the choice of word determines the thought—with special emphasis on theology. Its purpose is pragmatic: How can we, today, concretely reflect on communicative form in such a way as to improve the teaching and the practice of theology? The essay moves in three steps: First come some general comments on communicative form, bolstered by an historical review of the clearest form-content influences; next follow some remarks on contemporary communicative style and form; finally, some brainstorming about theological disciplines and communication concludes the essay.

From Oral Culture to Print Culture

Despite the potential novelty of its application to theology, the connection between form and content should not surprise us. Literary studies and aesthetics have acknowledged it, literally for centuries. For example, one can say things in a lyric poem that do not fit prose. Recall Macleish's famous line, "A poem does not mean but be." Conversely, prose expresses meaning and argument in ways unsuited to poetry or music. Orators choose rhetorical forms in accordance with their theme and purpose. Artists, sculptors, composers and, more recently, film makers do the same. Neil Postman stresses this point in a negative form when he writes, apropos of television and evangelical religion:

> Most Americans, including preachers, have difficulty accepting the truth, if they think about it at all, that not all forms of discourse can be converted from one medium to another. It is naive to suppose that something that has been expressed in one form can be expressed in another without significantly changing its meaning, texture or value. Much prose translates fairly well from one language to another, but we know that poetry does not...To take another example: We may find it convenient to send a condolence card to a bereaved friend, but we delude ourselves if we believe that our card conveys the same meaning as our broken and whispered words when we are present. (1986, p. 117)

The form in which theology (or anything else) resides affects what can be said, how it is said, and how people perceive it.

A larger (cultural) question arises with a consideration of communicative form as opposed to literary or presentational form. Historians of communication have noted an association between the style of communication and and cultural styles. Harold Innis, one of the first to comment on this, points out that cultures which choose "time-binding" communication (permanent materials) tend to develop locally while those which choose "space-binding" materials tend to spread out more widely (1951). Others examining how cultures without time- or space-binding materials could still maintain their level of development over centuries argue that oral cultures have highly developed means of retaining and retelling their deposit of knowledge.

Walter Ong (1982) summarizes much of this discussion by dividing the occurrence of communicative form into four overlapping periods, which succeed one another temporally (at least in the West), each giving rise to a different kind of culture: oral culture, chirographic (written) culture, print culture, and secondary-oral culture. The communicative form of each culture influences the patterns of consciousness of the members of that culture through what Ong terms the "psychodynamics" of the form. These patterns of consciousness include not only how people think but also what they think about.

Oral culture (the predominant culture from which the Bible emerges) depends on recall: People only know what they can remember. Names become especially important and powerful, for without a knowledge of names one has no knowledge at all. To know a person's or a thing's name is to have the power of understanding that person or thing. Patterns of recall also take on great importance: Rhymed verses, formulaic utterances, and proverbs both format knowledge and constitute thought (p. 35).

Other psychodynamics of orality appear more clearly in contrast to the psychological structures fostered by literacy. (1) Oral thought and expression (inseparable in practice) follow an additive style in which the speaker joins ideas or events by a series of "ands." On the other hand, chirographic and print structures subordinate one idea to another, using a variety of clauses and conjunctions. (2) Oral styles aggregate clusters of terms (the rosy-fingered dawn, wily Odysseus) and employ parallelisms, epithets, and antitheses. Once the culture creates these clusters they tend to stay clustered; to the literate ear, they seem clichés because literacy fosters analysis and the originality of style that comes from taking received phrases apart. (3) The oral mind expends its energy in recalling the phrases; the literate mind has energy for analysis since the written text provides the recall. The economy of writing also allows a direct style; the reader can always turn back a page to re-read something. The oral style must provide a degree of redundancy to allow the hearer to catch what might not have registered on first recital. (4) In a similar way, the oral style must conserve past knowledge in its recollections; few new ideas emerge as the community depends on the wisdom (and memory) of its elders. Written style on the other hand fosters exploration of new things since writing frees the mind to move beyond what the culture knows without risking its loss. (5) The oral culture stays close to the human life world, speaking of everything in relation to the people of the tribe or group. Even something as potentially abstract as craft instructions come to the hearer in terms of the actions of a master carpenter, for example. Chirographic and print cultures simply move to the abstraction and illustrate their text with drawings or pictures where necessary. (6) Finally, oral thought is collective or participatory thought. Everyone in the group shares the thought since thought exists only in its expression. Moreover, narrators and hearers alike often take on the first person identities or personae of the heroes whose exploits they tell. In contrast the written culture promotes objectivity since writing establishes a distance (at least on the page) between the text and the reader. The content of the telling becomes foreign and object-like (Ong, 1982, pp. 36-70).

Oral and chirographic thought patterns correlate with particular kinds of consciousness. Members of an oral society tend to operate with situational or pragmatic thinking: Objects and people have value in terms of what they can contribute or accomplish. On the other hand, chirographic cultures produce formal logic which allows people to judge individuals or objects on the merits of abstract qualities or in terms of abstract categories. In other words, the oral mind depends on individual names whereas the mind supported by writing seeks definitions. Because of their orientation to particulars, members of an oral society tend to have an externalized consciousness. They know themselves in terms of their roles in society, in terms of their possessions, or in terms of their families. Members of a chirographic culture tend to possess a self-consciousness characterized by interiority. They know themselves as individuals with particular motivations, with their own thoughts, and with a certain choice of options. Finally, members of an oral society work from an operational intelligence—intelligence indicates ability in practical settings. For societies dependent on writing, intelligence indicates verbal ability—intelligence tests in our culture, for example, primarily measure vocabulary and verbal activities such as the logical combination of words (Ong, 1982). Each of these differences manifests what Denny has termed the move from contextual thought to decontextualization (1991, p. 78).

The switch from an oral culture to a chirographic culture did not happen quickly but took place over thousands of years. Contemporary scholarship suggests that certain periods of history show the strains of the change-over more than others. For example, in Athens of the fifth century B.C., Socrates and Plato wrestled with the growing abstraction and logic that writing permitted while at the same time they questioned the oral substructure found in Greek epic poetry (Havelock, 1963). Almost 800 years later, Augustine still stresses the important role of memory (a necessity to the oral psychology) but in terms of its role in self-consciousness (a development fostered by writing's distanciation).

Another 800 years later scholastic theology and philosophy reflect the appropriation of written logic by the intellectual elite. The schools produced marvelously complex systems of grammar, of philosophy, and of theology. However, one would at least expect some failure in communicating the fruit of these labors to an illiterate population. Stock (1983) outlines some of these tensions in terms of medieval heresies, popular uprisings, theological misunderstandings, and scriptural interpretations.

With hindsight, we can suggest two solutions to the problem of communicating medieval theology. First (the one deliberately chosen at the time): One could make use of oral forms to embody theology—hymnody, stories (the *Divine Comedy*, for example), the use of "heavy characters" (that is, characters who typify the abstract concepts we wish to convey, characters such as those abounding in hagiography), as well as images (Miles, 1985), architecture, and role-bound social interactions. Second (the solution that proved more long-lasting but less predictable): One could strive to develop some technique to foster universal literacy. Where writing took too long to produce the materials needed to teach reading, printing provided an inexpensive means for the rapid duplication of texts (Eisenstein, 1979).

Although the psychological impact of printing on the individual consciousness does not differ all that much from that of writing, it does differ dramatically in its effect on the collective life of cultures (Eisenstein, 1979, pp. 71-159). Printing fosters all the psychodynamics of writing but makes them available for everyone simultaneously. However, it also does more than make texts available for individual reading. Printing changes the nature of authority in a culture—individuals need not depend on elders, teachers, or pastors for knowledge since everyone has equal access to knowledge. For example, in religious belief, the Protestant Reformation stressed the priesthood of all believers since all had immediate experience of the Scriptures. One needed no mediator except Christ.

Printing also facilitates critical thinking by making texts common and involving more people in the the process of gaining and ascertaining knowledge. The availability of texts allowed cross-referencing and correction of errors from one edition to another. But scholarship also became more impersonal as reading replaced face-to-face dealings. A scholar no longer had to travel from one library to another but could now possess volumes at home. This gave the scholar more time for studying books but indirectly moved learning away from discussion, debate, and dialogue to study, thought, and writing. Careful (written) argumentation replaced rhetoric in the academic curriculum.

This scholarship also undermined the accepted notions of authority. Authority had belonged to ancient books (and still did), but textual criticism cast doubt upon the inerrancy of the ancient texts. (This is another reason for the resistance that Erasmus met in publishing his critical edition of the Bible.) Further, new books attributed their composition to personal authors who often contradicted one another. This gave people even more reason to doubt what they read and to insist on some method of learning or critical evaluation—something that only the individual reader could do.

Printing affected the culture of the West in other, more subtle, ways. Since printing standardized books and typefaces, it led to an acceptance of standardized or uniform practices in many other areas as well: handwriting, manufacturing, indexing. The latter activity profoundly changed how knowledge existed and how people used it. For example, the application of laws depended not so much on the memory of a judge as on the arrangement of the laws in standardized reference works. Knowledge became static even while it grew in volume.

Printing also affected day-to-day life in the culture. On the one hand it fostered a common culture as people from all over read the same materials and shared the same stories. But while this common culture grew, individuals became progressively more isolated. Reading is, after all, a solitary activity. One needs quiet for concentration. And so, another side effect of the spread of individual reading is "the development of the sense of personal privacy that marks modern society....Print created a new sense of the private ownership of words" (Ong, 1982, pp. 130-131). Ong puts this state of affairs even more dramatically:

> By removing words from the world of sound where they had first had their origin in active human interchange and relegating them definitively to visual surface, and by otherwise exploiting visual space for the management of knowledge, print encouraged human beings to think of their own interior conscious and unconscious resources as more and more thing-like, impersonal and religiously neutral. Print encouraged the mind to sense that its possessions were held in some sort of inert mental space. (pp. 131-132)

Besides these changes the very content of communication changes as well. When manuscripts were expensive and scarce, the culture passed on only the most valued materials (usually the Bible, theological works, important governmental documents, and some practical learning—note too that these items are the ones valued by those who control the means of textual reproduction). As printing brought the cost of duplication down, more things are printed besides those already mentioned: first scholarly works, then popular entertainments and self-help books, novels, literature, and so on. The privacy of print and the introduction of new "gatekeepers" also encouraged the printing of "private" materials like pornography.

When the churches took advantage of print, they did so in ways to provide necessary resources for the development of faith. The Lutherans stressed the Bible and produced not only vernacular translations but also materials to teach reading. Catholics maintained the importance of the hierarchical church and produced devotional materials for the faithful. Both groups produced catechisms for the uniform teaching of doctrine. This form, made possible by printing, had a profound effect on theology, for it demanded a particular kind of theological thinking to frame question and answer responses in order of ascending difficulty. Other theology became more popular as the churches moved into the publishing business in the 18th and 19th centuries: Religious presses produced popular books, pamphlets, hymnals, and even newspapers.

Television as a Communicative Form

The review of the effects of changes in communicative form from oral to chirographic to print overwhelms us with evidence that much of what we take for granted in our communication styles could be otherwise. However, the fact that we can comprehend oral and chirographic societies supports Ong's claim that we presently live in a "secondary-oral" culture, a culture which has returned to oral patterns as its communication styles move from print to speech based on printed scripts. The review also suggests that we should expect to notice similarly momentous effects in our culture as we incorporate new communication patterns and forms.

Television, more than anything else, characterizes contemporary communicative style in the United States. As a mass medium driven by commercial forces, it encompasses the effects of earlier mass media (newspapers, magazines, radio, and film); it shares in and supports the commodity structure of developed capitalism; and it combines the oral and visual qualities of earlier media but without demanding the concentration of reading or attentive listening. What, then, might television teach us about contemporary communicative style? To situate our answer, we will look at some social and psychological effects of television.

Television consumes time. People today spend, on the average, large numbers of hours watching television—averaging over four hours a day (Gerbner, Gross, Morgan, & Signorielli, 1986, p. 19)—time that in an earlier age they would have spent on other things. Recreational reading has decreased; so too has game playing and conversation. The demise of weekday devotions in churches may be as attributable to the television alternative as it is to changing popular piety.

Television partially supplants the family, the school and the church as the socializing force in American society (Comstock, 1978). By introducing a variety of images, statements, and values into the home, it proposes a wider repertoire of behavior to people than they would otherwise have. Television also provides basic knowledge about society, about right and wrong, about appropriate behaviors, and about the world at large. While families and schools still play a large role in people's lives (at least measured in terms of hours of contact), churches do not; even more critical to the churches is their practical disappearance from the television world.

Television concentrates economic and interpretive power in a society in which economic power reigns. Some, notably George Gerbner and his associates, have argued that this gives television the form of a dominant religion which defines the world, defines the worldview, and defines the successful values in the world. In addition, television interprets events and images in terms of its world in just the way the medieval church, for example, interpreted events for Western Europe. This gives television (and those who appear on television) an immense authority in contemporary society.

> Television provides, perhaps for the first time since preindustrial religion, a daily ritual of highly compelling and informative content that forms a strong cultural link between elites and the rest of the population. The heart of the analogy of television and religion, and the similarity of their social functions, lies in the continual repetition of patterns (myths, ideologies, "facts," relationships, etc.), which serve to define the world and legitimate the social order. (Gerbner, Gross, Morgan, & Signorielli, 1986, p. 18)

However, it is an authority gained not from any expertise nor from any civil or religious role but from the omnipresence of television.

All these factors work together to reinforce the status quo and to homogenize cultural groups. Television, then, adds stability to the national culture and provides common experience for millions of people. What McCombs and Gilbert assert of the news media applies all the more to television:

> Considerable evidence has accumulated since 1972 that journalists play a key role in shaping our pictures of the world as they go about their daily task of selecting and reporting the news....Here may lie the most important effect of the mass media: their ability to structure and organize our world for us. (1986, pp. 3-4)

Although we cannot measure it exactly, the form of this dominant means of communication does act on what we communicate.

Structurally, television has changed many elements and institutions in the United States. Its development shifted radio from a national medium into a local medium. Made-for-TV films have transformed the traditional Hollywood production houses and have advanced an independent book trade. More seriously, television has altered the shape of politics: Gone are the days of the whistle-stop campaign and hotly debated issues. A candidate's image often counts for more than the candidate's issues. Television has also reshaped religion. Religious television has done away with the community, with the sacred space of worship, and with the separation of sacred and profane (Postman, 1986, pp. 118-119). The same set that sells bleach now sells salvation.

Television also has psychological effects (Postman, 1986, pp. 92-107). Its pacing accustoms us to rapidly shifting images. What we gain in the ability to deal with visual complexity we lose in the ability to maintain an attention span over a long period of time. The nature of the medium suppresses content, particularly abstract content, in the name of visual interest. Because television must above all maintain interest, it opts for entertainment. And so, it confuses fact with fiction: We have news stories and docudramas, soap operas and happy news talk. Television avoids reflection, preferring instead presentation.

> The power of the media lies not only (and not even primarily) in its power to declare things to be true, but in the power to provide the form in which the declaration appears. News in a newspaper or on television has a relationship to the "real world," not only in content but in form; that is, in the way the world is incorporated into unquestionable and unnoticed conventions of narration, and then transfigured, no longer for discussion, but as a premise of any conversation at all. (Schudson, 1982, p. 98)

Stories develop in an uncritical manner—the pace counts, not the plausibility. This psychological formula has such power that the successful religious programming on television explicitly imitates it: There are religious entertainment shows, religious talk shows, and religious dramatic shows. Few, if any, of them demand an examined life of their viewers.

But we cannot claim that the communicative form of television supports only ill effects. On the positive side, it heightens our visual senses and sharpens our appreciation of symbols, particularly condensation symbols. It can restore a sense of presence and immediacy lost in writing or print. It touches emotions, bringing them closer to consciousness, restoring a psychic balance missing from linear or logical reasoning. By joining visual and oral communication into one image, it integrates the nonverbal with verbal communication. Finally, television can also promote an appreciation for more complex narrative structures. Television viewers generally watch stories with multiple plots and multiple perspectives (the varying camera angles, for example). More ambitious shows explore non-linear story lines and juxtapose events and images to create a feel for the characters and their histories.

In short, whether structurally or psychologically, television is a medium through which anything can come. And it is a medium, a form, that shapes its content, just like any other form. The nature of the interaction that takes place through television (and indeed through all the mass media) features entertainment, limited content, fragmentation of presentation (that is, variety of content), unidirectional address, a lack of reflection (or self-consciousness), and commercialism. The nature of the interaction also fosters an appreciation of symbols, emotions, nonverbal communication, and complexity of narrative style.

Theology and Form

Writing in *The Rhetoric of Religion*, Kenneth Burke, American rhetorical and literary critic, forcefully argues the validity of an analogical relationship between theological principles and the nature of language, between theory (if you will) and narrative. Implicit in his argument lies the claim that linguistic form can predict theological form. His argument nicely summarizes what we have considered in a roundabout way through the history of oral and written cultures. Narrative, he writes for example, expresses first principles in quasi-temporal terms—the Genesis accounts of creation and covenant deal with principles of governance (power and authority) in terms of the stories of creation and fall (1961, p. 180). This clearly reflects an oral background. Theology, in contrast, deals with logical firsts, with essences, distilling from the narrative of Genesis ideas of authority, order, and obedience. Writing and print, of course, facilitate this kind of analysis.

Burke also sounds a warning that the condensation of temporal sequences into their logical forms can lead to metaphysical problems. Using as an extended analogy the musical distinction between a dissonant chord and a melody consisting of the same notes, he writes:

> In keeping with our chord-arpeggio distinction, the metaphysical problem could be stated thus: In the arpeggio of biological, or temporal growth, good *does* come out of evil (as we improve ourselves by revising our excesses, the excesses thus being a necessary agent in the drama, or dialectic, of improvement: They are the "villain" who "competitively cooperates" with us as "criminal Christ" in the process of redemption). But when you condense the arpeggio of development by the nontemporal, nonhistorical forms of logic, you get simultaneous "polarity," which adds up to good and evil as consubstantial. (p. 229)

By the same token, logical analysis does not translate well into narrative. Logic gives deeper insight into motivation, relationship, human socio-political order, and so on. Despite its problems, logic (or theology) is more flexible and allows application to more situations than does narrative. The danger for theology (and for narrative) is the danger of its form, particularly for people who neither know nor understand the form.

What does all this mean for theology and pastoral ministry today? First, and minimally, we have seen that contemporary communicative forms move away from logic and analysis, providing instead an emphasis on symbol, emotion, and perspective. The theological preparation for pastoral ministers should then stress the translation of theological content into a form that neither betrays it nor alienates it from people's lives. But this must take place carefully, stressing an understanding of the form as well as an understanding of the content. Unfortunately, current educational practice tends to stress content over form.

But, second, because the current communicative culture participates in what has gone before it (because of its secondary orality), it can never force us to forego even partially our theological heritage. Past theology can well be understood and appreciated, given the necessary preparation. A reflection on its form may well help to understand its nature.

Third, we should expect theology to change and develop as it shapes itself to the communicative forms of the 20th century. Where this happens uncritically, as with the "theology of material success" of the television evangelists, the Church and its members will suffer (Fore, 1987). But when careful reflection leads us to use the newer communicative forms effectively, we can expect both a deepening of theological thought and a more profound effectiveness of theology in culture (much the same way that the theology of liberation has transformed some third world cultures).

What, then, might some tasks be for theology in the light of these reflections on communicative form? Here are some immediate thoughts about theological directions and disciplines from the perspective of someone working in the area of communication.

Somewhere along the line theology must recover its sensitivity to the analogical character of language. As theology has become more "scientific," it has become more sensitive to the critique of the linguistic analysts and seen its own task as one of explication, interpretation, and reasoning—in the manner of linear thought. And yet theology has an ally in language (communication) itself: There is a sacredness in language. Theological reflection shows an awareness of this sacredness from time to time, beginning with the Johannine prologue and continuing with subsequent wrestling with the notion of the *Logos*. The recovery of the communicative intensity of theology may well involve renewed meditation upon the *Logos* as a central theological category.

From this flows an interpretation and explication of the Word that takes advantage of our contemporary sensitivity to symbols. The study of Scripture can supplement its gains in critical analysis with new reflection on the multiple senses of Scripture.

Liturgy has retained its close association with communicative forms and liturgists have experimented with ways to recover more of its ritual roots in action, in music, in dance, and in drama. The task for liturgy today goes beyond this; now it must integrate a congregation which has accepted the role of an audience from all its usual communication fare.

Christology can greatly benefit from contemporaries' appropriation of condensation symbols since the image of Christ is such a symbol. While the Church's theological reflection must continue in its efforts to understand Christ, the Church should also exploit Christ as the symbol of the new humanity in its teaching and proclamation.

The theology of God (the Trinity) might add to its current focus material drawn from ideas of communication as relationship. Classical formulations of the Trinity use the language of communication. It may well be helpful to explore the analogy further, given today's new knowledge about communication.

Ecclesiology might contrast differing styles of communication. Mass communication clearly exhibits one-way styles; to the comfort of the Church, we can recognize that not even in its most hierarchical times did the Church ever approach the unidirectional monologue of television. Ecclesiology could include more specific considerations of dialogue as a communicative style. It could also add reflections on roles and leadership based on communication.

A theology of the human person should certainly begin from the experience of human community. As we move away from print-based ideas of culture, we can stress again the common basis of our humanity in language, in families, and in communicating groups.

Historical theology may find more light in a correlation of communicative styles and communicative form with theological conclusions. We have already gained an appreciation for the cultural embeddedness of theology; the addition of communication as a part of culture may add yet another dimension to that understanding.

Fundamental theology might also benefit from this meditation on communicative form since its purpose is to prepare the proclamation of the Gospel by addressing issues of culture, authority, and interpretation.

This brief review of topics in theology barely scratches the surface of what might happen when an appreciation for communication interacts with theological disciplines. As an exercise in brainstorming it suggests the possibilities. Best of all for teachers and students, it requires no additional courses for pastoral ministry. However, it does require something much more difficult: a rethinking of theology's treasures in the light of our new communicative forms.

The hope is this: to become like the householder who brings out from the storeroom things both old and new (Matt. 13:52).

6

Ministry in an Age of Communications

Robert F. Leavitt, S.S.

The phenomena of mass communications have created an entirely new situation for evangelization in the modern world. Vatican Council II's *Decree on the Instruments of Social Communication* forms the contemporary equivalent of Trent's having issued a decree on "printing." The Church, in effect, has recognized that changes in the media of communication such as we have seen in the modern period present totally new conditions, opportunities, and problems for proclaiming the Christian faith.

Evangelization undergoes much more than a change of "vehicles" of communication when culture's dominant communications media shift from from oral to textual to electronic forms. It essentially submits itself to a new pattern of social relationships, subjective awareness, and even to a new epistemology. The medium has its own message which interacts dynamically with the messages it carries.

In this essay, I will reflect on the new conditions and issues facing ministry in a communications age. Starting with the "ministry of the Word" as my fundamental category for ministry, I will attempt to enlarge its range of application to all ministry and to the media of communications. This will lead to a philosophical reflection on how three different interests shape knowledge and its communication and how these interests relate to the ministry of the Word. Finally, I will conclude with a series of opportunities and challenges facing ministry in an age profoundly influenced by modern communications.

The Ministry of the Word

In my opinion, theological reflection on ministry in an age of communications properly starts with the ministry of the Word. I will begin, then, by analyzing this concept and expanding its application from proclamation to sacramental and pastoral ministry.

Vatican Council II defined the priest's ministry using the classic tripartite division: Ministry of Word, Ministry of Sacrament, and Pastoral Ministry. The Council made a significant new assertion by identifying the Ministry of the Word as the priest's primary ministry. Its primacy logically depends on the nature of Divine Revelation that, in Scripture, is understood as God's Word. And, since the mission of the Church is to serve and proclaim that Word, its first and essential ministry must be a ministry of the Word.

I emphasize the ministry of the Word, a "communicative ministry," within the threefold ministerial pattern because the theme of the "Word" links critical theological categories like Revelation, Scripture, Tradition, Kerygma, and Incarnation. So, logically and naturally, this central theme should also define our notion of ministry.

From the start, however, I wish to assert emphatically that an approach to ministry in general through the angle of the ministry of the Word does not imply any diminution of sacramental or pastoral ministry. On the contrary, I believe that the motif of the "Word" brings out the depth and unity of all ministry—precisely as a service of God's revelation—whether that ministry occurs as preaching, liturgy, or pastoral care.

After the council, the primacy of the ministry of the Word was taken to mean that priests should have (1) a deeper knowledge of Scripture and (2) a greater competency in preaching. These two emphases have shaped priestly ministry so much in the last generation that one could say that the axis of the priesthood has now shifted from a predominantly cultic to a communicative mode.

This shift in the priestly axis has had an influence on other ministries as well. The emphasis on Scripture and the pastoral priority of evangelization now virtually characterize all ministries. But, it would be a mistake to limit the ministry of the Word to Scriptural knowledge or preaching. Instead, we should expand the concept to unify a whole variety of ministerial actions.

(A) I would first expand the meaning of the ministry of the Word in a broadly hermeneutical direction. One always presumes in biblical knowledge and preaching the ability to interpret Scripture and the situation of the Church. Christ's final commissioning of the disciples in the Gospel of Matthew is "Go teach all nations." This missionary call has a deeper hermeneutical challenge buried in it. For "teaching" implies interpreting a message, and teaching the "nations" presumes interpreting their cultures.

We can easily forget that the historic process of interpreting the Gospel has literally produced the Christian tradition. Tradition itself is essentially an ongoing development and application of foundational revelation. The Word of God, as Vatican II understands it, embraces both biblical foundational revelation and the revelation that occurs through the processes of tradition. Layers of tradition are secreted by the Church's historic effort to communicate and practice the Gospel in each culture. In the Roman Catholic view, this "traditioning" process is itself a vehicle of God's own self-communication inspired by the Holy Spirit.

Tradition, of course, largely occurs through the ministry of the Word in all its diverse forms. It occurs in prayer, preaching, catechesis, biblical commentary, creedal formation, theological reflection, and doctrinal definition. It achieves its most profound expression in liturgy, which celebrates God's Word, and in witness, which gives it existential and moral specificity.

Various kinds and levels of interpretation, then, constitute what we call "tradition." Knowing the biblical Word, in the Catholic sense, implies also knowing the Word of tradition. Knowledge of these two "words" means following the Christian interpretative process as it unfolds in history. The ministry of the Word, from the earliest Kerygma to Vatican Council II, embraces the breadth of Christian faith.

(B) The ministry of the Word, as we have said, is not limited to proclamation, nor is it confined to the diverse hermeneutical activities which constitute tradition. It can be expanded to include sacramental ministry as well. Since the time of scholastic sacramental theology, we have affirmed the essential role of the word in sacramental experience. The word is a constitutive element of the sacramental sign. Prior to catechesis or proclamation, we find a word at the interior of the sacramental sign as such. Whether or not we speak of this as the "form" of the sacrament, the sacramental word constitutes a ritualized first level exegesis of the sacramental symbol. The union of visible symbol and sacramental word constitutes the nature of the sacrament. So, I would claim that the ministry of the Word appears within the sacramental ministry itself.

(C) Finally, we can explain how pastoral ministry also connects to the ministry of the Word. I regard pastoral ministry as a specific hermeneutics of the Gospel primarily employing the grammar of action to interpret the Christian message. Actions themselves speak, and often more powerfully than words do, because they embody complex physical and social commitments. They communicate pragmatically and symbolically at once.

So, one could say that Christian meaning threads like an implicit proclamation through all pastoral activity. The ministry of the Word links up in many ways to pastoral ministry. Pastoral counseling, for example, consists essentially of a communicative therapy designed to uncover and resolve emotional problems. In it, the language of feeling, with its own logic, joins to the language of faith recast in psychological terms. Spiritual direction, to take another example, uses the metaphors of faith as an exegesis of the existential realities of human life. Finally, group communication in all its forms is one of the most important aspects of contemporary pastoral ministry. It requires skills for enabling group processes to take place effectively and for interpreting the results of group interaction.

In virtually every form of pastoral activity, then, we discover some communicative dimensions—proclamation, interpretation, celebration, and mediation. One could even view pastoral ministry as a hermeneutics of pastoral action modeled on the hermeneutics of religious texts.

To go one step further, the expanded application of the ministry of the Word resembles what Lonergan (1972) calls "communications" in his list of theological functions. He regards communications as the critical activity in engendering and preserving community. So, all ministry is in some way "communicative" since it aims not only to interpret the Gospel but to serve the community of faith itself.

It is my conviction that just as the philosophy of language has come to occupy a central place in our theory of knowledge and subjectivity, not to mention action, it also can help us unify our concepts of revelation and ministry. Ecclesiology, and its subcategories like ministry, needs the resources of language-theory, symbolism, and hermeneutics to develop a full picture of the Church's life. That is why I believe that the ministry of the Word, in all its forms, supplies an important thread in the fabric of ecclesiology, especially when the Church seeks to proclaim the Gospel in a culture like ours so shaped by communications media.

Yet, while I wish to integrate different Church ministries in the theme of the Word, I do not wish to imply that the life of faith can ever be reduced to language. Speaking certainly accompanies life, but without exhausting it. A word-centered theology and ministry easily stumbles into verbal quicksand. This happens, for example, when a constant liturgical "chatter" voices over sacramental experience and gluts it with excessive commentary. Or, when a sort of pastoral verbosity accompanies the dense symbolism of direct service. The preferred language of revelation and faith is the language of metaphor. As we have rediscovered the centrality of parable, story, and narrative in Scripture, we need to keep these modes of discourse in mind for liturgical and pastoral life as well.

Our emphasis on the ministry of the Word, therefore, does not mean that faith is always a talking faith. Speaking with God and about God ultimately serves living for God. The Kingdom of God may be announced, but it arrives as an event in the lives of people. Ministry of the Word must identify symbols of the Kingdom in the midst of human life so the people can recognize and respond to this "event" of grace and its analogues. God's Word comes to us like the rain, making a new life possible in the tissue of our earthly existence.

Having expanded the idea of the ministry of the Word to mean the "communicative" dimension of all ministry instead of simply a limited repertoire of homiletic or catechetical activities, we can now move to consider the communicative situation facing ministry today. I propose to do this using Jürgen Habermas' theory of human interests to give a philosophical focus to this discussion.

The Theory of Human Interests

Jürgen Habermas, in *Knowledge and Human Interests* (1971), argues that there are three classes of human knowledge, and that each class is grounded in and controlled by a specific human interest. (1) Scientific-technical knowledge is guided by an *instrumental interest* in controlling and manipulating reality; (2) humanistic knowledge is shaped by a *communicative interest* in understanding human culture; (3) social-critical knowledge is motivated by an *emancipatory interest* in overcoming ideologies and distorted communication.

I propose to use Habermas' schema of interests, and their corresponding classes of knowledge, to focus the tasks of the ministry of the Word in modern culture. These tasks, it seems to me, fall into one or another of these three interests and their related knowledge groups. Ministry today clearly adapts to a technological culture and takes advantage of technical instruments in carrying out its mission. It is also obviously concerned with interpreting and applying its religious tradition in the contemporary world. And, finally, ministry ultimately hopes to contribute to the redemptive liberation of human beings and their culture. Thus, the *communication* of a faith-tradition for the sake of genuine *salvation* using the *media* of modern communications effectively defines Church ministry. Reflecting on technology, tradition, and emancipation is one way, then, to appreciate the different challenges our culture poses for the ministry of the Word today.

The interest in technology

The scientific-technical fields include the hard sciences, the applied sciences, and the new knowledge-groups related to communications, systems, and management. These fields are linked together by their common interest in expanding our ability to manipulate the physical or social world. They enable us to understand certain phenomena because we want to control a specific environment.

The field of communications technology, in particular, rests on modern discoveries in physics, electronics, optics, and laser technology as well as on linguistics and language-theory. Today, we understand better than ever before how human communication works and how to manage the media of mass communications to accomplish specific objectives. The technologies of television and computers, now being merged in a new hybrid with immense implications for culture, support and influence this. Video tapes keep expanding our capacity to preserve and transmit information and entertainment. Teleconferencing makes possible a new dimension of human dialogue among subjects separated by thousands of miles. We already live in the age of "desk top printing," and may soon see the era of personal producers of programs.

The discovery of superconductors will vastly change the present generation of communications technology in the years ahead. The fantastic capacity for speed and miniaturization that new conductors provide essentially makes this communications revolution possible. Minute conductors, which can code much more data, have established the conditions for advanced communications systems. The transistor, quaint as it now seems, was the first letter in a new alphabet of communications technologies and possibilities.

The technology of the instruments of communications (television, computers, graphics, etc.) and the sciences of human communications (linguistics, rhetoric, advertising, etc.) have created the conditions for mass culture. This has unpredictable and far ranging effects on human activities which are primarily communicative: entertainment, politics, commerce, and religion. These spheres of human activity have been altered significantly when the primary communications medium of culture has shifted, first from an oral to a written, and then from a print to an electronic system. Each shift has introduced a set of technical advantages (face-to-face immediacy, preservation, dissemination in space, instantaneous and entertaining dissemination in space and time) along with a corresponding set of epistemological preferences (talk, reading, scholarship, entertainment) (Ong, 1982).

The ministry of the Word has adapted to oral, written, and print communications media. Now, the issue is how it will adapt to an electronic medium. This is not a mere horizontal substitution of one medium for another, but the addition of a new level of instrumental effectiveness along with a new set of communicative biases. These biases represent the ideological dimensions of mass communications or its inherent capacity to distort human communication in a certain way because its own structures require it (Innis, 1951). Writing, for example, removes the process of question and answer which is inherent to human dialogue; it compensates for this by requiring "more writing" in the form of rejoinder or commentary. Television, on the other hand, restores visual contact but is shaped by the requirements of transforming all content into an entertaining mode. The technology itself dictates the shape and style of the content it transmits. This raises the question of what happens to the religious phenomenon when its leading communications style moves from oral (or print) media to electronic media.

The interest in understanding

The second knowledge group consists of the humanities (history, literature, philosophy, the arts). These disciplines express the universal human interest in communication itself. I speak, though, of the communication of ideas and understandings. The arts and humanities promote the acquisition and interpretation of varieties of cultural meaning: historical events, classical texts, philosophic ideas, and aesthetic works. These form the substantive records of human culture in which we can understand ourselves. They are the evidence of the meanings and purposes which human beings have discovered in the course of history.

Since the end of the 19th century, numerous social philosophers have attempted to unify the theory and method of the humanities under the rubric of hermeneutics. Hermeneutics refers to a general theory of interpretation of signs. Because there are different kinds of signs, however, we need different kinds of hermeneutics (legal hermeneutics for law, biblical hermeneutics for scripture, historical hermeneutics for history, etc.). Hans-Georg Gadamer, in *Truth and Method* (1960/1975), has developed a broad hermeneutical theory intended to inform our experience of history, language, and art. His central doctrine holds that human beings are essentially constituted by their traditions and that their subjectivity is so deeply interwoven with their history, language, and art that being human really means living out and recognizing the tradition that has made us. We may study our tradition as if we existed above or beyond it, but we are more creatures than students of it. Hermeneutics, then, really means knowing that we are grasped ahead of time by cultural symbols that shape the consciousness we have. To know ourselves, we have to know our works, symbols, and great texts.

The centrality of the "text" has occupied the attention of another modern scholar in hermeneutics, Paul Ricoeur (1974). For him, the pivotal concern in hermeneutics is the universal phenomenon of language. This unique instrument of consciousness enables human beings to develop a culture and keep expanding the experience of ordinary language into other realms which require special languages (art, science, religion).

However, the changes which spoken language undergoes when it is written particularly interests Ricoeur. These changes make historical and literary hermeneutics necessary since the author is no longer present to interpret his or her work. In effect, the work itself creates both new opportunities and difficulties for interpretation that spoken communication does not.

Linking Gadamer and Ricoeur, we can see that all human traditions survive by taking the form of texts. Art works, of course, endure through the material substance which constitutes them. History can only be reconstructed from the records of events. Language leaves its own signature in writing. So, the "text" forms a kind of model for the transcription of human meaning allowing it to be preserved, interpreted, re-worked, and applied.

In the Church, we understand ourselves by interpreting and applying the tradition of our faith. That tradition comes to us in the dominant religious texts we use: Scripture, Liturgy, Theology, Magisterium. It is interpreted through various kinds of biblical and theological hermeneutics which seek to make us aware of the forgotten levels of meaning buried within the tradition. The ministry of the Word serves faith, then, precisely as a hermeneutics of revelation. But, the fullness of revelation necessarily includes tensions among the great religious symbols deposited in the tradition. Thus, contrasts and conflict always mark theological hermeneutics. The Word of God is too rich for any system or set of categories, and yet we must interpret it and seek an inner logic to the data of revelation.

In the interpretation of the faith, we do not accord equal prestige to all positions. The Magisterium, the official teaching office in the Church, may decide which ways of interpreting revelation are faithful to the Word of God and which are not. This decision inevitably creates problems associated with the exercise of authority and the limitation of expression. Power and force, of any kind, establish conditions that require the resources of another kind of human knowledge, namely, the critique of ideology. It has an interest not so much in understanding a tradition as in analyzing the distortions of human communication.

The interest in emancipation

Habermas calls the third class of knowledge the social-critical sciences. They deal primarily with the problem and effects of repressed or distorted communication. The paradigmatic examples of this knowledge-type are psychoanalysis and ideology critique. One analyzes the domain of psychic forces and the other the world of social and political force. They each contend that truth falls victim not only to mistakes and malice, but also to illusion and the need to justify institutions. So, the social-critical sciences do not aim so much to "understand" a tradition as they do to "deconstruct" it into the disguised forces which operate through it.

As we know, the interest in emancipation goes back to the Enlightenment with its aim to establish a rational society which would break the irrational hold that myths and dogmas had on human intelligence. Freedom of thought, of speech, of assembly represented new social and political objectives. Rigid social stratification (aristocracy and monarchy) and authoritarian religion marked the *ancien regime*. These traditions stood in the way of scientific and social progress by branding certain ideas heretical and forcibly outlawing them. Outdated institutions, the Enlightenment held, could only maintain themselves by force and fear. Once this spell was broken, they would fall and a new order emerge.

The philosophical lessons of the great revolutions of the 18th century gradually took hold. Human emancipation requires a searching critique of the forces which distort free communication and action. Only by unmasking the psychological and social mechanisms which distort thinking and speaking, can people find true liberty. The new philosopher as critic of ideas, dreams, and economic arrangements was born.

While the critique of ideology has largely concerned itself with the subterfuges of the unconscious and false consciousness, it is not limited to that. Habermas himself wants to extend it to that realm of human activity which more than any other characterizes modernity, viz., technology. The distortion of technology, so to speak, results from its rejection of all other forms of knowledge except scientific-technical knowledge as either false or meaningless. The success of technology in the material sphere has allowed it to gain virtual philosophic hegemony in the ordinary consciousness of modern men and women. Truth is scientific truth. Everything else is just opinion. And, all opinions are equal!

The task of the ministry of the Word encompasses not only interpreting a tradition, but unmasking ideology as well. Prophetic proclamation often seeks to identify and condemn an evil made plausible by some legitimation. We simply take evil like this for granted and integrate it into our way of seeing reality. Ideology critique, as part of the ministry of the Word, can be applied to communications itself in three ways.

First, technology (including communications technology) significantly shapes, and in its own way even distorts human communication. Neil Postman claims that television, for example, reduces all programming to entertainment and thus brands all program content with this communications bias (1986, pp. 83-88).

Second, cultural traditions often block discoveries of new social and moral truth and need to be analyzed for their ideological effect. But the interest in emancipation itself can also sweep aside substantive moral traditions in the name of a single tradition of thought, for example, one characterized by radical individualism which only retains procedural values. Such a reigning vision of emancipation is highly ideological.

Finally, the critique of ideology itself is not immune to the ideological virus. When it plays itself out as only a negative critique of other positions, ideology critique seems to avoid the necessity of affirming a position itself. But one cannot postpone moral commitments in the name of ideology critique. Such postponement establishes not true intellectual freedom, but its caricature.

In this part of the chapter we have reviewed three classes of human knowledge and three corresponding interests: technical control, hermeneutical understanding, and critical emancipation. The ministry of the Word has points of contact with all three in its use of media, hermeneutics, and the prophetic denunciation of ideologies. In an age of communications, ministry must understand more than ever the values and problems built into technology, tradition, and emancipation. These constitute its agenda for the present and foreseeable future.

Tasks for Ministry in a Communications Age

In this final section of the chapter, I want to describe some of the tasks facing the ministry of the Word in a communications age. These tasks flow from ministry which attempts to pass on a tradition of faith, for the sake of salvation, using the media of modern communications.

Understanding the epistemology of media

Ministry today at all levels has become wedded to the media revolution. Video tapes, teleconferencing, national televangelism—these form the new catechisms and pulpits of a media culture. The denominational avatars may vary, but the technology is the same.

One might imagine that communications technology, especially television, remains a neutral instrument of the "Word," a lens untouched by the

opacity of perspective or prejudice. But, current studies in the epistemology
of media challenge that. When communication shifts from spoken to written
to electronic forms, the gain in technical control goes hand in hand with
social transformations. Walter Ong, for example, describes the seemingly
innocent advance from oral to written culture as a "transformation of consciousness" (1982). George Steiner captures the nature of the contemporary
shift from a classical written culture (admittedly a class phenomenon) to a
modern entertainment environment:

> Self-bestowal on a text, the vertigo of attention which bends the
> scholar's back and blears the eye, is a posture simultaneously sacrificial
> and stringently selfish. It feeds on a stillness, on a sanctuary of egotisti-
> cal space, which exclude even those closest to one. Today's ideals of
> familial co-existence, of generational amity, of neighborliness are par-
> ticipatory, collective, non-dismissive. Music, performed or listened to,
> meets these social-emotive needs and aims as reading does not. The
> new humanistic literacies where we can fairly make them out, are musi-
> cal not textual. Eloquence is suspect, formal speech is palsied with lies,
> political, theological, moral, which it articulated and adorned. The hon-
> est man sings or mumbles. (1980, p. 10)

In short, entertainment—for that is what music essentially is —has become the modern ideal of communications.

This is precisely Postman's thesis about the nature of television. For
him, the epistemological traits of TV define it as basically an "amusement
medium": affect-centered, image-centered, present-centered, moralistic,
authoritarian, contemptuous of authority, discontinuous in content, immediately and intrinsically gratifying (1986, Ch. 5). These traits, some of which
are contradictory, indicate what a complex communications medium TV really is. These imperatives of the medium transform whatever content goes
on TV. Its structures requires that anything—news, weather, sports, liturgy—be made into entertainment.

Communications media are not value-free. They have their own built-
in epistemology. Polished, yet unobtrusive, the protective coloration of TV
permits it to conceal its own effect on consciousness. It is surely no accident
that the studio layout of the TV evangelists resembles the set for the "To-
night Show." This results less from a conscious choice than from a TV media imperative: Make the set interesting. The eye of the camera lays down
the commandment "thou shalt entertain." It requires this in order to hold the
foreshortened attention span of compulsive channel-changers roaming the
networks for something interesting!

But, some essential features of sacramental religion—like silence and
community—don't play well on TV. Silence is pretty costly and'"viewing"
it is largely pointless. Community participation becomes either the "studio-
audience" or the "audience-at-home." TV makes liturgy into another "show"
one watches. And, at home, on the couch, one's posture and the ritual on the
tube have no essential correspondence.

Religious illiteracy

If communications media impress their own epistemology on religion, the media-curriculum has other implications for ministry as well. The discussion about "cultural literacy" (Hirsch, 1987), for example, has its religious counterpart. Today, schoolchildren can read, but they don't know enough to understand what words really mean. High school students who guess that "Latin" is spoken in Latin America or that Socrates is an Indian chief are culturally illiterate. Similar deficiencies exist present in the religious consciousness of our youth as well.

Believing they have to keep up with TV, schools today are tempted to strike a Faustian deal with communications technology. Perhaps schools can televise some content for students so they'll find it interesting. But, the medium always wins in the end. Detailed knowledge shrinks to "factoids," little information blips without any nuance or background. T.V. has even created print media to resemble itself, like *U.S.A. Today*.

What is happening in mass culture occurs in religion too. Despite the explosion of religious knowledge ordinary believers know less about their tradition. The bumper-sticker, the advertising slogan, the coffee cup, and the monogrammed tee shirt have replaced folk wisdom and religious proverbs as rules for living. Only shorthand can survive the immense bombardment of the mind and senses which modern media create. The slogan—quick, memorable, pithy, funny—copes best with our situation. A faith tradition which wants to give something more, must give it more slowly. Its gravy has to sink in gradually. But media are impatient with the schedule of such traditional fare; they want the novel, the interesting, the entertaining instead.

The unity of genre and message

Modern communications theory has taught us how much the medium influences the message. This principle, however, applies as much to literary media as to electronic media. Biblical studies have long emphasized that literary genres (forms) molded the Christian faith from the start. The Christian message even created its own form, the "gospel," which itself contains sub-forms—infancy narratives, miracle stories, etc. Narrative, prophecy, and proverb do not just express the same thing in three ways; three different literary genres, they capture in different ways the ebb and flow of religious experience. A proverb, for example, may summarize the point of a story, but cannot preserve its rich texture, subordinate messages, or sense of time.

The current interest in Jesus' parables has generated a corresponding interest in the "story form" for preaching and teaching. Traditionally, preaching borrowed classical rhetorical models, but now the narrative model seems to be gaining ground. The eloquent and well-crafted oration (the sermon) yields to the art of the storyteller.

But we should remember that the "form" of preaching always determines the content. The Bible contains at least five dominant genres—story, law, proverb, psalm, and oracle. Each of these genres has communicative potentials the others do not. We would lack a certain wisdom should we limit preaching to the narrative mode; instead we should expand it in the direction of all these genres: telling a story; explaining a principle of conduct; summarizing with maxims; using song, poetry, and prophetic announcement. Each genre adds something to the experience of God.

We should also not confine ourselves to the narrative mode because storytelling is a special art. Not every preacher has the kind of stories that will nourish people religiously. Lacking these, he may be tempted to tell his own story—such as it is—and we unwittingly create a new category of problem preachers in which personal bathos has free reign in the pulpit. More importantly, because religious language is the language of metaphor and symbol, a sense for this language is absolutely essential for preaching and spirituality. Homiletics requires a symbolic-religious sensibility above all. God-talk moves back and forth between the world of common sense and the world of the imagination. It mixes the references of communication so that the familiar/ordinary merges with the unfamiliar/extraordinary. Jesus says in his parables "the Kingdom of God is like..." and this tips us off that identity, dissimilarity, and analogical resemblance are fused together. In Ricoeur's terminology, the real is "metamorphosized" in the metaphor.

The language of ministry

Because symbolic language is central to biblical revelation and liturgy, ministers ought to familiarize themselves with the nature and operation of poetic discourse. By poetic discourse, I don't mean ornamental images which adorn a homily. I mean the sense of metaphor and plot, the world of the imagination which poetic speech opens up. In poetry, and in religious talk, we grasp reality through the prism of metaphoric twists. Religious poetics tries to pry a world open which is always close to collapsing as fact and common sense.

Pastoral ministers should be practical people, but they also need to be equally poetic. Only in this way can they maintain a spirituality integrating pragmatism and inspiration. Ministerial spirituality requires a sense of the depth in human life in order to do this. Good spiritual writers coin metaphors which communicate this depth. The metaphor of the "dark night of the soul" is not the same as the poetics of "compassion." But all ministerial experience is poorer if not nourished by these symbols. Those charged with the ministry of the Word should know the poetic language of faith.

The task of handing on a tradition

One of the major tasks facing ministry today is handing on the Catholic tradition. This includes the Bible, the heritage of the various periods of Catholic history, the teaching of the great councils, the liturgy, and devotional practices. The burden that falls on Catholic schools, catechetics, and adult education to make sure that this happens is enormous. But today both scholarship and technology complicate the problem. Historical research in the tradition has recovered so much detail and conflicting information that one has difficulty in seeing the forest for the trees. A Catholicism once encoded in the creed and catechism has disappeared. However, publishers of theology and religious education materials should not take its place. Vatican Council II should have issued an abbreviated and abridged catechism along with its 16 official texts. Therefore, I welcome the publication of the international catechism as well as a national catechism for the United States. To communicate a rich tradition in a communications age requires abbreviated and easily understood symbols.

Group process

The communications age brings with it an increasingly important feature of contemporary pastoral life: the group. The process of group communication increasingly overshadows the one-to-one communications of counselling. The various species in this "genus" show its inevitability: episcopal conferences, priests councils, pastoral councils, parish councils, finance committees, lay movements, single-issue constituencies. Most priests and pastoral ministers, comfortable with interpersonal communication or preaching, have not learned group dynamics. A new communication situation arises when one is being interviewed by a reporter or debating with an angry parish council. Good intentions alone won't suffice in such contexts. One must realize the different terms on which these kinds of communications take place.

Contemporary situations may require developing skills in group dynamics and media management, and who will deny that they pose new dilemmas for leadership? One now must assess how an issue will "play" in the press and larger community. Strategies of communication bring us far too close to the manipulation of half truths than we might wish to get. Public communications and privileged information, the stock conflict of political administrations, increasingly find their way into church life.

Emancipation and salvation

The ministry of the Word has as its ultimate goal announcing the message of salvation in Christ. Along with proclamation goes the task of interpreting salvation and relating it to the various human quests for liberation and emancipation. Since the Enlightenment, the theme of freedom has become the philosophic motif of all modernity. In alliance with other epochal symbols—equality, the individual, experience—freedom defines the horizon of personal and social hope in the modern period. The task of relating these Enlightenment themes to the message of Christ requires skill, for they not only are patient of religious interpretations, but of radically secular versions of reality as well. Increasingly, the Christian exegesis of modernity has become the prerequisite for relating faith to culture.

Many Catholics felt relief when Vatican Council II seemed to affirm the impulses of modern culture and identified itself with the "joys and hopes" of people. The Church had seemingly emerged from the ghetto and abandoned its negative apologetic. Others, however, question any unqualified affirmation of culture by the Church and even support a highly critical appraisal of the modern world. In essence, this appraisal hinges on the notion of what constitutes true liberation for human beings.

Modern society communicates its popular and elitist visions of liberation largely through the media. Between a chic materialism and a political radicalism, a whole spectrum of images of human emancipation clamor in the media marketplace. Ideology is the coin of modern intellectual commitment. Which party, which school of thought do you subscribe to? Argument and implication are subordinated to party affiliation. Since ideas have consequences, the politics of ideas has become our philosophy.

The ministry of the Word has to take part in the debates which engage our culture, but it also has to avoid the ideological allegiances which seem required to participate in the discussion. So, it must affirm and criticize the religious tradition it upholds without joining the movements where a preestablished doctrine and agenda demand wholehearted support. The prophetic freedom peculiar to the Church is the freedom to develop its teaching without paying dues or homage to the prevailing *zeitgeist*. Religious emancipation is not a rigid method, but a moral and spiritual quest requiring careful discrimination in the realm of ideas.

Above all, the ministry of the Word must understand the ideologies of "salvation" in our culture. For over a century, secularized eschatology and hope have replaced the traditional future-vision of the Church. The development of secularity has, as a matter of fact, contributed a great deal toward our understanding of human liberty and rights. Religious liberty, for example, though now found to be consistent with revelation, was first sketched out from a non-religious perspective. We can incorporate the progress of modernity into the doctrine of the Church, but it takes time.

Today, though, the temptation is to accelerate the Church's acquisition of cultural heritages, including their ideological perspectives. This runs an unusually high risk of sacrificing traditional wisdom and doctrinal centers of gravity. The Church's ministry must master its own wisdom, carefully and in depth, before adapting it to cultural heritages and current ideas. If not, we end up with mixtures of faith and culture which are not truly synthetic, but just popular and trendy. The modern period, with its advanced communications, and demand for novelty, easily reduces the religious phenomenon to another kind of intellectual or personal entertainment. "Do-it-yourself" and "throw-away" religion is truly state of the art! The calling of the ministry of the Word is to resist this reduction and still keep the interplay of faith and culture fresh and creative.

Conclusion

Ministry in an age of communications presents us with conditions, opportunities, and difficulties previously unimagined. We can be equal to the challenge if we seek to understand the epistemological gauze wrapping all knowledge up in interests and much of modern televised communications in amusement. The more self-conscious we become about the world of ideas and the means our world employs to spread, absorb, and criticize them, the more equipped we will be for service of the Word of God. The ministry of the Word consists not just of evangelization, but also of recognition, criticism, and discrimination. Exegeting the "signs of the times" is definitely the most difficult and far-reaching task of ministry today.

7

Models of Church and Communication

William Thorn

Linking models of Church and models of communication is important because the Church is communication, as theologian Avery Dulles has argued (1972). At the same time, political theorists argue that politics is communication; critics and devotees make the same case for works of art; educators echo the aphorism for teaching; and others from coaches to talk show hosts modify the formula for almost every imaginable human relationship. Communication came to be understood as so central to human activity that for a time it was fashionable to analyze every problem as a "failure to communicate." But the Church is communication: As an organization it depends upon communication to maintain a coherent presence among the faithful, and, endowed with supernatural means and ends, it depends equally on communication within the spiritual realm, particularly with the Godhead. The latter forms a crucial theological dimension of communication and Church, but one which this chapter will not take up except as it appears in ecclesiological models.

Both communication and Church offer models of independent phenomena within which the other can be understood as a portion or an extension of the central reality. In studying personal communication networks, for example, a scholar will note those elements of the network which deal formally and informally with Church or the broader construct of religiosity. Conversely, in studying ecclesiology, one can deduce the types of desirable communication patterns from the proposed model of Church (Dulles, 1989).

The problem becomes more complicated by the fact that both communication and Church have different analytical starting points, sometimes leading in quite different directions. The most common starting points for communication analysis can begin with the mass media system or with a specific medium or with the communicators or with the audience. Similarly, one can begin an analysis of Church from the perspectives of theology or sociology, among others. Each offers distinctive insights which, when integrated, provide a complex portrait of the interdependency between communication and Church.

To solve the complexity, this essay will review several communication models which have implications for Church, and then take up the sociological and theological models of Church as they bear on communication.

Communication Models: Communicator and Audience

Early scholars proposed and developed a mass media model oriented to communicators and the medium (Lasswell, 1948; Braddock, 1958):

Who says **What** in which **Channel** to **Whom** with what **Effect**?

(Lasswell, 1948)

The shortcomings of this simplistic theoretical frame became increasingly evident as scholars discovered that audiences are far more complex in their use of media, which forms but one of several factors involved in their acquisition of information and ideas and able to influence their world view and values. As Steven Chaffee (1986) noted, the ensuing model was oriented toward the audience:

Who hears **What** from **Whom** in **Which Medium** for **What Purpose**?

(Chaffee, 1986)

Inherent in the difference between these two models is the locus of power and the question of dependency. Both models arose from study of the relationship between mass media and individuals in the audience, but each begins with very different assumptions and assignment of control.

The first model, constructed against the backdrop of World War I and World War II propaganda, assumes that the communicators control the situation, using the tools of content and channel selection, and that the audience and its response result from the product of proper manipulation of the instruments. This model proved inadequate because the underlying assumptions about audience members were incongruent with reality. Indeed, this mass media model wholly ignored the important role of interpersonal communication, which proved far more powerful than early scholars anticipated.

The second model emerged from empirical research on the process of persuasion and the power of propaganda through media. Carl Hovland and his colleagues discovered that each individual approaches media with selective attention and selective perception. Selective attention describes a pattern of tuning in and out, thereby picking up only part of each message. Selective perception describes a pattern of personal interpretation based on psychological factors such as existing prejudice, wants, needs, and the like. Increasingly, research on persuasion demonstrated that individuals interpret media messages in the context of groups.

In a classic study of information flow, Elihu Katz and Paul Lazarsfeld (1955) discovered that self-nominated and group-selected individuals operated between media and individuals as personal sources of information and influence. Rather than a direct link between media and audience, the model which emerged through subsequent research had as many as 11 levels of personal contact:

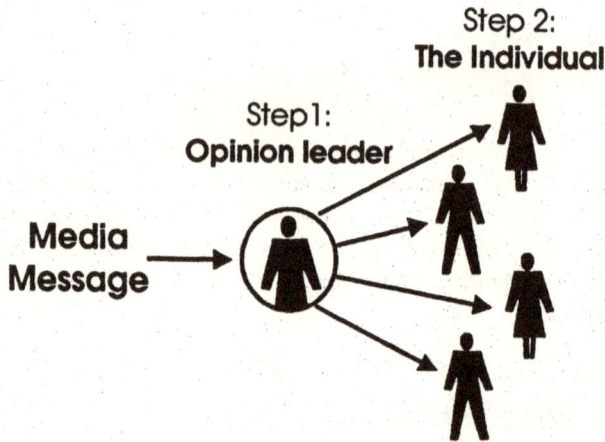

(Lazarsfeld and Katz, 1955)

Other studies reinforced the view that the locus of control resided with interpersonal communication rather than with the communicator. The results demonstrated that however authoritative the communicator, the audience member's response is powerfully affected by friends, co-workers, and family.

More recent research by Katz and others has demonstrated that each individual's use of media is far more complex, springing from personal psycho-social needs and linked closely to the uses of the content and the gratifications derived from them. Additional research has demonstrated that some audience members are active information seekers while others avoid new information or information that conflicts with strongly held beliefs. The resulting knowledge gap between the information rich and the information poor stems from personal choices based on interest in the topic and curiosity rather than the form or medium.

For the Church, the difference is crucial. As initiators of communication, the hierarchy, clergy, and other leaders may structure communication to the faithful with the assumptions of the first model and be surprised when it has little impact or effect. Indeed, until recently much of the commentary on Church use of media stressed mastery of the instruments as the key to reaching people (cf. *Inter Mirifica*; Baragli, 1974). The instrumentalist view, while leading the Church and its leaders to active participation in many forms of communication in the modern era, produced the same lack of impact which Lazarsfeld and others reported. This view spurred mastery of printing in the Middle Ages, the establishment of an active Catholic press, the formation of Vatican Radio, the programs of Fr. Charles Coughlin and Bishop Fulton Sheen, and the formation of the Catholic Telecommunications Network of America.

However, the underlying assumptions and the overemphasis on the power of the communicator and the message blinded everyone to the power of personal choice and interpersonal communication. Wilbur Schramm, after noting in a classic study that it was less what television brought to children than what children brought to television that explained its effects, went on to assess the communication roles and social environment of both communicators and the audience. His model, depicted below, made several key points.

First, both communicators and audience members have the same three tasks in communication: decoding, interpreting, and encoding. By this, Schramm meant that both communicators and the audience must first draw meaning from communication events and from experience, integrate the meaning with previous learning, and then formulate the result into some

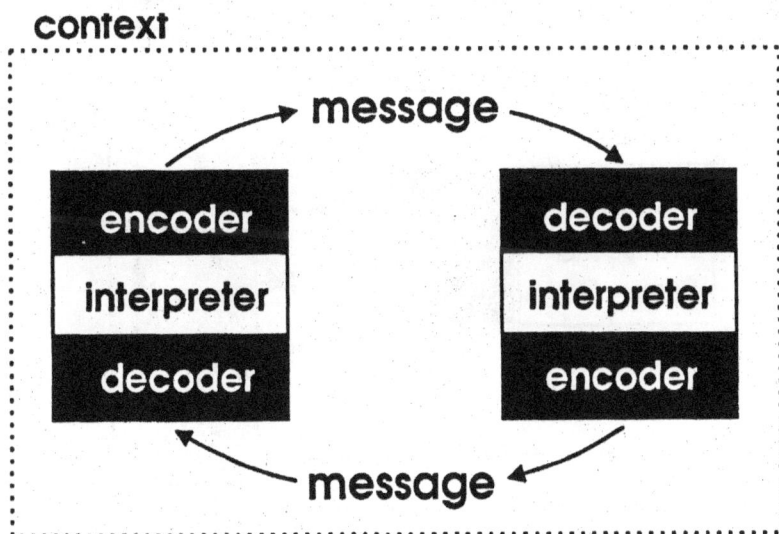

(Schramm, 1954)

expression. Any deviation between the encoding scheme of one person and the decoding scheme of the other proportionately reduces coherence and accurate interpretation.

Second, and perhaps more novel, was the observation that both communicators and audience members operate within social groups which strongly influence their interpretation and communication patterns. The role of primary groups was elaborated further by J. W. Riley and M. W. Riley (1951, 1959), who found that primary groups function as the single most important reference in interpreting information and encoding it. This means that Catholics will have diverse interpretations according to their frame of reference and non-Catholics, too, will have diverse interpretations.

Primary groups, then, have at least as much impact on an individual's perception of reality and derivation of personal meaning from media content as the communicator's skill with the medium. Moreover, as communicators reach beyond like-minded individuals to those whose primary groups are progressively different, their messages become proportionately less intelligible and even misunderstood. Communication through media must take account of the differences created by the prodigious subcultures in the U.S.

The actual relationship, depicted by the model below, demonstrates that the communication relationship is seldom one-way, but rather ongoing. In addition, it is seldom posed by one individual to another but rather runs between primary groups and their surrounding social structures.

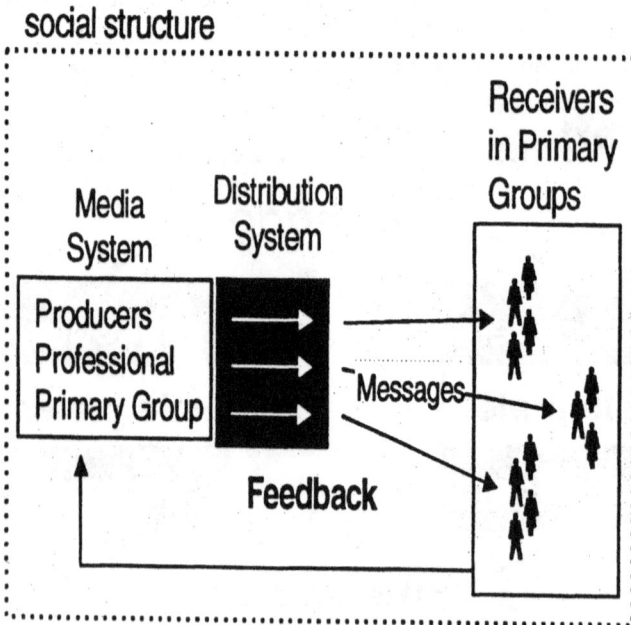

Riley & Riley (1959)

For the Church, this means that communication must take account of primary groups in both the way people understand messages individually and in the way people respond. With abundant subcultures and diverse values, the American context is replete with opportunities for miscommunication and misperception. Messages aimed at groups like those who create them may be disastrous for people from other subcultures who receive them but interpret from a different perspective.

The model's emphasis on primary groups should alert Church communicators to another dimension: dialogue as a way of clarifying misperceptions arising from divergent ways of understanding. The vast reach of electronic media multiply the difficulty, particularly as economic pressures reduce the amount of time available for full elaboration and public dialogue.

The full complexity of the relationship between communicators and audience members was elaborated by G. Maletzke (1965, as quoted in McQuail & Windahl, 1981), who summed up decades of research on communicators, media, and receivers with the model below. It is a complex model which details the various influences sociological and psychological studies had found to be significant to communication through mass media. In its complexity it reveals the dominant result of those decades of scholarship: Neither the audience nor the communicator is immune from numerous influences, each of which defies the concept of a simple and predictable effect from communication by mass media. The model shows how messages pass through what we call social filters (on the left) to reach a receiver, who in turn passes the message though a series of psychological filters (on the right).

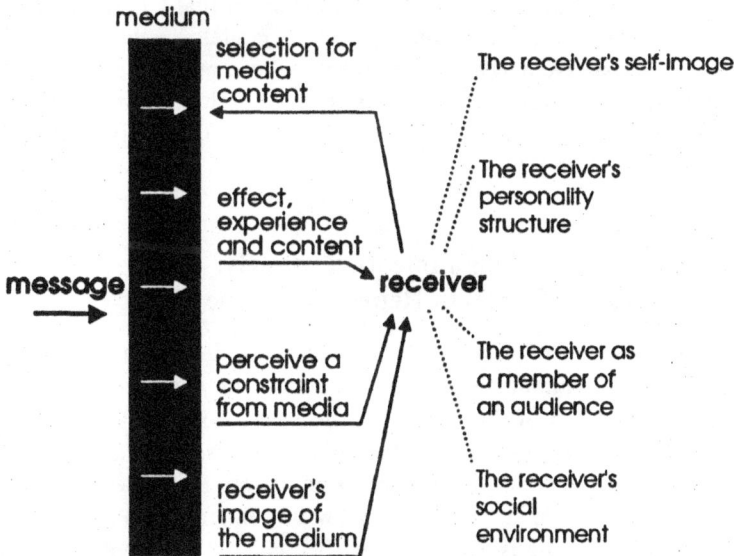

(Maletzke,1965)

Two communication strategies seem to have taken account of the complexities in achieving their effects: Sesame Street with children, and group communication with adults. Both provide group and individual discussions and activities in conjunction with media programs in order to insure coherence and integration of learning. Sesame Street, which was designed to bring underprivileged children closer to the level of their advantaged peers by kindergarten and first grade, was carefully designed on the basis of thorough and competent research.

Kits including workbooks, games, toys, and schemes for individual and group activities were provided for day care centers, preschools, and parents in Head Start programs because research had clearly demonstrated that such follow-up greatly increased a child's learning from a particular program. Adults in study groups were taught how to take advantage of the day's program and build learning activities around the content. The result was a phenomenal growth in learning of numbers, colors, letters, and the like. After a few years, however, the gap between disadvantaged children and their middle class peers entering kindergarten increased rather than decreased. The reason: Middle class parents more consistently bought the Sesame Street materials and followed viewing with interactive learning.

Group communication experiments with adults in India have demonstrated comparable effects. Explaining Catholicism has much greater effect when guided group discussion immediately follows videotape presentations. The role of primary group and discussion following a media presentation clarifies misperceptions, provides material essential for understanding, and reviews portions missed through selective attention.

Perhaps the single most important conclusion that Church leaders and educators can draw from the communication models is that the audience comprises both passive and active recipients whose primary group has enormous impact. This means that messages from Church leaders sent to a mass audience are as likely to be ignored, dismissed, or misperceived as they are to be sought out or understood.

Communication Models:
Role of Media in Representing the Church

Communio et Progressio, a post-Vatican II document which reflects the professional communicators' understanding of communication media, noted the significance of dialogue with the world outside the Church as an important media role. In doing so, the authors address aspects of two different communication models which bear examination. First, the media play so important a role in shaping the world view of contemporary Americans that appearance in the media is a sign of life. Second, dialogue with the community takes place most often in the media and through the media.

The first model is a re-examination of the classic question from basic philosophy: "If something occurs and the media don't cover it, did it really happen?" While primary groups shape our response to media content, the communication in which we participate triggers response and shapes the contours and horizon of our world view. To the extent that Church and religion are not part of the normal media content, they are less real and less discussed as part of the socially constructed reality. Church leaders in every denomination have complained at one time or another about their lack or manner of coverage. Whatever the justice of the specific case, the larger reality merits support: Appearance in the media raises awareness, heightens the sense of reality, and provides material for analysis by individuals and their primary groups.

The models above in no way deny media a powerful role in shaping and framing social reality. Numerous studies by various individuals and a variety of groups concerned about this role have demonstrated legitimate concern in at least two areas of interest: control of information, or gatekeeping, and control of images, or symbolic reality.

Selectivity is an underlying principle in news judgement, entertainment programming, and advertising design. The *New York Times*, for example has room for less than 1% of the information it receives each day, and even a large diocesan newspaper may have room for less than 5%-10% of the information received each week from Catholic News Service. Editors pick and choose, stress or de-emphasize their material in what is called the gatekeeping role. Professional judgement and experience guide these decisions, but research has shown that personal perspective dominates the decisions (White, 1950).

Communio et Progressio called for use of the communications media to engage the world in dialogue, to participate in the formation of public opinion, and to explain the Church to the community. Such participation in the public arena, while the norm in earlier times, diminished notably after Vatican I, although it did not disappear. For example, pressure on Hollywood led to the Legion of Decency; Catholic opposition to Communism, particularly Russian and Chinese communism, similarly influenced the press. With Vatican II, the Church once again moved into active engagement with contemporary culture.

Since Vatican II, the Popes and the Catholic Church—national, international, and local—have become major sources of religious news, receiving a disproportionately large amount of space in national news magazines. The roots of this may lie with the skillful use of news coverage by the liberals during Vatican II to explain their position on the issues and documents during the Council (Whalen, 1967). They also lie in the Church's focused opposition to segregation and racism, in its strong public stance against legalized abortion, and in its controversial pastoral statements on war and the economy. And, they lie in the skill with which American dissidents have used media since 1968 to broadcast their opposition to *Humanae Vitae* and other documents, official statements, and actions.

Whatever the roots, the continued reporting of news about Catholics by secular news media stems from demolition of old taboos against covering internal denominational conflicts and the newfound desire by Church leaders to speak publicly on a wide range of issues. From a journalistic perspective, once the Church actively becomes part of the public debate, its internal processes become legitimate topics of public information. The operant philosophy derives from U.S. Supreme Court decisions about libel, though few articulate it as such: By seeking a place in public debate and public policy making, an individual or institution simultaneously moves into an arena of increased public scrutiny. Individual Catholics, taking their lead from theologians and Church leaders, have publicly voiced their positions on internal Church issues from parish management to Papal statements. Even once unmentionable areas such as pedophilia appear in the news.

Church leaders have challenged the tone of the resulting coverage as adversarial or even anti-Catholic, and at times it has been (Lichter, Amundson, & Lichter, 1991). However, participation in debate on public issues becomes bruising, biased, and even vitriolic, as soon as one participant seeks advantage through distortion, appeals to prejudice, or outright smear. Archbishop Rembert Weakland, seasoned by coverage of the Bishops' pastoral on the economy, has noted that even parish level problems have become news story material because disgruntled parishioners prefer to go to the press in order to vindicate their position (1991). He would prefer the quieter route of internal conflict resolution away from the glare of publicity and public posturing.

However, communication researchers have found that news media have two divergent orientations toward reporting problems and handling conflict based on the diversity of the community (Tichenor, Donohue, & Olien, 1980). The smaller and more homogenous the community, the more likely the press will seek to maintain consensus by reporting after the conflict is resolved; the larger and more diverse the community, the more likely the press will report problems as a way of managing conflict by alerting the community to conflict. The editor in a small community is expected to help maintain stability by reporting an internal problem only when the solution is near or the community is openly divided. By not reporting, the editor permits the participants maneuvering room and quiet resolution. Reporting not only freezes people into positions and prohibits compromise, it significantly elevates the seriousness of the problem. Conversely, the large and diverse community depends on the press to report on problems and conflicts which threaten to disrupt social order. From this vantage point, internal Church problems differ only a little from problems within unions, political parties, or fraternal organizations which participate in debate on public issues.

In trying to understand the press, the Church seems caught between the models. Like people in a small, homogenous community, Church leaders seek a press role which maintains consensus and avoids escalating the conflict. Simultaneously, the Church is one more institution in a complex, diverse metropolitan community whose reporters remain alert for social problems and threats to stability. Moreover, individual Catholics, raised within a conflict-oriented role of press, will naturally seek to involve the press in resolution of conflict and will look upon press silence as conspiratorial.

At the same time, religion reporters have complained that their work is both undervalued by the news editor and revised by the editor to stress conventional news values such as conflict (Steinfels, Wycliff, Marin, Neff, Lehmann, & Marty, 1995). In addition, major religion stories which have a political or international dimension are often taken from the religion desk and moved to the a more prestigious desk, e.g., national desk. The low status assigned to the religion desk in almost every news outlet assures that the best and brightest are discouraged from staying with it long enough to develop the background essential to coherent reporting. Not surprisingly, then, secular coverage of religion tends towards the shallow, unreflective, and conflict oriented.

The Catholic media are often perceived as an alternative or sign of contradiction, but in every country and culture religious media are bound by the same professional practices, sociopolitical limits, and laws. Whether the editorial posture accords with or opposes the dominant world view, the expected role and limits for religious media differ little from those applied to secular media. The government establishes legal limits, social convention enforces cultural patterns, and individuals have fixed expectations. In the U.S., Catholic media develop their own stylistic variations on the current models of news, editorial, advertising, and entertainment drawn from print and broadcasting. They offer content different in tone and focus, but not significantly different in fundamental traits. As part of the American system, they meet readers' expectations by offering divergent points of view and they receive legal protection in criticizing political figures or governmental policies. The sole exception is the Internal Revenue Service's rule on political positions taken by publications of not-for-profit organizations. This rule threatens all not-for-profit organizations with loss of their status if they take a stance on a politician or political issue.

Under repressive regimes in single party states the religious press may be the only voice for the voiceless, tolerated because the rulers do not want open conflict with religious leaders or foreign supporters. Thus, during his ill-fated election campaign against Corazon Aquino, Ferdinand Marcos tolerated the newspaper *Veritas* and Radio Veritas rather than publicly oppose Jaime Cardinal Sin and Catholic leaders.

Because the style and form of the dominant media in large measure shape the media model expected by the people, each reader's judgment of merit is based on criteria formed through familiarity with exemplars. From conventions of format and style through taste to underlying philosophy of role, religious media products diverge from the dominant models at high risk of non-acceptance and economic failure. The message may be a sign of contradiction, but the models by which the form and style and symbolism are judged come from previous media experiences and the resulting expectations.

Models of Church: Implications for Communication

The alternative point of analysis comes from ecclesiological models of Church and the communication patterns which they imply, assume, or explicitly state. From this perspective, communication models derive from the theological and sociological constructs which describe and analyze the Church (Soukup, 1983). Theological analysis gives priority to the relationship between hierarchy and faithful and to the way the Church images itself: Bride of Christ, Mystical Body of Christ, People of God and so on. Sociological analysis provides ecclesiological models based on social structure: "Like other institutions, it is subject to the play of social forces in both its formation and its operation" (Moberg, 1984, p. 6).

Pope Leo XIII articulated this approach to ecclesiology in *Satis Cognitum* (1896/1981), wherein he described the Church as a divine society founded by Christ with supernatural means to reach its supernatural goals but equally a human society because it comprises men and women. The supernatural dimensions merit, because of their importance, a separate analysis. Thus they are not the focus of this essay, which concentrates on the organizational and structural implications of ecclesiology. Nonetheless, the depiction of the means by which God speaks to the Church has implications for communication. For example, *The Catholic Worker*, while abjured by mainstream Catholicism (including Catholics within the FBI) from the 1930's through the 1950's for its call to radical social justice and pacifism, was tolerated and defended by the hierarchy as a legitimate Catholic expression of the means by which we are called to serve God (Roberts, 1984, pp. 129-132).

The Church came into the 20th century struggling with two dominant models built around the nature of the papacy: monarchical and communal. Against the backdrop of anti-monarchical revolutions, the push for national churches, and assertion of civil liberties as fundamental rights, Joseph de Maistre and other theologians argued for *ultramontanism* (literally: beyond the mountains; figuratively: rule from Rome), a monarchical model with the pope as Supreme Pontiff over the entire Church. Johann Mohler led other theologians to consider a communal model which focused on the spiritual, internal side of the Church and thereby stressed the role of the Holy Spirit and the unity of the faithful as a primarily spiritual community.

The long dominant model was a monarchical one which incorporated both the spiritual and the temporal realms within the authority of the pope. The triple tier tiara with which popes were crowned until John Paul I replaced it with the miter symbolized this model: The pope was the ruler, the clergy were the court and local administrators, and the faithful were the ruled. Ultramontanism emphasized unity through the teaching authority of the pope in matters of faith and morals and transmitted through bishops, clergy, and religious to the faithful. This view emphasizes the juridical structure of the Church and embodies the Platonic concept of a wise king: one who protects the community from the assaults of enemies without and of heretical divisiveness within.

Four forces forged a monarchical model in the Church in the U.S., which endured until Vatican II. First, Vatican I adopted the ultramontanist view, declaring the pope infallible in matters of faith and morals when speaking *ex cathedra* as Christ's Vicar. At the same time, the Church in the U.S. was defending itself against virulent anti-Catholicism mounted as a reaction to the annual immigration of hundreds of thousands of mostly Catholic Europeans and to the image of Catholics as subservient to Rome. Third, Catholic bishops in the U.S. had to accommodate the highly ethnic Catholicism and nationalistic antagonisms which immigrants brought to the New World. Fourth, an overriding Protestant world view dominated American public life and led the bishops to establish the parochial school system in order to provide Catholic children a haven from the Protestant view. While this situation obtained in the U.S., the communal model continued as a counterbalance among European theologians, providing the inspirational force which set the roots for the new models which emerged from Vatican II.

The monarchical model established the Cardinals of the 19th century Church in the U.S. as the most authoritative echo of the Pope, followed by archbishops, bishops, monsignors, and priests. Internally, every aspect of communication from liturgy and press to schools emphasized the authority of Rome. The bishops designed it to transmit accurately the doctrines and dogma of the Church. With Latin as the global language of liturgical life, apart from sermons, some songs, and some community prayers, the monarchical model produced a top-down model of communication, as shown on the next page.

In communication terms, the top-down model resembles Lasswell's original formulation with an emphasis on hierarchical stature for credibility and manipulation of the instruments in order to reach the entire audience. As the model illustrates, all official information moves from the appropriate hierarchical level (pope, bishop, pastor, priest, nun) to the laity. Official reports move upward, but the upper levels of hierarchy are little available to communication from the laity.

The model applied equally to mission activities: carrying the Good News to those who had not heard it. While some adjustments were allowed in designated mission territories to accommodate local culture for the short

```
┌──────── Cultural and Social Context ────────┐
│        ↑              ↑              ↑        │
│    Official Church Communications/Media       │
│        ↓              ↓              ↓        │
│                                              │
│                                              │
C                                              M
o                                              e
m                                              d
p                                              i
e                                              a
t          Church Membership                   E
i                                              x
n                                              p
g                                              e
                                               c
S                                              t
o                                              a
u                                              t
r                                              i
c                                              o
e                                              n
s                                              s
│                                              │
└──────── Societal Media/Communication Systems ─┘
```

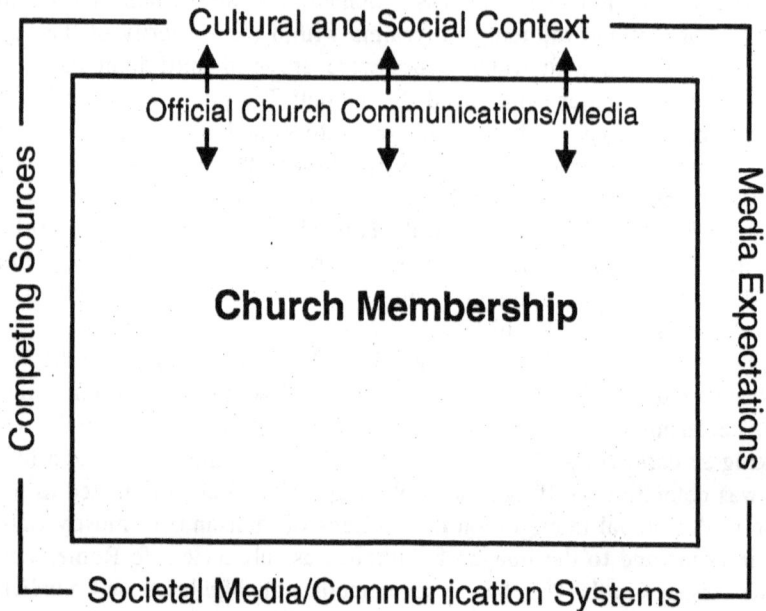

term or the long term, the operant model remained the same. The missionaries brought the official word, and they were allowed some modest adjustments to ensure ease and clarity of understanding.

To be fair, this model arose at a time when the vast majority of the immigrants were marginally literate and little schooled, and it continued to flourish in later generations because among literate and schooled lay Catholics few were learned in theology. Mission territory was by definition remote in culture from Christian Europe, thus unlikely to have much to offer which would justify anything other than communication through missionaries and their superiors.

With a poorly educated audience and modestly educated clergy, the top down model provides a highly effective means of dissemination. Coupled with an educational system which emphasizes the monarchical model, the system provides solid defense against both secular and heretical assault. The problem is that it has little ability to adapt to changes in the audience, and it cannot prepare the faithful for an alternate model without jeopardizing their allegiance to the institution and their very faith.

In the U.S. an active Catholic press defended Catholicism and proclaimed the official teaching, but it mostly operated independently of Church authority as for-profit commercial ventures. The result in larger communities was a dual communication system: the official structure and the multiple Catholic newspapers, many of which were non-English and all of which laid some claim to "official" status (Thorn, 1990).

At the Baltimore Councils, bishops complained about the divisiveness of the ethnic Catholic newspapers which brought national Church problems from the Old World into the multi-ethnic communities of New World dioceses. They also complained about the confusion which arose from diverse proclamations of "authentic" Catholicism. The divisiveness led bishops at the Third Baltimore Council (1884) to call for establishment of an official newspaper in every diocese. Leo XIII, upset by the divisiveness within the Church in the U.S., in 1899 wrote a apostolic letter urging journalists to treat bishops with the respect due their lofty positions and defined any criticism of them as injurious to the Church. The journalists obeyed, and bishops began a 40-year process of buying or starting newspapers to make them official church publications.

While effective for its goals—transmission of authentic teaching to the entire Church and defense against false teaching—the top-down model alienated educated Catholics because it closed off dialogue and it created a ghetto mentality among American Catholics. *America* began in 1909 as a bridge between the Catholic ghetto and public life. *Commonweal* emerged in 1924 as the urbane voice of loyal Catholics who refused to let criticisms of disloyalty cow them into silence. Dorothy Day offered a third alternative, exposition of the need for social justice, with *The Catholic Worker* in 1933. These publications provided an alternate model of communication—dialogue among the educated—within the dominant top-down model. More importantly, they emerged from the faithful who found top-down communication dissatisfying, even stultifying.

An important dimension of the Vatican I ecclesiology touched on ecumenism. In defining the Catholic Church as the sole means of salvation, the Council continued to hold closed the door of dialogue with other Christian denominations and non-Christian religions. Communication with the Orthodox, Protestants, Muslims, and other religions was marked by the same top-down mentality. Emphasis on the oneness and unity of Catholicism meant that external communication with other religions could only take place as a way of defending the teachings and proclaiming Catholicism's primacy.

Similarly, the ecclesiology of Vatican I essentially severed the Church's relationship with the world by declaring that the Church was supreme and self-contained, divorced from this world though in it. As a result, the dominant communication model was also non-dialogic. The Church defended itself against anti-Catholicism and falsehood, but it was a community of people who had little need to know about the world, and nothing to learn from it that it did not already know. At the same time, the Church sent missionaries into the world in order to proclaim the Gospel and offer salvation. Again, one-way top-down communication fits this ecclesiology.

Vatican II, the 21st Council, redefined the Church, and in so doing opened the door for alternative communication models. In calling the Council, Pope John XXIII sought a renewal, and Vatican II brought forth the most far-reaching statements of Church teaching in its long history. In its 16 documents, Vatican II rejected the dominant ecclesiology of the past by emphasizing the role of the laity, the integration of the Church into the world, an open-handed ecumenism, and religious freedom. After 25 years the reverberations continue as a new generation of scholars addresses the ideals and implications of the Council.

One conciliar document, *Inter Mirifica* (1962), directly addresses communication. Because of its approval early in the Council and its subsequent failure to reflect the ecclesiology developed in subsequent sessions, a postconciliar document, *Communio et Progressio* (1971), was commissioned as a more contemporaneous reflection on social communication. The ecclesiological models developed in Vatican II which significantly tie in with communication models appear in seven major documents: *Lumen Gentium*, the Constitution on the Church; *Gaudiem et Spes*, the Constitution on the Church in the Modern World; *Dei Verbum*, the Constitution on Divine Revelation; *Sacrosanctum Concilium*, the Constitution on the Sacred Liturgy; *Unitatis Redintegratio*, the Decree on Ecumenism; *Ad Gentes*, the Decree on Mission Activity; and *Dignitatis Humanae*, the Declaration on Religious Freedom.

Before moving to a broader consideration of these documents, it is important to quickly summarize the dominant ecclesiology and implicit communication models they present.

Lumen Gentium, the most fundamental statement defining the Church, refers to it as the body of Christ: Though many, all the faithful are one in Christ united invisibly in the spiritual realm and visibly in the social structure of the Church. All are called to it without losing their individuality, and many degrees of incorporation are possible; but full incorporation into the people of God results from visible communion with the Pope and bishops. Thus the Church develops missionary activities to bring the Good News to nonbelievers. Pope and bishops comprise the authoritative body, and bishops are the teachers. Laity are called to give testimony to their faith and, because they have a right to the spiritual goods of the Church, ought to make their needs known to their pastors.

This calls for a complex communication model which includes both internal and external subsystems. The internal communication system must be both authoritative in order to serve the teaching function of bishops, and reciprocal so that the needs of the laity can be expressed and addressed. It must also express the differences inherent in individuality of person and perspectives but be characterized by charity and respect. Externally, the communication system must participate in the public milieu in order to proclaim the Good News to everyone and emphasize the essential diversity and individuality of the audience.

In his analysis of the documents of the Council, Dulles identified five models of ecclesiology which lead to divergent models of communication:

hierarchical, herald, sacramental, community, and secular-dialogic (1989; see also Dulles, 1988, chap. 3).

The first two models, hierarchical and institutional, represent variants of the model of the Church as the religious society descended from the apostles and charged by Christ and with continuing the salvific mission with the assistance of the Holy Spirit. Both models, which originate in the differing definitions of Church found in Vatican II documents, can lead to the Lasswell model through their heavy emphasis on the communicator and message.

The hierarchical model, derived from *Gaudiem et Spes*, gives priority to the transmission of precise statements of the magisterium, from Pope and bishops to the rest of the Church. In this model the content originates with God and moves through the Pope and hierarchy outward through reliable communicators to the faithful who will accept it as an obligation of faith. This is the Lasswell mass communication model with an emphasis on *Who* says *What* in official channels, and it seems to assume the faithful will automatically receive the message and submit their intellect to it because of their faith. Skilled teaching of the official word, if incorporated into the model, would give greater stress to audience understanding and comprehension than this model seems to have on its face. Stress on the audience's understanding of official teaching would transform this to an audience-centered model. However, Dulles points out this ecclesiology stresses hierarchical sources and accurate transmission of the magisterium, i.e., communicator and message.

The herald model of Church originates in *Dei Verbum* and *Ad Gentes*, particularly the citation of the Church's mission as fulfilling Christ's charge to proclaim the saving truth. This model casts both the hierarchy and the laity as the communicator, the Good News as the primary content, and those inside and outside the Church as the audience. The desired response is conversion. When concern for conversion is emphasized, the herald model more readily leads to a communication model which begins with the audience or the process rather than the communicator.

The sacramental model moves beyond words to incorporate symbols, gestures, and interpersonal communication into a full range of communication through individuals and events. Found in *Ad Gentes* and *Sacrosanctum Concilium* and rooted in the fact that Christ communicated by what he did as well as what he said, the sacramental model considers how individuals and the Christian community provide a sign of Christ's presence in the world by the way they live out the faith. This model illuminates the communicative power of liturgy in different aspects:

- the expression of faith,
- the saving effect of Christ working through the sacred signs, and
- the possibility for entry into the mystery of the living Christ.

The communion model is a dialogic model like that of Riley and Riley, slightly relabeled to indicate parts of the Christian community in dialogue rather than as communicators and audience. Based on the value of common witness to central beliefs and exploration of points of difference and difficulty, this model arises from concern about ecumenical dialogue in *Unitatis Redintegratio*. The communion model has as its goal mutual profit from diverse insights which could lead to broadened areas of agreement and a stronger community. Internal to the Church, the communion model offers an approach to the full range of differences and divisions arising from culture, tradition, perspective, and personal experience.

Dulles' fifth model, secular-dialogic, explores how the Church can enter into dialogue with the non-Christian and secular world, not so much to convert as to learn with the hope of joint witness of human and religious values. An extension of the communion model, the secular-dialogic provides a route for discerning the signs of the times and making common cause on issues of justice, peace, and human solidarity. *Gaudiem et Spes* acknowledges how much the Church has learned and continues to learn from the development of human science and culture, and *Dignitatis Humanae* anchors the matter of religious freedom in the rising consciousness about human dignity. *Nostra Aetatae* points out that non-Christian religions have heard God's voice in the discourse of creatures, and that they often reflect a ray of Truth. Thus the Church is able to deepen its own understanding of God's plan by open dialogue.

Dulles concludes with a balanced perspective on the potential and risks of mass media and a theological *caveat*:

> The effectiveness of the apostolate in every age has depended on the Church's ability to make use of the dominant forms of communication. In the words of Paul VI, "The Church would feel guilty before the Lord if she did not utilize these powerful means of communication that human skill is daily tendering more perfect" (*Evangelii nuntiandi*, 45). Doctrinal or practical decisions that rested on faulty communications, or were incapable of being successfully communicated, would be pastorally unwise. Yet the criterion of successful communication should not be elevated to the status of an absolute. Not everything that is congenial to the mass media is consonant with the gospel of Christ. Sometimes God is more effectively sought in privacy and silence than in the blare of publicity.
>
> In the perspectives of theology, therefore, communications, like every other human reality, has to be interpreted and evaluated in the light of the gospel. Concern with the techniques of communication must always be subordinated to the primacy of the Christian message. Vatican II, while it had little to say directly about the media of communication, provided a theological vision that we shall do well to ponder. (1989, p. 546)

The range of models identified by Dulles calls for an expanded rather than limited model of communication, one which incorporates a reliable means for transmission of authentic teaching; a means for proclamation of the good news to those inside and outside the Church; and a means of dialogue with three disparate groups: those within the Church, those in other Christian denominations, and non-Christians. Moreover, Dulles' call for subordination of communication techniques to primacy of the message raises the question of the appropriate style of communication within the context of communication models.

The media society within which the Church exists, as *Aetatis Novae* (Pontifical Council for Social Communications, 1992) stresses, means that any effort to deal with communication within the Church must incorporate the larger cultural phenomena of multiplicity of sources. The reality for the institutional Church is one of competing, sometimes contradictory, sources of information which claim a Catholic identity and inspiration. Similarly individual Catholics can choose from a wide and expanding array of media from both religious and secular sources. In other words, the very nature of the mass media society makes it essential for the institutional Church to compete for audience attention and equally essential for individual Catholics to develop sufficient media literacy to locate and distinguish reliable sources. Moreover, the media society of each country sets the legal and economic boundaries for communication, and the media industry sets the standards and style against which all media products are judged.

The following model locates the Catholic community within the larger framework of the culture and society, and it provides emphasis on the communication relationships. The social and cultural component of that framework comprises several systems which set the boundaries, standards, and customs for communication: the political system, the economic system, social mores, and culture. Within this framework the Catholic community is

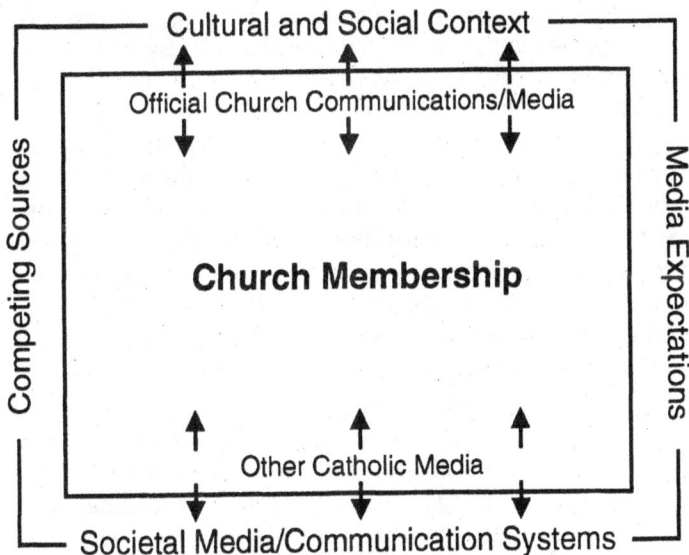

portrayed in three distinct segments: the official Church media, other Catholic media, and the general Catholic population. The Catholic population is further divided into three large groupings: autogenic, pneumatic, and institutional. Each will be discussed in turn.

The **political system** provides the legal framework and the operational norms for communication. The legal framework includes the First Amendment guarantees of freedom of expression along with other aspects such as licensing of broadcast stations and regulation of cable systems, standards for libel and slander, copyright protection, and controls on falsehood in news and advertising content. Legal norms set by the Internal Revenue Service regulate the freedom of expression on political issues and political candidates permissible by media of tax exempt organizations. Since most Catholic media are produced by not-for-profit groups, tax regulations set an additional standard.

The political society presents norms integral with the democratic culture which has grown up in the United States. Established by both legislation and accepted practices, the norms include open debate of public issues, virtually unrestrained commentary and reportage of public officials, those involved in public issues, and any group receiving public funds. The U.S. Supreme Court is the major arbiter of the boundaries of expression, and in its famous 1966 decision, *N.Y. Times vs. Sullivan*, set the standard for political discourse as "robust, even vitriolic" and allowed that in the heat of debate the allowable language would not be that which a cautious individual would choose. This operational norm can be seen in the vitriolic attacks on the Catholic Church on issues such as abortion, refugee asylum, and opposition to nuclear weapons. In recent years the norms seem to have expanded enormously into reporting of titillating tidbits from the private lives of elected and appointed public officials. Detailed press coverage of pedophilia, unthinkable a generation ago, reflects a major change in the norms: growing openness to detailed accounts of sexual matters.

The **economic system** sets the fundamental conditions of business in society, including the basic structure of the media industry. Economics establish the financial determinants for participation in the media. In the United States this means a competitive system in which the vast majority of media production is supported by either advertising or by private contributions; a small proportion is publicly funded. It also shapes the organization of networks, press associations, media production houses, and distribution systems. The economics of the media affect Catholic communicators with the same inexorable force that they apply to any participant. Financial risk is part of the system, as failed Catholic publications and broadcast programs attest. Catholic and other religious participants have depended heavily on foundations and direct subsidies, particularly in broadcasting. All religious groups, which have tried to compete in the commercial television system, have discovered that the economic system shapes their options with the same inexorable force it exerts on every other participant.

Social mores, which vary considerably across subgroups and between regions within the United States, provide both a basis for designing communication and a set of behaviors and attitudes which can be the content of media messages as well. The number of elements included in the area is vast, ranging from appropriate body distance in conversations to the boundaries for depiction of violence and sexual expression. Changes in mores, reflected in media content, create debates which tend to focus almost exclusively on media depictions. Research generally agrees that the mores represented by dominant film and television portrayals reflect the social mores of those who fund and produce rather than the audience. Stein (1979) reported that a group of Hollywood elite define the mores and values that are written into films and television programs, and that those who disagree with their commonly held assumptions are dismissed as ill-informed. The mores which pervade prime time television content, for example, are presented as acceptable or at least inoffensive to the broad majority. However, many do not accept these values and many people and groups no longer expect that mainstream entertainment media will represent their social mores. This perception underlies the drive of evangelical Christians and other religious groups to establish alternative media options.

Culture, broadly defined, is the way a people know themselves and their location in the world around them. In this context, culture provides the basic values and world view through which experience is interpreted and by which actions communicate meaning. The disparate cultures of immigrants to America and the relative newness of American culture seem to make it more a set of shared ideas about democracy, individual rights, and free market competition than an established culture. Mass media content inevitably and necessarily presents cultural norms and values to the audience, because culture is the common basis for understanding a people. For example, the media portrait of Catholics and Catholicism shapes the way others in the culture understand the Church. This shaping is part of the cultural process, whether Catholics agree to it or not. Some Catholic media efforts have been aimed at clarifying the history and nature of Catholicism.

So powerful have mass media become to the culture that George Gerbner has argued that it is no longer the hand that rocks the cradle but the hand that writes the TV scripts which shapes the nation. The most common cultural experience of grade school Americans comes through the television: Sesame Street, Mr. Rogers, Teenage Mutant Ninja Turtles, and Power Rangers. Television is not alone as a cultural source, though it is the most accessible medium, for popular music, books, movies, and magazines all carry cultural values while building from a common cultural base. Those who have studied American media find the culture presented one of capitalism, which celebrates competition, ownership, and individual strength. The winners are the strong and the aggressive, the prize is wealth and possessions. In his analysis of news stories, Gans (1979) found a pattern of underlying values which prized competition and capitalism.

Within this cultural and social framework the Church is hardly a monolith, whatever the stereotype presented by media or imagined by others. Classic sociological analysis of church membership has been built around the level of commitment exhibited by individual members. The levels included the most committed for whom the Church was the center of their social life and free time through the active members to the marginal. The language of Catholics includes adjectives like *practicing* and *lapsed* to describe the same phenomenon. While the classic analysis accurately describes the level of membership, it gives no attention to how people integrate the Church into their faith life and world view. In addition, the Catholic community in the United States is further demarcated by ethnic and linguistic boundaries.

John Haughey (1973) undertook a different perspective, how Catholics, whatever their level of membership, define the role of the Church in their lives; and he proposed that they have three very different kinds of spirituality: institutional, pneumatic, and autogenic. The three circles at the center of the model illustrate the fact that the Catholic community is not at all homogenous in terms of the role of the Church in its members. Indeed, there is little overlap and profound division in the fundamental self understanding of the role of the Church. Haughey believed these differences would explain the bitter divisions which mark the Catholic community on

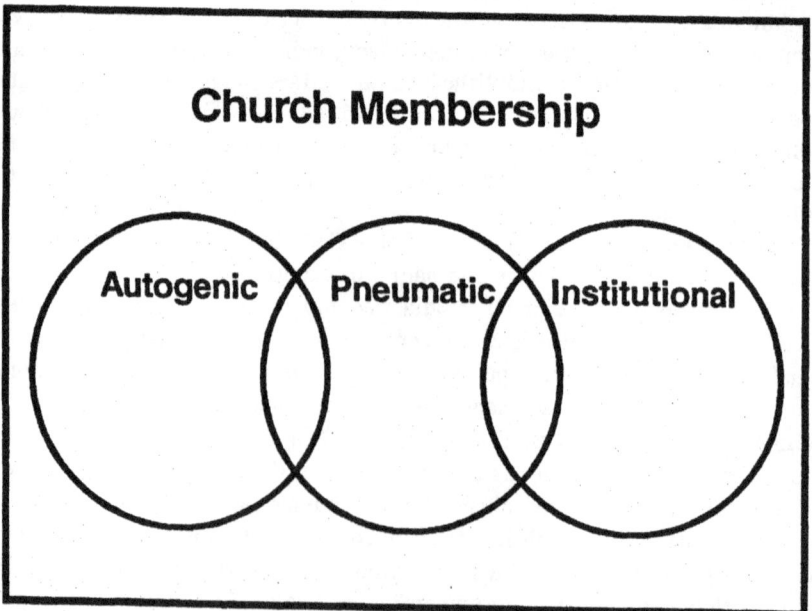

Church Membership

Autogenic   Pneumatic   Institutional

social issues such as abortion and social justice and on theological issues such as papal infallibility and moral teaching. My own subsequent research has demonstrated that these groups exist almost as Haughey perceived them and display markedly different patterns of media usage for information about the Church.

Institutional Catholics are those for whom the Church is the primary source of understanding about God and matters theological. Marked by loyalty to the pope and hierarchy, institutional Catholics seek to conform their behaviors and conscience to the teachings of the Church. They seek out and trust official Church sources for information and answers to their questions, and they mistrust secular sources. Institutionals expect loyalty to the pope and hierarchy from other Catholics, and they seek to know Church teaching on a wide array of issues.

Pneumatic Catholics have spiritual growth as their primary activity, and they define the role of the Church in their lives as nourishing and supporting spiritual growth. Contemporary social and theological issues take a distant second place to development of the relationship with God. This group is not coextensive with either charismatics or cloistered religious, though it contains both. Pneumatics pay less attention to media than do their counterparts, gleaning most of their information from books and seminars and discussions with others.

Autogenic Catholics bring democratic values to the role of the Church in their lives. They understand the Church as a divinely inspired institution founded by Christ which can help them live out a Christian life, but they also recognize that the Church is governed by imperfect humans. They thus encourage democratic process as a means to hold the Church authorities accountable. Autogenic Catholics take full personal responsibility for their own religious development, thereby diminishing the moral authority of the hierarchy and Church in their lives. They look upon Church teaching as one source of information among many about moral issues with which they are wrestling. Parish is the level of Church to which they are committed, so they pay scant attention to the diocese or to Rome. Autogenics believe they can trust secular coverage of the Church as unbiased, and they believe Catholic media operate only as public relations efforts which cover up the faults of the institution.

In addition to these groupings, there is another way to understand the Catholic audience. In a study of Catholic magazines, Berchmans (1988) found significant differences in attention to Catholic media based on individual's internal and external religious life. Internal religious life comprises private prayer, Bible reading at home, and private meditation. External religious life comprises going to Church on Sunday and being active in parish life. Those who rank high on internal and external religious life are the most active consumers of Catholic media. Those who have a high internal life but a low external religious life, i.e., those who no longer attend Church with much frequency but continue to pray privately, are the second most active consumers of Church media. They use Catholic media to monitor the Church and to locate themselves within it. Catholics with a high external religious life and low internal life rank third as active consumers.

There is yet one more substantial difference to be considered: generational differences. In his analysis of Irish Catholics, Gallagher (1988) found what he described as profound difference in the concepts and language of faith between the older generation raised in a rural society and the younger generation raised in an urban society. The difference is so profound, Gallagher wrote, that one could not use the same logic or language with both. Whereas faith questions for the rural generation means asking what the Church taught, for the young urban generation it means asking how Christ is relevant to life. In the extreme, the faith question became whether it makes any difference if God exists. Whereas Church for the rural generation was a source of community and an expression of shared meaning, for the urban generation it was simply one option (and usually a boring one) among many for a weekend. Whereas for the rural generation the Church's moral teaching, particularly on sexual matters, set the social standard, for the urban generation it seemed hopelessly archaic and irrelevant. Whereas for the rural generation familiar liturgy and music brought comfort and security, for the urban generation they seemed old fashioned, out of date and unmoving.

Thus it is clear that the Catholic community is far from a homogenous audience patiently waiting for the latest official information and ready to take action as directed by the hierarchy. The profound differences based on the perceived role of the Church and personal religious life demand a sophisticated, multi-pronged approach.

But Catholic communications are themselves quite complex. In addition to standard public relations work, they include ongoing publications, broadcast programs, instructional media, occasional films and tapes, and collaborative efforts in film. These also originate from three distinctly different sources: the official institution, subgroups with the Church, and Catholic media houses.

To reach this community, the Church generates official media through diocesan newspapers, broadcast programs, and special materials. In addition the institutional Church participates in the public dialogue through its official media and through public relations efforts. At the top of this model, official Church communications aim both ways: to the Church overall and to the larger American audience. The official Church produces an enormous number of publications ranging from weekly newspapers through newsletters, pamphlets, documents, and books. It also produces or sponsors local radio and television segments, and some dioceses run cable and instructional broadcast operations. For special situations like the pastoral on the economy, the Church generated a wide array of instructional aides. Every diocese has a communications director charged with developing relationships with local media.

Each segment or subgroup of the Catholic community produces its own media materials in the form of newspapers, newsletters, magazines, and tapes which express and communicate a view of the Church which is consonant with the perceptions and priorities of that group. As the model points out, the autogenic, pneumatic, and institutionals each have their own publications.

Commercial Catholic media houses produce all of the national Catholic newspapers and the majority of Catholic magazines, radio and television programs, films, and books. Each of the commercial Catholic houses creates media primarily for the Catholic community but with the larger society in mind, and each must identify the market and the audience before moving to production. Each must generate revenue to meet expenses. All are part of the Catholic community, though the perspectives they bring vary with the mission and tradition of the house. None can speak officially for the Church, though all can convey official teaching and information. For immigrant Catholics, these houses may in fact be outside the United States and their material may be shipped into the country, creating yet another dimension of Church communication.

Thus the Catholic community has at least three types of sources for information within the Church in addition to secular media portrayals and reports. The complete model, then, depicts the challenge facing Church communicators and the array of sources available to the Catholic community.

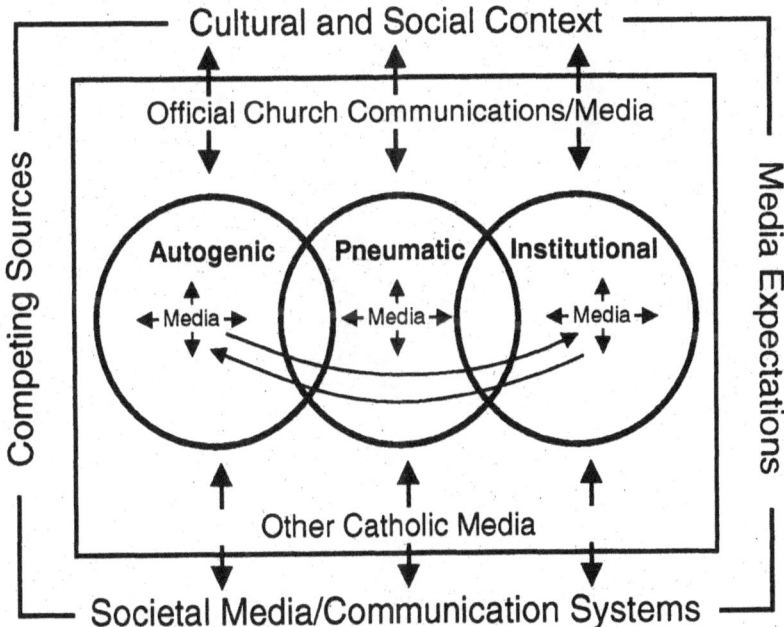

The model does not incorporate, nor does this chapter address, a further and growing element: communication from evangelical Christians to the Catholic community and Catholics who tune to evangelical Christian media. Research evidence clearly demonstrates that Catholics watch and purchase media created by evangelicals, and that evangelicals include Catholics among their intended audience.

The models of communication illustrate and depict different aspects of communication in the Catholic community, but they do not provide a complete portrait. As Dulles warned at the outset of *Models of the Church*, a model is a simplified depiction of selected aspects of the Church. The reality is far more complex.

III

Practices:

Worship, Homiletics, Teaching

8

Religious Symbolism and Mass Communication

Peter Mann

The Challenge: Living in the Age of Media

The German teenager told me he was bored with going to Mass—"It feels like the same movie every week." His comment was significant. I signified a *loss*—a loss of connection to the religious community and the communal celebration of worship; a loss of that *experience* of awe and praise which gives meaning to worship; perhaps the loss of a wider spiritual story, a living cosmology, which would provide hope and vision. Yet his comment may also have signified another kind of *belonging*—to the stories and experiences and worldview of mass communication. The challenge of living in the age of media is to understand this loss and this belonging out of a renewed experience of religious symbolism and story.

For the reception of the Gospel begins in experience, as it did for the first Christians and for people throughout the ages of the Church. If people's experience today lies elsewhere, if they are attuned to something else, they will not the able to hear the Word of the Gospel nor see what religion is all about.

Today, people are immersed in media and the age we live in is shaped by mass communication. Baudelaire said: We walk through a forest of symbols. Today we walk through a forest of media images and sounds. We turn a page, turn a dial, or turn a corner and experience illustrations, photographs, films, billboards, music, radio, and especially television, with satellite and cable bringing in multiple channels. We are flooded with images and sounds.

The potential

As a technology, television has an enormous power and an incredible potential. It can function as an instrument of collective awareness, both on a national and global level, which goes to the heart of what it means to be a people. Think of that moment when we watched through television the tragedy of the Challenger explosion. This was a collective shock, a national grief. We witnessed it as a people. Media are incredibly powerful instruments of shared celebration and grief.

The same holds true for the global community. A piece of BBC film picked up by NBC via satellite showing children starving in Africa galvanized people to action. This is the strength of television. As a worldwide communication system it spans the globe and connects together the world community. It brings us almost instantaneously gripping and troubling images of freshly breaking news. It works best when it communicates events, stories, and symbols which evoke powerful feelings (Mann, 1987a). It can become an instrument of solidarity between peoples. Television could become that integrating force which Siegfried Kracauer once envisioned in film and photography. He saw film especially as making us aware of the basic matrix of life which supports our human journey and the common life of humankind on earth: "The task of rendering visible mankind on its way toward this goal is reserved for the photographic media; they alone are in a position to record the material aspects of common daily life in many places" (1965, p. 310; cf. Mann, 1983, p. 4). The telecommunications revolution adds a potentially universal extension and accessibility to this power of the photographic image to explore physical reality and penetrate to its spiritual meaning. As an educational medium, in its documentary and news function, television has had some success in this endeavor: Witness the space bridge projects, the dissemination of health care and agricultural information in third world countries, the use of satellite communications for peaceful purposes (Mische, 1985).

The problem

At the same time, more and more voices warn of the dangers in our immersion in media words and images. Even as a news medium, television fails to show the connection between events, the relationships between its images and the political, social, or economic nexus which undergirds the news. The attention span of commercial television is too brief, its themes exhausted too quickly, its obsession with packaging and entertainment too paramount for it to become in its present state an ongoing pathway to a deeper understanding. According to Neil Postman, the visual language of television destroys interconnectedness, needs neither context nor history, and works against complexity and coherence (1986, Ch. 6, 7).

Postman's thesis is that television information packages everything as entertainment, rendering information simplistic, nonsubstantive, nonhistorical, and noncontextual. Stanley Aronowitz writes of the "mind set" of students who are immersed in mass media:

> Most students go through their classes as if in a dream. They are bemused by daily interaction as if it were the unreality. Many of them live for the spectacle of the television show, the rock concert, the record party, and other mass cultural activities. The spectacle appears as the

real world in which they wake up and participate in the process of living, and their non-media world is the fiction. (1981, p. 281-288)

Aronowitz claims that mass audience culture has colonized the social space available to ordinary persons for reading, discussions, and critical thought. One of the most dangerous effects of this in his view is an increasing tendency among young people to "literalness," to identifying thought with its object. They "seem unable to penetrate beyond the surface of things to reach down to those aspects of the object that may not be visible to the senses" or may even "controvert appearances" (pp. 282-283). Since the ability to abstract is crucial to self-awareness and critical thought, there are obvious dangers to democracy and powerful opportunities for manipulation in this immersion within images.

A further danger arises from the connection of media to the market and its consumerist agenda. Advertising images and television commercials are *behavioral scripts* (Mann, 1984, p. 30). United flies the friendly skies. GE brings new things to life. Work ends with Miller time. The night belongs to Michelob. We all become potential actors in other people's scripts for action. Advertising employs the symbols of culture, religion, and myth so that the images may plunge into the psyche, through the conscious into the subconscious mind.

Warnings

This immersion in images is obvious when young people watch MTV (which provides some of the most interesting television images from an aesthetic viewpoint): When asked about the "sex as violence" images they view, they seem totally unconscious of the issue or unable to articulate it.

Already we have received multiple warnings that the media world contains built-in addictions, consumerism, narcissism, instant gratification, and, in their wake, depression and violence.

Heidegger (1977) warned us of the danger that a scientific and technological transformation of the world into "representation" or "image" would lead to an increasing domination and exploitation of nature. As electronic media and technology shape life in our advanced Western societies to its roots, the possibility of the world transformed into image becomes increasingly near. We face the menace of the cancerous image—a world full of hyperactive, uncoordinated images bringing excessive information, intense optical stimulation, and an overwhelming flood of impressions. Instead of leading to a deeper knowledge of the real world and to a renewed commitment to this world, the cancerous image becomes a substitute for reality. As Roland Barthes has said, "everything is transformed into images; only images exist and are produced and consumed....It [the image] completely de-realizes the human world of conflicts and desires, under cover of illustrating it...the so-called advanced societies consume images...[not] beliefs" (1980/1981, p. 118). The increasing tendency for political campaigns to become media campaigns with vast sums of money spent to create the right images and perceptions bears out Barthes's thesis.

Susan Sontag connects images to the dynamics of capitalist society, of production and consumption:

> A capitalist society requires a culture based on images. It needs to furnish vast amounts of entertainment in order to stimulate buying and anesthetize the injuries of class, race, and sex. And it needs to gather unlimited amounts of information, the better to exploit natural resources, increase productivity, keep order, make war, give jobs to bureaucrats. (1973, p. 157)

She sees the camera defining reality in two ways essential to the workings of an advanced industrial society: as a spectacle (for masses) and as an object of surveillance (for rulers). The production of images has an ideological function also. A change in images replaces social change and society equates freedom itself with the freedom to consume images and goods. She therefore speaks of the need for an "ecology of images" as well as of real things (p. 158).

Recovering Religious Meaning in the Media Age

According to the analysis so far, mass culture means being immersed in media images, which can connect us to others but often work against interconnectedness; which can penetrate to the depths of reality but usually stay on the surface; which can communicate knowledge but in fact prevent it; which are potentially tools for self-awareness and participation with others but instead tend to isolate people in a consumerist way of life where happiness is equated with possessions and freedom becomes the freedom to consume both images and products.

This situation poses an extraordinary challenge to mainstream religion. It leads to a "displacement of attention," away from religious symbols and values. It functions as a major factor in what some have called "the loss of Catholic memory" in children and adults. Their imaginations and feelings are elsewhere. They see and hear something else. The Churches face the task of clearing a space within this new world for the preaching of the Gospel. The Church must communicate the Gospel in symbols, models, images, and words which are accessible to this culture and understood by it. Otherwise the Gospel does not get communicated at all. At the same time, this must be a *critical* communication, opening up the culture to the truth of the Gospel and learning to reread the Gospel through the new awareness given in our culture.

The image, the visible and concrete rather than abstract knowledge, fascinates people today. This means that we have to recover the image dimension of the Gospel. The word which moves, attracts, and empowers people today is not abstract doctrine but instead the word of story, metaphor, and the imagination. We must recover this liberating word within all aspects of our religious experience. Since events, not ideas alone, attract people, our proclamation must bring out the event character of the Gospel. Since this world in all its variety and change fascinate people, we need to see religion within the real world (Mann, 1983, p. 2).

The only viable strategy, it would seem, is what John Coleman has called Catholic "resourcement," openness with roots (1982, p. 165). This would mean seeing Catholicism not only as the identifiable Catholic Church with its institutions, doctrines, representatives, and rites, but also as a particular way of being religious, as a Catholic vision of life. In *An American Strategic Theology* Coleman summarizes Langdon Gilkey's argument on the five major strengths typical of Catholicism:

> (1) a high regard for rationality and the role of reason in public life, (2) a sense of mystic interiority and the legitimacy of mysticism in the spiritual life, (3) a deep sense of the symbolic, especially as mediated in liturgical and sacramental life, (4) the ability to generate loyalties to a transnational community, and (5) the sense of the role of moral norms and principles—as against situational intuitiveness—in public and personal life. (p. 178)

These words provide signposts for ministry in the media age which would be authentically Catholic. Ministry must be holistic, seeing the whole person with mind and body and spirit. Religion must be seen within the whole of life, in all its dimensions. Catholic ministry in the media age should recover the resources of our extraordinarily rich traditions of prayer, spirituality, worship, and art, as well as our sense of belonging to a worldwide Church. Our ministry would show a commitment to Christian moral values within the Catholic tradition, as well as to authentically secular values and human rights.

Catholic means universal, which we would see today as both global and directed to the interconnectedness of life. The Catholic vision is incarnational, accepting the many dimensions and levels of life. It is historical and visionary alike, binding together past, present, and future. Catholicism sees the interdependence of person and community, of this world and the next. All these aspects are shaped by God's grace and self-communication. This is not something purely invisible, but rather—as the Catholic theologian J. B. Metz has pointed out—takes on visible expression:

> In the biblical narratives and events, grace is encountered as a sense-related, historical-social experience. It is encountered in stories of awakening and exodus, of conversion and liberation, of discipleship, and of faces lifted up in hope. These stories are not additional embellishments upon an invisible event of grace; not at all. In them grace itself comes to expression, for example, within the historical-social life of a people in exile, in the experiences of discipleship undergone by a young community, of resistance to the representatives of Rome's political religion,

or of solidarity with the least of the brethren. In all this, grace is being "seen"; it is visible and sense-related grace. (1980/1981, pp. 53-54)

This joy of the senses and the spirit—part of Catholicism as a religion of Word and Image, of the Word made flesh, not of the Word alone—should lead naturally into a ministry appropriate to the media age. It should lead into a celebration of life, an awe before the mystery of life in which God is communicated to us. It leads just as naturally into the power to lament or mourn the violence and evil which hold back the reign of God (Mann, 1983, pp. 43-44).

Obstacles to a symbolic awareness

When we look at various functions of ministry in a Catholic context— theological education and spirituality, leadership and interpersonal skills, preaching, liturgy, and evangelization—we see that they cannot be grasped, interiorized, or developed without understanding and using religious symbols. However, we find an increasing blindness to symbols at the very time that we move through the forest of symbols. Three forms of this blindness are:

1. Immersion in symbols. We have already seen this immersion in the symbolic world of mass culture. This could affect ministry in two ways. First, if the attention of the church community is displaced into the symbolic world of mass culture, there may be no resonance to the human, religious, Christian, and Catholic symbolic world used in ministry. Second, the process by which the symbol enters into awareness—"gives rise to thought," in Paul Ricoeur's phrase—is blocked.

2. Standing outside the symbolic world. The opposite kind of blindness results from a rationalistic mind set which is closed to the symbolic, metaphorical language of Scripture, liturgy and faith. This often occurs among ministers who, self-conscious about symbols, surround them with explanations and words. To explain to a community that some gesture or object will be a "symbol" for something else, and then to use this very self-consciously in a ceremony or ritual, is to pretend that things become symbols by our talking about them. (The American flag works perfectly well as a symbol without anyone needing a commentary on it each time it is used).

This self-conscious attitude to symbols lies at the root of excessive commentaries and explanations before Scripture is read in liturgies. It is also present in what Joseph Campbell calls, in a devastating phrase, the "Julia Child" approach to celebrating liturgy:

> Institutional religion has lost a sense of art, has disowned some of its great artistic masterpieces. These include Gregorian chant and the Latin mass. The Latin mass is far more a work of art than the new mass with its celebrant acting like Julia Child and its banal music. Churches, if they are to open the hearts of persons, if they are to translate a spiritual realization of the universe, must return to an understanding of metaphor as that which enlivens the object used as a metaphoric image. But when

the object is taken to be the end term, then it loses its radiance. (Kennedy, 1987, pp. 7-8)

3. Fundamentalism: the literal symbol. Fundamentalism, which exerts an amazing attraction on Catholic communities today, takes the symbol *literally*. God's Word is present in God's own words, not in human words. Scripture is true in a literal, not a literary sense. Adam is back there at some fixed point in space and time, and Christ is ahead of us at some other fixed time to be calculated according to apocalyptic codes and nationalistic politics:

> Similarly, in decrying the rise of communist expansion, televangelists ensure [sic] their audience that Jesus, if he was around today, would support the MX and Pershing II missile systems. Calling on the God-fearing, Bible-toting America of old, televangelical fundamentalists urge Washington to launch search and destroy sweeps in Central America, Africa, Asia, and the Caribbean to mete out fire and brimstone to all the communists, crazies, and other infidels threatening America. (Luke, 1983-1984, p. 210)

After Oliver North's success as a media event, one can understand how calls such as this resonate among the public instead of being seen as apocalyptic ravings. There is a great deal of violence in all this (I once worked with someone whose car sported the bumper sticker, "IN CASE OF RAPTURE THIS VEHICLE WILL BE UNMANNED!").

Televangelism, which as Postman shows, packages religion as entertainment, succeeds because it wholeheartedly embraces the methods and values of corporate culture. In Luke's words, televangelical viewers are admonished to "get to know Jesus," in accord with the same code of product promotion that sells laxatives, the prevention of forest fires, and more life insurance:

> It appears that no substantive system of values completely can escape commodification in the society of corporate-planned consumption. Worship, reverence, and devotion as such are repackaged electronically into *special events* rather than as *habitual practices*. These events, in turn, fit into the corporate society of spectacle as telecast or teleprompted rallies, crusades, conferences, and revivals that can be mass marketed like the Superbowl and passively experienced on endless rebroadcast. Televangelism, then, necessarily transforms its sect into a market, its believers into consumers, and its message into products. (1983-1984, p. 206)

The very success of televangelism and fundamentalist ministries makes it one model of ministry that makes inroads both into Catholic media and into some aspects of Catholic ministry. In the name of Catholic resourcement, this should be resisted.

Symbolic Renewal

Paul Ricoeur has shown that symbols are *signs with multiple meanings* which disclose their hidden meanings in and through their immediate meanings (1970, pp. 12-16). Symbols disclose but also disguise these hidden dimensions, and thus need to be deciphered through a process of interpretation or reading. This multiple meaning is present in all the *zones of emergence* of the symbol.

- It is present in *cosmic symbolism* where the elements of the world around us—the heavens, the oceans, the earth and vegetation, the living creatures—become signs of the Sacred and of our own inner life.
- It is present in the *oneiric* or *dream world*, the symbols of which point backward into our hidden desires and yet also forward into our future possibilities.
- It is present in the world of the *poetic imagination*, which is not simply the power to form images but rather that fundamental power of language able to express the cosmic, the oneiric, the Sacred—and via these our deepest possibilities—through the medium of images.

Symbolism and *language* interact. As Ricoeur puts it:

> There is no symbolism prior to the man who speaks, even though the power of symbols is rooted more deeply in the expressiveness of the cosmos, in what desire wants to say, in the varied image-contents that men have. But in each case it is in language that the cosmos, desire, and the imaginary achieve speech. (1970, p. 16)

Thus we are led toward the cosmos as "sacrament" of God through the psalmist's hymn, toward the mysteries of the psyche and cosmos through the word of the poet and prophet. Further, these many levels and dimensions of the symbol need to be deciphered, and this deciphering and interpretation take place also through language, through the exegesis of the psalm, the dream, the poem, and the prophecy. We reach toward and into the symbol's meaning through the text in which it is expressed (Mann, 1980).

In entering these symbolic worlds of the Sacred, the cosmos, and the psyche, we become aware of the enormous power they have to renew our understanding and praxis of ministry. As Joseph Campbell says, "quite ordinary people understand that religion is meant to open their hearts, to help them realize the meaning of their experience" (Kennedy, 1987, p. 8). He warns that religions that hold on to the literal meaning of metaphoric concepts lose their relevance at a time of enormous change such as ours when we have entered the space age, when our culture is polarized between two attitudes—of suspicion and recovery—which call in question religious truths and yet provide a new possibility of understanding and living these truths. We live in the conflict between *suspicion* and *recovery*, between a movement of thought (and attitude also, for we are confronting ways of living as well as patterns of ideas) which presupposes, on the one hand, that all traditionally received meaning must be a false meaning, and another movement of reflection—*recovery*—which seeks, on the other hand, to restore meaning and sees in our belonging to traditions a life-giving and humanizing potential (Ricoeur, 1974). In the final section on soundings in religious symbolism, I shall indicate some possibilities for a "hermeneutic of recovery," within American culture today and taking into account the power of mass communication.

Soundings in religious symbolism

Our age has a broken relationship with religious symbolism. On the one hand, religion seems no longer a mystery. We point to particular religious persons and institutions, sacred rituals and events, church buildings. Yet for all those whom the familiar signs of religion reassure, others see in religion only fixed rituals, dead traditions, and empty forms. This is one sign of the culture of suspicion.

In this situation we need to recover a wider and more mysterious sense of religion as our connectedness to a deeper dimension of existence. Our life contains *limit-situations* of birth and death, love and suffering, struggle and celebration that open onto a deeper ground of meaning, into the sacred dimension of life (Tracy, 1978, pp. 105-109). In these situations we touch something transcendent, the extraordinary present within the ordinary. In this wider sense, religion expresses those situations which are totally human and yet more than human. Religion is the spirituality of the human situation. This is the implicit God-dimension of human existence.

This wider sense of religion can transform the meaning of religion in the narrow sense. We find in religious traditions, although in different language and formulations, the basic truth of an openness of human life to God and the groundedness of the world in God. This aspect of religion can say a great deal to media because these "limit-situations" are the stuff of story. Religion in this perspective also challenges the vision of televangelism because it brings God within the whole of life.

Cosmic symbolism and the sacred

Religious tradition continually expresses a cosmic symbolism of the world as sign of God. The sea, rocks, clouds, trees, earth, and sky are "sacraments" of the Holy. God is the rock of salvation, there is the "oceanic" experience of God, God guides Israel in the Exodus through cloud and fire, religions speak of the cosmic tree, the heavens express God's infinity, and so on.

In my experience Catholic people hunger for this sacramental awareness of God in the cosmos, in the signs of earth. In using these signs, we enter into the collective symbols of humanity—the water, the cave, the mountain, fire, space, the mandalas, and the images found in nature or created by the imagination—through which the religions of the world have expressed their encounter with God. At the same time, people have rediscovered the enormously rich tradition of Catholic spirituality and theology, with its images and symbols drawn from the worlds of nature, culture, and the psyche. This cosmic symbolism is healing for an American culture which has reached a certain end point in its scientific and technological exploitation of the earth. This religious symbolism also subverts a media world which uses all aspects of the natural world to sell products.

The human person

The human person forms, in a special sense, the "sacrament" of God. In our mind and body, in the journey into inner space as well as outer space (Ps. 138), we encounter the mystery of God's knowledge and love. We are in the image of God (Gen. 1:26); in the image of Christ (2 Cor. 3:2-4; 3:18; 4:6). In the age of mass communication, this relationship to God as creator seems especially powerful. We make images, not simply consume images. We participate in life, not observe it. We have no fixed image, being in the image of God, and therefore we cannot be fixed in media scripts or corporate strategies.

As we discover the world of the psyche through depth analysis, and discover our connection to the universe (the human person is the universe conscious of itself), we see in a new way that we can understand human life only in terms of the universe and its creator. The human person and the infinite longing of the "restless heart" (Augustine) is the first referent of all symbolism. Through the response which the symbol evokes in us, we discover our hunger for God.

God

The Catholic community hungers for a language and for symbols in which its relationship to the "ever greater God" can be expressed. Adoration, praise, worship—the mystical and sacramental—lie at the heart of Catholicism. Part of the identity crisis of the Catholic community since the Council may stem from the fact that this awareness of God did not receive adequate expression.

We see ever more clearly that there is no direct expression of God or direct presence of God. Even the symbol of "the burning bush" only indirectly shows the presence of God. If the symbol becomes an object, that is idolatry. But the heart endlessly hungers and the mind ceaselessly questions. It is said that God is revealed in three books: in the book of the universe, in Scripture, and in ourselves. All these three books provide words, images, symbols, and stories of God. In that sense they respond to the orientations of the media age.

Yet as we experience that God is the Mystery which cannot be captured in our concepts or manipulated by our schemes (God "on our side"), we become free to receive that Mystery as God's self-communication in unconditional love. This is healing for a culture which wants to produce and control everything. It is also saving for the same culture that we find God at the deepest part of ourselves, that—in Rahner's phrase—God's divinity is revealed in the mystery of our own life and our own becoming (Mann, 1987b).

Christ

Aspects of our proclamation of Christ which would be particularly relevant to the age of mass communication include Christ as Word; Christ the Storyteller; the Cosmic Christ; and the new awareness of Christ, which develops within the Church as we begin the difficult task of integrating the message and impact of Jesus of Nazareth, as these emerge through critical exegesis of the texts, with the wider awareness of Christ in the life and worship of the Church. This is a necessary task, against the literal reading of the texts in Fundamentalism. It will be painful for those many Catholics who still think we have a documentary report on Christ in Scripture. But it is a task which will be ultimately liberating for the Catholic community. A work such as Marcus Borg's *Meeting Jesus Again for the First Time* (1994), which shows Jesus as both subversive wisdom and the wisdom of God, and as challenging the politics of purity with the politics of conversion, has tremendous implications for living in the age of media in an open yet critical way.

Church

Finally, symbolism can give us a better awareness of the church community, its struggles, and its needs. The explicit sacraments and rituals of religion, the sacred places and persons of religious tradition, reacquire their deeper meaning through this symbolism of the Sacred, the cosmos, and the self. A church building, for example, does not exist solely as an edifice marked out for a religious purpose. It is meant to be a microcosm of the macrocosm, the center of sacred space and time, the *axis mundi*. Further it is not only a cosmic space but also a psychic space, where we journey inward and communicate with the Sacred as we move into the heart of the church.

It is in this area of church structure and liturgical renewal that the struggle between suspicion and recovery has been most bitter within the Church. When the "Old Liturgy" of the Pre-Vatican II Church was dismantled in the wake of the Council, this signified and effected for many people a loss of symbolic meaning. Even though this symbolism was, in a sense, secondary—the "mysterious" Latin language, the position of the altar, the sense of sharing in an unchanging, "timeless" ritual—such symbolism nevertheless mediated for people something which was indeed primary. For people felt themselves initiated through this action into sacred space and time, into a mystery of language and silence, into a ritual of sacred signs that brought the Holy into their midst. This symbolism affects people deeply. It reaches into the emotions, into the core of the person, the "heart," and, beyond this, into the deepest sense of belonging to a wider world in time and space and the imagination.

The "New Liturgy" which came into being failed wherever it only translated or adapted the old one. Many Catholics experienced this new liturgy as full of words and activities but without symbolic depth, for their experience of the actions and, in a sense, of the "actors" and participants had changed. We cannot simply go back to a former symbolic action. With our deepening awareness of religious symbolism perhaps we can recover that symbolic depth in our worship and community life.

This community experience will be healing for the culture of American individualism, which has deep connections to media, of which Robert Bellah and his colleagues have written in *Habits of the Heart* (Bellah, Madsen, Sullivan, Swidler, & Tipton, 1986; see also Bellah, 1985, pp. 13-21). It is also important for an age in which televangelism has often transformed worship into a television show that Catholicism recovers its own authentic sacramental tradition.

9

Communication and the
Art of Presiding

Dennis C. Smolarski, S.J.

Several years ago, I gave the homily at the funeral of my college room-mate's mother. I had never before preached in that church nor had I met most of those present at the funeral. At the reception following the liturgy, one of the mourners told me how much she enjoyed the homily. Her enjoyment resulted, not from any brilliant insight I passed on to the assembly at that Mass, but rather from the fact that I spoke distinctly and clearly: Thus, for the first time in a while, she was able to hear and understand what was being said in the homily! The clergy at that parish focused their homily preparation on content, i.e., the *what* to communicate. Evidently, they had not reflected on whether what they said was being heard well, that is, on *how* they communicated.

This essay deals with liturgical communication—not only the special oral communication that takes place in the homily but also the other moments of communication that take place verbally through the presidential greetings, instructions, and prayers (particularly the eucharistic prayer), and nonverbally through the demeanor, style, and gestures of individuals and through the ambience and the use of physical articles in our religious rites.

By reason of their ordination, bishops, priests, and deacons are entrusted with the work of communicating God's message to the Christian community, that is, of spreading the word about the Word of God. Unfortunately, individuals often try to do this through multiplying words (unwittingly becoming more and more wordy), and the one Word gets lost among the many words. In many churches, the liturgy might dramatically improve if the ministers reduced the number of spoken words, proclaimed the remaining words with more dignity, and placed more concern on nonverbal aspects of worship. One might say that the liturgy would improve if we paid more attention to the *mode* and *medium* than merely to the *message*. Many leaders and planners of worship need to (re-)capture a sense of celebrational style rather than solely concentrating on rubrical correctness; they need to

121

put more stress on the *nonverbal* "matter" of the sacramental celebration rather than solely worrying about the *verbal* "form."

The proverbs "one picture is worth a thousand words" and "actions speak louder than words" both capture the spirit of a renewed concern for nonverbal aspects of worship (and of human intercommunication in general). Our religious heritage has long held the nonverbal aspects of our tradition in high esteem—for example, gestures (the laying on of hands, the *orans* prayer posture), physical matter (holy water, blessed oils), sacred symbols (incense, the altar). However, most worshippers have witnessed clergy who make use of the nonverbal in liturgy as if it were a curse rather than a blessing. For example, one still all too commonly finds celebrants who "greet" the assembly with hands tightly clasped and eyes fixed on the book or on someplace other than on the people they are supposedly greeting. The words may be saying: "The Lord be with you," but the body says: "I guess I'm supposed to say this at this time, but there is something else I'd rather be doing." In some churches, so much clutters the altar that one can hardly see the primary elements of "the one bread" and the one cup (cf. 1 Cor. 10:17) on the "table of the Lord."

Most regular Church-goers can relate other stories of ecclesiastical mis-communication. The fact that people do remember nonverbal details yet (in most cases) not remember what was said at the services, emphasizes that *how* one proclaims a message (through symbol, demeanor, gesture) may in many cases matter more than the message itself. In other words, those entrusted with conveying the message should not easily overlook the *manner* in which it is conveyed. Human beings communicate in a multitude of inter-related ways. Unfortunately, the style of many liturgies sometimes suggests that those leading them assume that ESP is the primary, if not the sole, mode of communication!

Biblical Roots and Recent Heritage

Scripture reminds us that the verbal and the nonverbal have always been united in our history of ministry and worship. In the Old Testament, kings and prophets were anointed for their ministry. Jesus himself used to lay hands on the sick and spread mud on the eyes of the blind. Paul exhorts worshippers to "offer prayers with blameless hands held aloft" (1 Tim. 2:8).

However, the prime paradigm of the union of the verbal with the nonverbal is the person of Jesus—God's Word who became flesh. The liturgy celebrates the Enfleshed Word in our midst and helps that Enfleshed Word come alive in our midst and through our lives. In Jesus, the Word of God became one with our human nature. Material creation was not "frosting on the cake" of the divine soul of Jesus. It was intimately knitted into a wondrous union of the divine with the human. Jesus still remains the paradigm for sacramental life in the church—word still joins with material substance and human action and through that union is God's sacramental grace conveyed to human beings. With Jesus as our model, our words in the liturgy must also be enfleshed—borne out in the seen and felt along with the heard.

Because of the Incarnation, we can never consider the (nonverbal) material objects and physical gestures merely "frosting on a cake" whose substance is words. Rather, we should consider the non-audible parts of ministry and worship as the visible, tangible, indispensable expressions of the content of what any audible words say. At the same time, however, most would rightly warn against those who so concentrate on externals that they unwittingly turn worship into "all show and no substance." The advice given by St. James in his letter about the indispensable union of faith and works also applies to our worship (cf. James 2:14-26). James says that "faith without works is as dead as a body without breath." In a similar unity, our tradition of worship has joined audible, visible, and tangible dimensions together to form one coherent act of praise to God.

The presence of sufficient nonverbal material objects and physical gestures does not of itself automatically guarantee prayerful and fulfilling worship, no more than the mere reading of Shakespeare's text guarantees a superb performance of *Macbeth*. The leaders of worship must handle both the verbal and nonverbal dimensions of the rite with a care, concern, and reverence that bespeaks the holiness and seriousness of what takes place. One might call this aspect of worship an appropriate "ministerial style."

The two letters of St. Paul to Timothy both exhibit the deep care and concern of Paul for Timothy, whom Paul saw as an adopted son. He had put Timothy in charge of the local church, in a position of ministerial authority. In each letter Paul makes reference to what today might be called an "ordination." The rite included the nonverbal laying on of hands (central to modern day ordination rites) which Paul considered to convey a divine gift. In 1 Timothy 4:14 we read, "Do not neglect the gift you received when, as a result of prophecy, the presbyters laid their hands on you" (cf. 2 Tim. 1:6).

If one understands these Pauline passages as referring to some sort of ministerial initiation, then the rest of the letters contain advice for a new minister. The advice given can be classified as advice about "style" rather than "content." In 1 Timothy 4:12, Paul wrote: "Let no one look down on you because of your youth, but be a continuing example of love, faith, and purity to believers." Part of this verse is frequently inscribed on the back of the pectoral cross worn by Russian priests. It summarizes a key description of what a minister should be: "a continuing example of love, faith, and purity to believers."

This does not passively describe desirable physical qualities or necessary job skills. Neither should we read it as an exhortation to cultivate public relations and "showmanship" qualities, helpful in the world of sales and business. Too often the "smooth" qualities of television personalities are thin veneers that have little underlying substance. Rather, Paul's words describe key ways that human beings see one another as living out a union with God. The minister should shine forth the love, faith, and purity that come from the depths of his being and are nurtured by prayer with God. These qualities should be part and parcel of a personal ministerial "style," both in the role and function as leader of prayer during a formal liturgical celebration, and also in the day to day informal situations in which communication also occurs, such as when counseling distraught and bereaved individuals or congratulating those experiencing great joy.

Several years ago, Father Robert Hovda wrote a short, but substantial, booklet on celebrational style entitled: *Strong, Loving and Wise* (1980). This title comes from 2 Timothy 1:7, where Paul gives Timothy this advice: "The Spirit God has given us is no cowardly spirit, but rather one that makes us strong, loving, and wise." Father Hovda uses these words of Paul as a description of ministerial style, and he sees in them the key qualities that should be evident in a minister both when leading an assembly in prayer or when speaking to another person one on one.

Unfortunately, too often we see ministers that do not appear to be strong, but rather timid or overbearing. Some of these ministers are easily overwhelmed by "bossy" parishioners or else run such a tight ship that they appear unwilling to accept any suggestion from anyone. They seem not loving, but oblivious, rude, or condescending. Some of these ministers affect a "clerical" air about them that puts others off rather than invites them in. They do not appear wise, but rather appear as know-it-alls or as out of touch with reality. Some of these ministers often treat their parishioners or coworkers as uneducated grammar school children, who could never hope to understand the complexities of ecclesiastical or spiritual affairs. Style does matter, for the wrong style can inhibit God's Word, the two-edged sword, from entering a person's soul to do its work.

A good presidential style can engender an openness on the part of those in the assembly to accept the message being communicated. A poor style can stifle that message. Eyes can become blind and ears become deaf if the leader of prayer overlooks some of the basic tenets common to all human interpersonal communication. The U.S. Bishops have included thoughts similar to these in two of their major documents. In *Music in Catholic Worship* (1983), we read,

> Good celebrations foster and nourish faith. Poor celebrations may
> weaken and destroy it....Since liturgical signs are vehicles of communi-
> cation and instruments of faith, they must be simple and comprehensi-
> ble....They must be meaningful and appealing to the body of worship-
> pers or they will fail to stir up faith and people will fail to worship the
> Father. (No. 6, 7)

In *Environment and Art in Catholic Worship* (1978), we read, "gestures...done by the presiding minister...can either engage the entire assembly and bring them into an even greater unity, or if done poorly, they can isolate" (No. 56).

A tradition of sensitivity to style and to nonverbal aspects of the liturgy that was alive for centuries in the Western Church was slowly lost. However, this sensitivity remained alive in many Eastern European and Eastern rite Churches. As the modern languages developed in Europe and people and clergy alike understood less and less of the liturgy, a conscious celebration of God's presence among them was replaced by a rote rite of getting through the mechanical gestures and verbal text prescribed by the liturgical tomes. In those countries in which the rise of Protestantism led to persecution of Catholics, style in worship was considered a non-essential that people could easily dispense with. When people risk imprisonment by attending Mass, their concern is not usually about an endearing style or the ingratiating personality of the priest. In these cases, they could tolerate a certain "minimalism" in liturgical rites and in presidential style, simply because pageantry and pomp could easily lead to arrest and execution. In these situations, of greatest need were the correct words and the minimally necessary actions (Day, 1990, p. 20).

Unfortunately, this ritual minimalism became the norm in many places at the early part of the 20th century even when persecution ceased. Many people had no idea that it was possible and even desirable to celebrate the liturgy in ways other than those learned as children in their native lands. Over the centuries persecution, the loss of the vernacular, pragmatism, and other factors (such as the American work ethic) all led to an impoverished view of the liturgy that differed distinctively from the fullness of communication evident in the Scriptures and the earliest traditions. This rigid, narrow understanding of liturgy also became the one commonly taught to several generations of priests. In all fairness, this approach to liturgy did guarantee a unity in the format of worship, something that comforted many a troubled worshipper in a world of change and persecution. It also enabled many an unschooled cleric to serve the church as a minister of the Lord. As long as they followed the rules, priests and people alike could be assured that grace was conveyed and God was somehow praised.

The liturgical training common prior to the reforms of the Second Vatican Council consciously and unconsciously influences many of today's priests. That training emphasized "validity" and the correct execution of the many rubrics. As long as they performed with rubrical correctness those things minimally required for validity, they had correctly celebrated Mass (or the sacrament). For many generations, Catholic priests learned the message and meaning of the Latin phrase, *ex opere operato*. Whenever the sacrament was celebrated correctly (that is, the words pronounced and the action performed), grace was conveyed. One need not consider "style" because style never entered into the equation for a grace-producing sacrament. There was no real concern for "style," except perhaps that since it was unseemly for a celebrant to trip on the alb (or a dangling cincture) in the sanctuary, he should avoid doing this too often.

However, we now realize the forgotten truth that style *does* matter in liturgy. Father Virgil Funk (1990) has suggested that different styles of worship reflect different liturgical values. He further suggests that when someone experiences an unappealing liturgy, it may be because the liturgical style emphasizes values that contrast with the liturgical ambience and the needs of the individual. An informal folk Mass with senior citizens in a gothic cathedral is probably as incongruous (and unsettling for the assembly) as a sung Mass with Gregorian chant and incense in the common room of a college dormitory. The style used for the liturgy and the style used by the priest can and does influence the prayerfulness of the worship taking place.

The Second Vatican Council tried to change the mentality that centered almost exclusively on the correct execution of the rubrics by the priest and seemed never to take the people into account. The often-quoted paragraph 14 of the *Constitution on the Sacred Liturgy* speaks of the "full, conscious, and active participation" of the faithful in liturgical celebrations. Elsewhere, in paragraph 11, we read:

> Pastors of souls must therefore realize that, when the liturgy is celebrated, more is required than mere observance of the laws governing valid and licit celebration. It is their duty also to ensure that the faithful take part knowingly, actively, and fruitfully.

The "more" that is "required" beyond the "mere observance of the laws" involves issues of style for the celebrant, a style that fosters the knowing, active, fruitful, full, and conscious participation of the rest of the assembly.

"Secular" and "Sacred" Communication Skills

People in many professions often learn fundamental advice about interpersonal communication. This same advice applies to anyone who must regularly deal with other people, yet, based on the way that many ministers conduct themselves during a worship service, it seems that some of them never absorbed this advice during their seminary training. The advice is this: *since studies show that more is communicated nonverbally than verbally, one must always be aware of what is being communicated nonverbally.* Sales representatives know that they can do more selling by their manner and style than by sophisticated arguments about the quality of their products. Even college students are coached on how to "sell" themselves when companies interview them for a prospective first job. In an article geared for graduating engineers, Carolyn Kues suggests that "what is said in a conversation or interview conveys only 7% of the total message. The other 93% is communicated nonverbally" (1990, p. 39). She suggests that any job applicant should pay attention to (and practice) several nonverbal ways that communication takes place between individuals, especially the handshake, appearance, body posture, gestures (especially appropriate "mirroring" or matching the other person's gestures), facial expressions, smiling, head nods, and eye contact. Other authors may debate the figures given by Kues, and more people may agree with numbers such as 33% for verbal and 67% for nonverbal, but almost all would agree that more is communicated nonverbally than verbally.

How often do we experience our colleagues in the ministry (or even ourselves) overlooking and contradicting these principles in liturgical settings? Our words may say "yes," but too often our bodies say "no," and people do "listen" more to our bodies than to our words. As a case study, let us again reflect on the opening rite of the Mass, specifically the *manner of greeting* and the *location* of the presiding priest.

At the liturgy, certain "greetings and responses" occur between the priest who presides at the assembly and the people gathered in prayer. In non-liturgical settings, when one person greets another, there is usually eye contact between the two, a posture of openness, and an occasional hug or two. However, in churches, some celebrants still "greet" the assembly with hands tightly clasped and eyes fixed on the book. Even though the priest's words are trying to convey God's presence, his body is conveying a certain discomfort with the assembly.

Location is another important factor in communication (Hall, 1959). The sanctuaries of many churches only partially accommodate a post-Vatican II liturgy, in that they have never thoroughly actualized the vision of the present Missal in the placement of altar, ambo, and chair. As a result, some priests still follow the rubrics of the Tridentine Missal and stand at the altar (or ambo) whenever they speak to the assembly. However, the present Missal envisions that for the Opening Rite of the Mass (and also for the Profession of Faith, the General Intercessions and the Concluding Rite), the presider stands at a chair that is visibly (and even physically) accessible to the assembly. The introduction to the Lectionary even allows the presider to be seated at the chair while delivering the homily. Ideally, the chair will enable the presiding priest to be seen and heard, and will symbolize his leadership of the assembly and his accessibility to its members. A well-placed (and utilized) chair will aid the communication taking place during the liturgy.

However, often one witnesses celebrants who place themselves behind a sturdy pulpit or a solid altar during the initial greeting and other opening rites, as if to make sure that some strong barrier lies between them and those they are welcoming. Locating the chair behind the altar, even though an old tradition, often has the same disadvantage, particularly if the chair is close to the altar or on the same level as the altar. Symbolically, in these situations something exists between the assembly and its president at a significant moment of verbal communication. Some might (unconsciously) interpret this as saying that the presiding priest somehow fears the people of God and is trying to keep his distance by ensuring that something substantial separates him from them. In a non-liturgical situation, such as a visit to someone's home for dinner, when guests arrive at the house, the host doesn't hide behind a chair or peek out partially from the doorway (Hoffman, 1988, p. 191). If a host were to do this, the guests probably would get the hint that they are not really welcome.

By keeping a barrier between two people during a greeting, the body says: "I don't want to be close to you" or "I'm glad there is something between us because I feel safer that way" even though the words convey a sense of welcome. A presidential chair mis-used, mis-placed, or ignored by the presiding priest can communicate all the wrong messages!

The "How" of Verbal Communication

In *You Just Don't Understand*, Dr. Deborah Tannen (1990), a professor of linguistics at Georgetown University, writes about differences in conversational style between men and women, and how that affects their relationships. She has tried to study the "language beyond the sentence," and how the use of intonation and pauses can be just as important in conveying meaning as the words in a sentence. She writes, "much—even most—meaning in conversation does not reside in the words spoken at all, but is filled in by the person listening" (p. 37). Liturgical ministers can learn from reflecting on the works of such scholars. The words we read from the Lectionary or Sacramentary convey only part of our message to the rest of the assembly. Our "style" carries a significant amount of meaning and, in some cases, the personal "style" can be at odds with the official verbal message.

Those who proclaim the Scripture at worship need to take Tannen's findings seriously. In many places, the quality of readers is mediocre because people are not accustomed to proclaiming a text meant to be heard by a large group of people. Readers often read God's Word with as much life as they would read sections of the morning newspaper. However, this need not occur, since there are numerous helps available. For example, Liturgy Training Publications of the Archdiocese of Chicago annually publishes the *Workbook for Lectors and Gospel Readers* (and a similar Spanish book, *Manual Para Proclamadores de la Palabra*). This book prints the readings in sense lines with pause marks and indications as to which words readers should stress. In addition, a brief commentary on the Scripture text assists the reader's comprehension of the text, in order that the "style" of the reader can aid the message being conveyed.

People in other disciplines who take their work seriously often learn about communication methods much better than communicators of God's message, i.e., better than the clergy. At a recent mathematical convention, Dr. Paul Halmos, noted American mathematician and author of numerous books and articles, was invited to give a major talk. In order to make sure that his message reached the assembled delegates correctly and in all its fullness, Halmos practiced the talk 19 times in front of a mirror. Halmos is over 75 years old and has been teaching, giving short lectures, and presenting major addresses for over 45 years. Yet he felt this occasion important enough to practice and practice his presentation so that he communicated the message without hindrances. How many clerics have ever practiced a homily or even have enough courage to volunteer to let themselves be videotaped while celebrating an actual (or "pretend") Mass (and then analyze the tape afterwards)?

Practical Advice—Ministerial Mis-Communication

I would like to offer three extended examples of how mis-communication takes place during the liturgy and an additional list of questions suggesting other similar examples. All are examples of symbols and words used during Mass. These and other occurrences of mis-communication usually involve both a consciously intended message and an unconscious second message sent by the nonverbal behavior of the ministers or the arrangement and presence of the physical necessities for the celebration. The three main examples involve (a) altar bread, (b) missalettes, and (c) informal greetings. Let us reflect on these examples one by one.

Altar bread

The Tridentine Missal gave rise to the custom of a two inch host for the priest and one inch host for distribution to the people. Partially prompted by the rubrics of the Missal and partially influenced by eucharistic devotion, it became the standard practice that the priest would consume all of "his" host and distribute small hosts (separately consecrated in a ciborium or even previously consecrated and stored in the tabernacle) to the people. This older custom led many people, even after the publication of the revised Missal in 1970, to assume that priests should always be allocated newly-consecrated large hosts and people should normally receive small hosts (often consecrated at other Masses).

A careful reading of the present Missal reveals a significantly different custom, but, judging from practices witnessed in many a parish, the new custom has not supplanted the old. In paragraph 283, the *General Instruction of the Roman Missal* (Sacred Congregation for Divine Worship, 1974) prescribes that the bread for the Eucharist should be made in such a way that the priest is able to break it into a number of pieces, so that he might distribute them to at least some of those present. It also suggests that one large vessel might be appropriately used to contain all the altar bread together (par. 293), rather than separating the priest's host from those pre-pared for the people.

The intention of the revision was to emphasize a unity. The bread is one—therefore the community assembled is made one in Christ (cf. 1 Cor. 10:17). The former rite did not highlight and thus often ignored this aspect. What therefore seemed to be emphasized (by default) was a separation—the priest's (large) host versus the people's (small) hosts. To fulfill the prescriptions of the revised Missal, extra-large hosts (about six inches in diameter) are commercially available. Although sometimes called "concelebration"-size hosts, they should not be limited to concelebrations. These extra large hosts enable a celebrant to fulfil the requirements of the Missal to distribute some of the broken bread to those assembled.

Although the revised rubrics seem reasonable and sensible, I have rarely found churches which regularly implement them. When visiting a church at which I am to celebrate Mass, on occasion I have had to request specially that the sacristan place the large host prepared for me into the same vessel as the hosts prepared for the assembly. It seems that people have been brainwashed into believing that "Father's" host must for some reason always be kept separate from the hosts for the people. I have also had to specially request the extra-large hosts. What I request is (in my understanding) "standard operation procedure." It should not be seen as out of the ordinary, but too often it is.

Unfortunately, we have become so accustomed to communicating separation that we find it difficult to break those old customs and instead continue to communicate to people (nonverbally!) something contrary to scriptural tradition!

Using missalettes at the ambo

The throw-away "missalette," made of newsprint, originated in the years immediately after Vatican II when churches had to provide English texts for the people to speak their parts during the Mass and hymnals that contained appropriate hymns. Since there was no recent tradition of respecting the importance of symbol during Mass, many people saw nothing wrong with proclaiming the readings from the ambo from a missalette or even from a xeroxed or type-written page. That it might be more appropriate to proclaim the sacred Word of God from a sturdy, well-bound Lectionary never occurred to them! God's Word may be eternal, but in the missalette the people see something that is "here today and gone tomorrow." Although most people would probably be aghast at the suggestion that one could use a disposable paper cup to hold the blood of Christ in lieu of a golden chalice, many of the same people would see nothing wrong with reading the words of Christ in the gospels from a disposable missalette.

Informal greetings

Almost everyone has heard a celebrant begin a Mass by saying "Good Morning!" rather than the formal "The Lord be with you" or "The grace of our Lord Jesus Christ..." Certainly the celebrant should introduce the liturgy in a warm, friendly, and human manner. However, what is communicated in the phrase besides the two words "good" and "morning"? First of all, the phrase—an informal greeting, in common use even by strangers on the street—conflicts with a situation where everything else (the building, the clothing [i.e., vestments], the "script") speaks of formality. The nonverbal associations of these two (otherwise innocuous) words communicates something distinctly out of sync with the nonverbal communication of everything else around. Professor of Music Thomas Day calls it "that moment of supreme emptiness" (1990, p. 54). American liturgist Ralph Keifer even suggests that an informal greeting treats the assembly "as if they were bored or ignorant" (1980, p. 109; Smolarski, 1982, p. 39) because it implies (nonverbally) that the celebrant thinks that the assembly cannot fathom the depths of the formal words of the ritual greeting.

Other points

What does a homilist communicate by putting the homily notes on top of the Lectionary containing God's Word? What is communicated by putting the Lectionary on the floor or under a chair instead of in a special place (is the Eucharist ever put on the floor or covered with parish announcements)? What is communicated when a reader uses a small lectern for the non-gospel readings, but the deacon or priest uses a large pulpit (is the lay person not holy enough for the pulpit, or is what they read less important than the gospel)? What is communicated when in the middle of praying to a timeless God, a modern watch on the arm of the celebrant becomes visible to the assembly? What is communicated at marriages when only the bride and her female attendants walk down the main aisle and the men must magically appear from the side door or the sacristy? What is communicated at marriages when the mothers of the bride and groom are prevented from accompanying their children in the entrance procession? What is communicated when churches still have barriers (altar rails) keeping the sanctuary (psychologically) off limits to the assembly? What is communicated when national flags (e.g., American and Vatican) are prominently displayed in places of honor in church sanctuaries? What is communicated when the presider greets "each and every one of you" rather than "you all" (St. Paul emphasizes that we form one body of Christ!)? What is communicated when the presider blesses "us" rather than "you" (is the presider that uncomfortable with his liturgical role as leader of prayer and intercessor on behalf of those assembled)?

In these and many similar situations, we may communicate much more than we intend. The alert priest will take time to reflect on all that is communicated and adjust if necessary to make sure that he does not hinder God's message from taking full effect because of the nonverbal messages that contradict his words.

Conclusion

In Jesus, God has enfleshed the Divine Word with material Creation. Because of the Incarnation, God continues to convey power and divine presence through visible and tangible realities. That is the ultimate meaning of the sacramental tradition in the Catholic and Orthodox Churches. Communicating the Word does not take place solely through human words. Much communication of the Word can and does take place nonverbally. Those entrusted with leading the worship of the community have the particular obligation and duty of making use of everything at their disposal to help communicate that message. Leaders of worship also have the obligation and duty to make sure through ambience, posture, body language, demeanor, and style, that God's Word is not hindered from performing its task.

10

Preaching the Gospel in a
Video Culture

Robert P. Waznak, S.S.

Of all the senses, trust only the sense of sight.
— Aristotle, *Metaphysics*

If you want truth, don't come to us. We'll tell
you anything but the truth. Go to God. Go to
your gurus. Go to yourselves. But don't come
to us....Your lives are real, we are the illusion.
— Howard Beal in Paddy Cheyevsky's *Network*

The homiletic reforms of the Second Vatican Council obliged preachers to
take seriously both the biblical text and the cultural context in which the
Gospel is proclaimed. In the "Dogmatic Constitution on Divine Revelation,"
the Council insisted that preaching "should be nourished and ruled by sacred
Scripture" (*Dei Verbum*, No. 21. All quotations of the Documents of the
Second Vatican Council are from Flannery, 1992.). The homily was to take
"into account the mystery which is being celebrated and the *particular needs
of the hearers*" ("Instruction on the Proper Implementation of the Constitution on the Sacred Liturgy," No. 54. Emphasis added). The "Decree on the
Ministry and Life of Priests" insisted that preaching "expound the Word of
God not merely in a general and abstract way but by an application of the
eternal truth of the Gospel to the *concrete circumstances of life*" (*Presby-
terorum Ordinis*, No. 4. Emphasis added).

At the same time that the Council was seeking to renew the preaching
of the Church by a communication system suited to the needs of our con-

Sections of this chapter first appeared in "The Church's Response to the Media:
Twenty-Five Years After *Inter Mirifica*," *America* (January 21, 1989) and "Preach-
ing the Gospel in an Age of Technology," *New Theology Review* (November, 1989).
They are printed with permission of the author and respective editors.

temporary culture, it was also grappling with the most pervasive force in our culture, the mass media. Vatican II's "Decree on the Means of Social Communication," *Inter Mirifica*, sought to formulate the Church's position on the mass media along with proposals for their employment to spread the Gospel.

Three decades have passed since the promulgation of the first two documents of the Council, "The Constitution on the Sacred Liturgy," *Sacrosanctum Concilium*, and *Inter Mirifica*. We now have insights from both preaching and media scholars that were not available to those who wrote the conciliar documents. In this chapter, we will explore these insights and their implications for preaching the Gospel in a media culture.

Preaching the Homily

The Second Vatican Council did not introduce a new preaching form but returned to the spirit of an old preaching form, the homily, which was once an integral part of the liturgy. The earliest liturgies manifested a unity between the scriptural texts of the day and the sacramental·action that followed. The liturgical renewal of Vatican II signaled a turn from the "traditional" sermon where moral and dogmatic topics were presented in the defense of the Catholic faith, to the ancient biblical homily.

Much of Catholic preaching prior to the Council amounted to not much more than a retelling of the gospel story with some moral exhortations. If the scripture readings of the day were referred to, they were used to prove some doctrinal point or moral teaching. The unfaithful Jews of the Old Testament texts were often presented as foils for the faithful disciples of Jesus.

A corrective to this mode of preaching came from the new biblical commentaries that were being published at the same time that the Church was calling for a return to biblical homilies. Modern biblical scholarship promised to tell us what the text meant, which seemed like an indispensable step toward the homily, which was supposed to tell us what the text means for us today. Thus, a homiletic method began to emerge wherein the preacher attempted to apply the discoveries of modern biblical scholarship to today's community of faith. While this new method was an improvement, it sometimes resulted in a lecture rather than a homily; it was an explanation, rather than a breaking open of the Word of God. Donald Senior, acknowledged this didactic tendency when he wrote

> Nothing is deadlier than a sermon or a homily that turns out to be simply an analysis of the biblical text....Very often articles and commentaries on Scripture are exegetical in nature—they may not even bring up the question of what the text might mean for a believing Christian today. That is one reason why preachers can be frustrated when they look

for homily ideas from exegetes. Good homily ideas will usually come from preachers rather than exegetes. (1986, p. 16)

Without abandoning the contributions that modern biblical scholarship can offer to authentic biblical preaching, today's homiletic literature encourages homily preparation where the preacher first listens and dwells with the biblical text in prayerful imagination before consulting biblical commentaries. *Fulfilled In Your Hearing: The Homily in the Sunday Assembly (F.I.Y.H.)*, the document on preaching produced under the auspices of the National Council of Catholic Bishops, urges homilists not to run first to the "experts." "By doing to, we block out the possibility of letting these texts speak to us and to the concerns we share with a congregation" (Bishops' Committee, 1982, p. 32).

F.I.Y.H. goes beyond the restrictive definitions of the homily found in the first document of the Council, *Sacrosanctum Concilium.* It incorporates the "reading of the signs of the times" motif found "The Pastoral Constitution on the Church in the Modern World," *Gaudium et Spes.* This last document of Vatican II defined "reading the signs of the times" as a task of "the whole people of God" (No. 44); it is a process of discernment by which the Church pays serious attention to "the events, the needs, and the longings" of our time so that we may be able to discover "genuine signs of the presence or of the purpose of God" (No. 11).

Assimilating these theological insights from *Gaudium et spes* and from *Dei verbum, F.I.Y.H.* presents the homily primarily as an interpretive rather than an instructional event. In the homily, "the preacher does not so much attempt to explain the Scriptures as to interpret the human situation through the Scriptures" (Bishops' Committee, 1982, p. 20). The object of the homily is an unveiling of meaning. The preacher is not primarily a teacher, but a "mediator of meaning" who attends to the present moment as revelatory of God:

> The preacher represents this community by voicing its concerns, by naming its demons, and thus enabling it to gain some understanding and control of the evil which afflicts it. He represents the Lord by offering another word, a word of healing and pardon, of acceptance and love. (Bishops' Committee, 1982, p. 7)

The "other word" that the preacher presents is an alternative way of looking at our world. It is the biblical alternative that both affirms the afflicted and confronts the comfortable. Walter Brueggemann has proposed that contemporary preaching should be viewed as "a poetic construal of an alternative world." He defines the preacher as one who "mediates what is true about us as it is known and sounded in the texts" (1989, p. 6). The Bible offers a compelling alternative to many of the myths of our culture. The biblical worldview challenges our *quid pro quo* world view that values only what is knowable, manageable, and predictable. In the biblical alternative, graciousness is valued over what is earned, mystery is cherished rather than explained, and transcendence replaces a world where everything must be controlled and manipulated. The biblical alternative offers healing and life where all seems broken and impossible—which is why we call it good news (Brueggemann, 1977).

The Bible, therefore, is not the preacher's "how to" book. The Bible is the Church's book of poetry that raises the questions of why. Canonical critics remind us that the stories in Scripture were remembered and "canonized" because they told people about their lives and at the same time told them there was something more to their lives.

The primary goal of the liturgical homily is not to repeat or explain the biblical text but to spark the imagination of listeners so that they will read the signs of the times in light of the alternative world of the Gospel. In *Dei Verbum*, the Bible is compared to "a mirror, in which the Church during its pilgrim journey here on earth, contemplates God" (No. 7). The vocation of the preacher is to hold up that mirror in an imaginative way so that, despite our sinful lives and our anguished world, we can see ourselves as graced and interpret our times as Good News.

Before leaving this section on our present understandings of the liturgical homily, let us briefly consider some contemporary insights about the homily's form. Because the "traditional" sermon, prior to the reforms of Vatican II, was more didactic than interpretive, a deductive form of preaching dominated. There was an introduction which proposed a dogmatic or moral thesis, "points" (usually three) and illustrations to prove the thesis, and a final exhortation. Today's "new homiletic" scholars (Craddock, 1978, 1979) challenge this homiletic form which is more suited to a lecture than a homily. They have also been stressing the importance of creating homilies in words and images that the assembly will recognize. The "new homiletic" encourages preachers not to use scripture to prove a point or hammer out a lesson but to disclose a new way of looking at life, an alternative vision. An inductive form, which moves like a story rather than a lesson, seems more appropriate to a media-bombarded society. A television commercial, for example, is a condensed parable. It does not begin with a thesis, but a human situation. It does not contain three points but gets to the point. A commercial does not tell people what to believe or do but offers an alternative to the way things are. That is why many of today's homileticians advocate an inductive or narrative form with attention to images. These forms are similar to the biblical form of story and also seem more appropriate to today's video culture. They are analogically designed to enable listeners to recognize a living word of meaning in the "concrete circumstances of their lives."

Preaching and the Media

It is an irony that *Inter Mirifica*, which dealt with the most pervasive force in our culture, became the least significant document of the Council that sought to "read the signs of the times." Bleak assessments of the decree began to surface a month before it was promulgated. At a U.S. Bishops' press panel, Gustave Weigel, S.J., said, "The decree does not strike me as being very remarkable. It is not going to produce great changes. It does not contain novel positions but gathers and officially states a number of points previously stated and taught on a less official level" (Abbott, 1966, p. 318).

The council fathers were told on November 21, 1962, that the communications schema would be considered just two days later. Some believed that this would be an easy document to deal with and would provide a welcome respite after the stormy debates on the sacred liturgy and sources of revelation. Cardinal Fernando Cento, president of the commission for presenting schemata, asked the fathers for their good will in dealing with a schema that was not strictly theological in substance but was pastorally important since the new mass means of communication could prove to be either a great blessing or a terrible curse both for the Church and the faithful (Vorgrimler, 1966, p. 90).

The most stimulating of the discussions on the schema came from Bishop François Charriere of Lausanne and Fribourg and Bishop Herbert Beduorz of Katowice in Poland who acknowledged that the times in which we live are influenced more by image than by abstract thought. Some bishops, like Manuel Fernandez-Conde of Cordoba, Spain, and William Godfrey of Westminster, took a suspicious stand toward the evils of the entertainment media. Although the United States was the center of modern mass media, the only American to speak on the schema was Cardinal Francis Spellman of New York who praised the usefulness of the schema but was bothered by its length.

A month prior to the final vote on *Inter Mirifica*, a group of Americans produced a statement that was not in favor of the decree. The statement, issued on November 16, 1963, was issued by experts in the mass media. It received public support from three council theologians, American John Courtney Murray, S.J., Frenchman Jean Danielou, S.J., and Argentinean Jorge Meiga. The American document stated that the schema reflected

a hopelessly abstract view of the relationship of the Church and modern culture....No decree which the Second Vatican Council has yet discussed could touch the lives of contemporary men (sic) so directly. And yet this decree, as it now stands, may one day be cited as a classic example of how the Second Vatican Ecumenical Council failed to come to grips with the world around it. (Abbot, 1966, pp. 332-333)

Another statement protesting the schema emerged from 26 bishops of the Council. They argued against the promulgation of the decree because it was written by people with little knowledge of the mass media. Despite these last minute attempts, the communications schema passed by a relatively narrow margin of 190 votes above the minimum required for a two-thirds majority. Both *Inter Mirifica* and *Sacrosanctum Concilium* were promulgated on December 4, 1963.

It was unfortunate that the council fathers did not have the benefits of insights of scholars like Marshall McLuhan (1962), who, while the Council was in session, were predicting that the media would eventually change our whole perspective of the world. As early as 1969, William Kuhns was high-lighting media's impact on the world of faith:

> The entertainment milieu has transformed the ways in which we believe and are capable of believing. An absolute kind of belief, as well as a belief in absolutes, becomes increasingly difficult as the entertainment milieu trains people to believe tentatively and with elasticity...the very concept of faith—to believe in that which you cannot see and cannot understand—comes with difficulty to a generation that has depended, as perhaps no generation before, on its senses. (1969, p. 165)

It was also unfortunate that *Inter mirifica* was one of the first documents of Vatican II. Lacking the wisdom and theological embrace of the later documents of the Church and its relationship with the world, the decree was isolationist and utilitarian in its approach. Avery Dulles has noted that *Inter mirifica* represents the institutional model of the Church as authoritative teacher (1988, p. 122). The decree is filled with presumptions about the power of the Church to control and influence the mass media. Its authors failed to understand that unlike previous times, the Church was now entwined and dependent on a channel of communication, which was outside its control.

One of the major reasons that *Inter Mirifica* proved not to be an influential conciliar document was because it was written by people who knew little about the topic. Toward the end of their debate on the schema, the bishops realized that they were confronting a topic beyond their expertise. That is why they mandated a pastoral instruction on communications in article 23 of the decree. That instruction, *Communio et Progressio* (1971) was written by media experts and is a more intelligent and practical document than *Inter Mirifica*. The Pastoral Instruction of 1971 incorporates such themes as ecumenism, personal freedom, and dialogue that were not firmly established at the time of the writing of *Inter Mirifica*. Its emphasis is not on the Church's use of media but on the contribution of media to human progress. *Communio et Progressio* describes today's world as "a great round table" at which a worldwide community is being formed through an exchange of information and cooperation (No. 19, 73).

More than three decades after the Council, we have a convincing body of literature that demonstrates how the media, especially television, has become an alternative to religion. If one agrees that religion is a statement about life and tackles the ultimate meaning in life, then television is religion. Television seeks to define our world, to tell us how it works and what it really means. The world of television cultivates habits of the heart by defining roles and telling us who is important and who is not. George Gerbner, former dean of the Annenburg School of Communication in Philadelphia, puts it this way: Television acts as "the cultivator of our culture." Gerbner reminds us that "what people learn best is not what their teachers think they teach, or what their preachers think they preach, but what their cultures in fact cultivate" (quoted in Fore, 1987, p. 21).

Like our preaching, the task of television is "to read the signs of the times." Television attempts to define our world and tell us who we are. Like preaching, it mediates meaning. Like preaching, television offers an alternative reading of our lives. Television is not a neutral communication medium but an integrated symbolic world of myths. Empirical research of television's myths suggests a consistent value system. Gerbner's research demonstrates how television portrays a world in which two-thirds to three-fourths of the important characters are male, America, middle class, unmarried, and in the prime of life—and they are the people who run the world (quoted in Fore, 1987, p. 63).

Studies of religious television by Gerbner and Gallup reveal the fascinating fact that the "sins" of religious programming are similar to general television productions. In both, men outnumber women three to one. Men are dominant in both. Non-whites are underrepresented in relation to their actual numbers in society. Children and elderly people are also underrepresented. "In both prime-time drama and religious programs, blue-collar workers, the unemployed, the retired and housewives are practically invisible" (Gerbner, Gross, Hoover, Morgan, Signorielli, Cotugno, & Wuthnow, 1984, Vol. 1, p. 52).

Religious people, including preachers, have long been concerned about television's ability to project a world where promiscuous sex and gratuitous violence are taken for granted. Television programming portrays stories where the only people who do not participate in sex are those who are married. Although TV sitcoms profess to mirror real life, it is a rare episode where people go to church or pray (which does not reflect the actual statistics of American religious life). Martin Marty (1967) has observed that the "proper" opinion always dominates on television, and the Christian view is always "improper" opinion. Marty notes that only during Christmas and Easter week is there any authentic reflection of people's Christian beliefs and practices. He has referred to this phenomenon as television's "Be Kind to God Week."

Besides these obvious challenges to the preacher, William Fore, Assistant Secretary for Communication in the National Council of Churches of Christ in the United States, believes that there are other dominant myths in television programming that should also be of concern to church people. Fore lists a few of televisions's central myths and values:

- The fittest survive.
- Happiness consists of limitless material acquisition.
- Property, wealth and power are more important than people.

- Everything can be purchased to satisfy our narcissism and immediate gratification.
- Progress is an inherent good. (1987, pp. 64-67)

Fore claims that the media "seek out and detect those values and assumptions which appear to be acceptable in the culture. This is done without regard for any moral or religious considerations, since the media are a part of The Technique which is interested only in *what works*" (1987, p. 43). What works is what sells. The life-blood of television is advertising. Advertisers spend billions of dollars each year to get their message across. The ultimate question of television is not how this will affect people's lives but how this will make a profit. The automobile industry combines two related strategies: annual model changes and advertising cars less as tools of transportation than as freedom of choice. These two advertising strategies convince us that we are what we own, but what we currently own is not enough.

Like the preacher, the television advertiser employs behavioral scrips: "Datsun saves and sets you free." "Buick is something to believe in." "The night belongs to Michelob." "Work ends with Miller time." "Coke is the real thing." Peter Mann (1984) has written how we become unwitting actors in these behavioral scripts which effectively employ the symbols of culture, religion, and myth so that the images plunge into our psyches. Recent homiletic literature has focused on the necessity of the preacher to fashion homilies in a fashion congruent with the immediacy and imagery of today's media world. Thomas H. Troeger has suggested "a cinemographic technique, which includes leaping through spans of time without the sustained development of a logical argument" (1990, p. 48).

Television advertising also tells us from childhood that we are despicable and inadequate because of the products we lack: curly hair, sweet breath, slim bodies, sexy clothes, zitless skin. That is why preachers must not mute the clear biblical message that existence means not what we have or what we can do but who we are as Covenant partners with God. The Bible provides an alternative way of discerning our identity and relating to our world.

While the preacher can gain much from a serious critique of television as an alternative religion, there is much to be admired about its potential for good. While we should be critical of television's reading of the signs of the times vis-à-vis the Gospel alternative, we must not become paranoid. Television has demonstrated a unique power to challenge our parochialism and to help us see our interdependence in the world community. Günter Virt has observed that our "mass-mediated culture for the first time offers humans the possibility of global participation in the sorrows as well as the values of various cultures. Thereby, the truth about the humane enters our consciousness more colorfully and diversely" (1994, p. 66). NBC picked up a piece of BBC film via satellite showing children starving in Africa and people all over the globe were galvanized to action. The image of Chernobyl powerfully revealed our universal vulnerability to nuclear technology and our shared fate with the future of humanity. In the watershed year of 1990, we were struck with the images of people in Eastern Europe demonstrating for democracy in the non-violent manner they had seen on U.S. television. They joined hands and sang, "We Shall Overcome."

While it is true that television talk shows have attained new lows in tasteless exhibitionism, they have also sometimes focused on topics of concern and ultimacy that people rarely hear talked about in the pulpit, like abused children, the homeless, religious hypocrisy. While it is true that television ordinarily does not allow for what Jürgen Habermas calls "unconstrained communication," there are exceptions. On the evening of the 20th anniversary of our landing on the moon, a viewer of the *MacNeil/Lehrer NewsHour* could listen in on a stimulating conversation with James Michener, Maya Angelou, and Isaac Asimov. Michener represented the technological person and contended that we should continue to explore space because it was there. He asked,"*How* could we do it?" But Angelou asked the questions all poets dare to ask, "*Why* are we doing it?" She wondered how President Bush's program to explore Mars will cut into our social services for the poor. Asimov wondered why our space expeditions should have to settle on either exploring the universe or helping the needy. He questioned instead the senseless outlays of money spent on weapons of destruction like the B-2 stealth bomber. The conversation was rich and rewarding. It forced us to look at our world and ask not only *how* but *why*.

Not all television is vacuous or opposed to the Gospel alternative. Sometimes, in a story, there is a compelling portrayal of our limited horizons. The German homileticians have a word for this human point of vulnerability, *anknupfungspunkt*. This point of vulnerability and a search for grace in the world in often captured imaginatively on television. The preacher must learn to glean the good grain from our video world and separate it from the chaff.

It is true, therefore, as we are told in *Gaudium et Spes* that our new video culture offers both a conflicting alternative to the Gospel and also the possibility of a universal human solidarity (No. 53-55). Authentic preachers of the sacred text cannot ignore the video context in which they now preach. Our video culture must be affirmed when it makes possible a more effective revelation of the Gospel but also challenged when it offers cheap grace.

From our exploration of contemporary understandings of both the liturgical homily and our video culture, two major convictions emerge:

1. *The preacher's need to recognize the video culture.* The homiletic reforms begun by Vatican II and developed in recent years by homileticians and biblical scholars urge preachers to consider the new world context in which the Gospel is proclaimed. Echoing the call of Pope John XXIII to "read the signs of the times," Pope Paul VI counseled preachers to proclaim

the Gospel not in "an old, abstruse way, cut off from life and contrary to the tendencies and tasks of today" (quoted in Burke, 1978, p. ix).

Whether we like it or not, we proclaim the Gospel in a video culture. In the words of *Network's* Howard Beal, television is "the most awesome, the most powerful force ever unleashed." Today's preachers cannot claim that they are somehow immune from our video culture. Some preachers may consider television a medium of mindless entertainment, a secular trash machine that churns out worthless images and dangerous values. Since some preachers do not watch television, they wonder why it should matter to their preaching ministry. They fail to recognize its pervasive force in today's world both for good and evil. They fail to realize that their congregations are more powerfully influenced by television than by the Church. The television set in the average American home is on seven hours and seven minutes a day. The average viewer watches about four hours and 30 minutes each day. "Aside from eating, sleeping and working, most people in the United States spend about 80% of their entire lives in the world of television rather than in the real world" (Fore, 1987, p. 16).

In today's video culture, listeners are accustomed to getting information quickly and thus their attention span has contracted. The 30-second commercial, the 10-second sound bite, the three-minute news report, the 10-minute entertainment slot are serious challenges to the long-winded homily. Television powerfully communicates not just with words but images, not just with messages but stories. Unlike the homily with three points (which only the homilist remembers) television commercials have one point: "The best part of waking up is Folgers in your cup!" Our video culture challenges homilies that are instructional rather than interpretive, cognitive rather than evocative, deductive rather than inductive, predictable rather than imaginative.

2. *The preacher's need to proclaim the biblical alternative in a video culture.* Virgil and Cicero used the word *cultum* in the context of worship. Culture is a revelation system. Culture effectively transforms, provides heroics, organizes our world, suggests human fulfillments. Culture is a gospel; it reveals an alternative way of looking at ourselves and our world. Culture creates in us habits of the heart. In this chapter we have seen how television rather than the Church is becoming more effective in creating habits of the heart. People find in our video culture a world view which reflects ultimate values and a way of life.

We have seen how there are times when television courageously offers new possibilities of viewing our lives in images and stories that are paradigmatic of the Gospel. We have also seen, how our video culture's value system clashes mightily with the Gospel alternative.

We have seen how the authors of *Inter Mirifica* failed to grasp the fact our video culture is not just a challenge to religion, but a form of religion. It, too, reads the signs of the times. Preachers today must not only find clues from the media on how to preach the Gospel more effectively, but also have faith in the Gospel alternative which offers a fresh new way for looking at our lives in terms of God.

In *Fulfilled In Your Hearing* the object of the homily is an unveiling of meaning. The preacher is described as a "mediator of meaning." Asserting the authority of the Church, the Bible, or biblical exegetes will not unveil meaning nor help listeners to read the signs of the times. An imaginative presentation of the Gospel as an alternative vision to many of the myths of our culture is what is needed.

Postscript

Caring preachers have always picked up the Gospel with this world in mind. From the beginning, the Gospel was preached not in sacred languages but in the language of the people. Jesus spoke Aramaic, Paul used *koine* Greek, Origen chose not the stylized rhetoric of the academy but the familiar discourse of his culture. We too must proclaim the Gospel in our own day in words, images, and forms that are called for by our video culture.

The bishops of Vatican II sensed that the media were offering new challenges and blessings to the Church. They grappled with the fact that people today are influenced more by image than abstract thought. Preachers today are in a more advantageous position than the authors of the documents of Vatican II. They can benefit from the insights of today's homileticians and media scholars who have demonstrated how our video culture has shaped and challenged the way we proclaim the Gospel today.

11

The Use of Media in the Teaching of Church History

Robert J. Wister

The first day of class for incoming students in schools of theology always produces a wealth of anecdotes in the faculty lounge. Professors
encounter once again a diversity of ages and backgrounds in the classroom. They deplore how many students come with little or no understanding of Catholic traditions that, in years past, provided a foundation
of habits of life, knowledge of doctrine, and understanding of Christian
principles. They express concern that since increasing numbers of students have so little grounding in these traditions, professional education
might easily lapse into adult catechesis.

Professors of church history may be relied upon to recount some of the
most interesting tales, often the most discouraging. While theology professors might lament the weakness of the religious education background of
their students, church history professors too often encounter not a weak
background in their field but no background at all. Precious few of the students in theological schools are history majors. Sad but true, one can earn a
bachelor's degree at many colleges and universities without ever taking a
course in world history, much less the history of the Church. Unfortunately,
some even see history as an intrusion which takes valuable time from pur-
suits perceived to be more important and more practical.

One professor who combines excellence and humor in the conduct of
his classes has told his colleagues that "Today's first year students envision
the history of the world as divided into the past and the present. The present
includes people who are alive and the past includes people who are dead.
Abraham Lincoln, Julius Caesar, Pope Pius XII, Moses, James Dean, St.
Peter, Henry VIII, Socrates, John Kennedy, Hammurabi, St. Francis, Cleopa-
tra, and George Washington are among the dead. They all lived in the past
at indeterminate times and in indeterminate places."

The *tabula rasa* which confronts the professor of history presents several challenges. The integrity of church history as a graduate discipline is
difficult to maintain in the face of so scant a foundation on which to build.

144

Graduate theological education involves more than imparting information. The most effective teaching takes place in an informed dialogue between students and teacher. It presumes a relatively elevated level of reflection on culture, a capacity for clear and reasoned argument, an acquaintance with the cultural history of Western civilization, some facility with more than one language, a background in the history of Western philosophy. It requires that the student analyze and synthesize information gleaned from primary as well as secondary sources. The lack of any of the above makes this task difficult. When confronted with students who may lack a structure or framework in which to relate new learning, it can be discouraging indeed.

Yet today's students are not intellectually less gifted than their predecessors. They have had a variety of learning experiences, formal and informal, structured and unstructured, traditional and non-traditional. The teacher must accept the backgrounds and talents of the students and the potential difficulties they will encounter and adjust course materials accordingly. The effects of technology and television have altered students' expectations in every level of education and, if we ignore them, our teaching will suddenly become not simply outmoded, but actually ineffective. The teacher who ignores the reality of students' learning modalities might end up teaching students who aren't really there.

The use of technology in classrooms has not replaced the teacher. Rather, the teacher is challenged to use the technology available creatively to excite students about learning and to increase their capacity to understand and to discover. In all cases, the technology is only as good as the teacher. Of all the disciplines taught in graduate theology, church history most easily adapts itself to the use of media. A wide variety of media are available and relatively easy to utilize.

Classroom Media

From the earliest years of teaching, one may imagine the passing on of myth, legend, tradition, and history by referring students to paintings and statuary illustrative of the story being recounted. Later, engraved illustrations and woodcuts would acquaint students with the physical appearance, real or imagined, of major historical figures.

More recently, professors have used slides and short films in the classroom to illustrate lectures and arouse interest in a particular issue or subject under discussion. They have also employed a variety of documentaries but, I believe, with very limited success. No matter how well done, documentaries rarely entertain or engage the audience. Quite often, they are little more than expensively packaged illustrated lectures.

In the last two decades, assignments may have included the viewing of historical series, such as those produced on BBC and elsewhere including, for example, *Elizabeth R; I, Claudius; The Six Wives of Henry VIII;* and

A.D. Many of these feature careful research and present an reasonably accurate historical picture. Glenda Jackson and Derek Jacoby give memorable performances as the "Virgin Queen" and the hapless but shrewd Emperor Claudius. Yet they suffer from a number of disadvantages. All are rather rigid chronicles in which the characters and the plots develop at a very slow pace. *Elizabeth R* presents a portrait of a fascinating woman, a political genius who dominated the course of British history for generations, but neglects many issues of importance for the teaching of church history. *I, Claudius* and *The Six Wives of Henry VIII* take on a melodramatic air and slip into the style of the evening soap operas of the 1970s and 1980s. Each becomes a sort of *Dallas* on the Tiber or the Thames. One must admit that this might not be the fault of the television writers since both Suetonius' writings and Henry's life lend themselves to this genre. These and other such series are also rather long and require up to 12 hours of viewing time. Although they may be entertaining they are not really useful for advancing the cause of Clio.

Today a number of computer programs assist in developing basic skills in geography and other sciences ancillary to the teaching of history, church or other. Interactive multimedia and historical simulation programs replicate events of the past and allow the student to interact with the program. Computer assisted research tools also connect libraries and provide access to materials at a distance. Many of these computer programs hold great promise for the future but at present are not within the financial reach of most schools or have not been adapted to the specific needs of teaching church history.

With what does that leave us? Documentaries contain much useful information but are often boring. Television historical series are entertaining but over-long and rarely focused on important issues. Computer programs are still in their infancy and too often out of the financial reach of theological institutions.

The Feature Film

An often ignored and often misused resource does exist—the feature film. A number of feature films can be used to great advantage in stimulating interest in history and, with imagination, can serve the goals of classroom instruction. Feature films have several advantages over other types of film such as documentaries. They contain very human stories and conflicts that the documentaries often lose. In many cases, they are visually appealing, having been produced at astronomical cost. While not perfect in every historical detail, their defects provide an opportunity for critical discussion.

The feature film is a means to an end, not an end in itself. It cannot replace classroom activity or reading assignments. It is merely an aid, albeit a most effective aid. Feature films are most useful when teachers allow them to do what they were intended to do—to entertain. An unfortunately large portion of students have had very little background in historical studies. In addition, many have had unfortunate experiences in history classes which have caused them to discount or avoid the study of history. The feature film provides an opportunity to *engage* their interest in specific historical questions. The splendor of the production, the quality of the acting, and the very human conflicts of the film achieve this engagement in a way that a lecture or a reading would find difficult, if not impossible. This engagement serves as an opening wedge to stimulate questioning, and hopefully, further study and research.

These films give an opportunity not only to present to the student and to analyze the historical issues and questions that the specific film includes but also to show how human beings faced with crises, struggling with their consciences, seeking answers to questions that are perennial confronted these issues. Films give the professor the opportunity to instill a proper understanding of history as the story of humankind, a story in which real people grapple with the events of their times, succeed or fail in being faithful to their principles, and have an impact on the course of events. An individual such as Thomas More failed to influence the course of his contemporary world as he wished but the example of his fidelity to his conscience has overshadowed the "winners" through the centuries. Films can also assist in moving the student, who in most cases is a "beginner" in historical studies, from being a simple recipient of historical data to becoming a critical analyst of a presentation of history, here presented not in traditional form but through the medium of film. The beginning of this critical skill, if one can awaken it early in the course of studies through criticism of a film, can be further developed. The film breaks the ice in a way because of its familiarity. Students are used to film and television and they have opinions on what they see. Teachers can assist the step to a more professional degree of analysis by giving the students the opportunity to critically approach history through the use of this medium.

Before presenting a film teachers should set forth relevant pedagogical goals. Students should complete appropriate reading assignments geared to the topic or topics that the film illustrates before the viewing. Teachers should provide questions regarding the film in order to direct the students' focus and to stimulate subsequent discussion. This will raise particular issues and enable them to look for things which otherwise might escape their attention. It can also lead to the introduction of other related topics and stimulate interest in other areas. The preparation for the viewing of any other feature film should also include an explanation of the goal of the film within the course, its place in the history of American movies, and the context of the period in which it was produced.

Films that can be used successfully in the teaching of church history include *Quo Vadis, Becket, A Man for All Seasons*, and *The Mission*. I even venture to suggest that *The Bells of St. Mary's* and *On the Waterfront* can be used with profit. It is obvious to all that none of these films is historically accurate in every detail but they can serve our purposes. Let me briefly illustrate each as a classroom tool.

Quo Vadis

Quo Vadis provides an excellent example of using film to *engage* the student. At first instance, such a film might evoke ridicule from historical sophisticates. After all it recounts just a legend, whose written basis did not make it into the canon of Scripture. Even worse, it was done in the 50s, a period of unsophisticated popular religious enthusiasm. It seems to fall into that genre of film that includes *The Robe, Ben Hur*, and other costume dramas of the period. Yet it is something more. Peter Ustinov's Nero is an unforgettable character, a mixture of pathos, madness, and evil that at some moments even evokes sympathy. The love story of the Christian maiden Lygia and the Roman general Marcus Vinicius contains the same problems faced by interfaith couples today and presents opportunities to ask many intriguing questions about early Christian life. And much more.

This film provides presents an opportunity to introduce a wide variety of topics relevant to a course in early Christianity and also topics not immediately related to this period. What is *Quo Vadis*? It is a 19th century novelization of a story of the early Church found in the apocrypha. Its origin in the apocrypha means that, more than just a legend, it forms part of the attempt of early Christians to understand their origins and to understand themselves. The apocrypha refer to a body of literature stemming from the earliest traditions of the Church, and thus reflect a part of "Tradition" writ large. The film serves as a vehicle to introduce students to the apocrypha and to the concept of tradition itself. Used properly it can evoke deeper interest in early Christian writings and in the period of the early Church itself.

Before viewing *Quo Vadis*, the students should become familiar with the body of apocryphal literature; they might also read the *Acts of the Holy Apostles Peter and Paul*, in which the basis of this story is found. The viewing of the film should be the responsibility of the student and listed among course requirements like any reading assignment. (*Quo Vadis* and the other films mentioned are readily available for rental on cassette.)

Knowing the context of the film will also help the students. *Quo Vadis* comes from the early 1950s, a period of national confidence and a period when people still regarded the "main-line" churches as the trendsetters for the nation. Hollywood produced such films because of a demand for them. They made money. Would they today? What has changed?

The story purports to take place around 65-70 A.D. (C.E.). This very significant period in the growing self consciousness of the early Christians included the time of the Jewish rebellion, which culminated in the destruction of Jerusalem by Rome. The movie contains anachronisms as well as accurate portrayals of the period. Teachers should have students record mis-representations of the period as well as accurate presentations.

In the film the Christians appear as separate and apart from the other citizens of Rome. This raises the issue of whether or not first century Christianity was engaged in a battle with Roman society. Was it counter-cultural? If so, to what degree? A profitable discussion of the relation of Christians to contemporary society and its laws could then ensue.

Early in the story the emperor is referred to as "Supreme Pontiff." This is an obvious opportunity to present the significance of this title and its eventual adoption by the popes. It may seem trivial but why are Peter and Paul portrayed as they are in the film? What did St. Peter and St. Paul look like? Do we know? What do they look like in the movie? Christian art attributes certain physical characteristics to both of these men which perdure through the centuries. Is this an accident?

Paul is a very important character in *Quo Vadis* and the fact of his Roman citizenship is mentioned prominently. What was the significance of Paul's Roman citizenship and where in Scripture do we find indications of it? Would the author of the apocryphal "Acts" in which our story appears have been aware of it and what does this tell us about the relation of the canonical Scriptures and the apocrypha?

In the film an existing Christian community in Rome awaits the arrival of Peter. Who were they? Where do we find information concerning the Jewish community in Rome and where do we find indications of an early Christian community there? If there were Christians there before his arrival, can we say that Peter founded the church at Rome? What significance does their presence have with regard to the Primacy of Peter? The Christians in our film use signs to identify one another. In our era, which spurns the study of the classical languages, this gives us an opportunity to explain one of the earliest Christian symbols, the word "ICHTHUS."

Probably the visually most impressive, and the most expensive, scene is the triumphal return of Marcus Vinicius, the Roman general. In the scene of the triumph an individual tells the triumphant general, "Remember that thou art only a man." This little ceremony has a later echo in the ceremony of the coronation of the popes when a monk would precede the new pope being carried in triumph to his coronation. Three times he would burn a piece of flax and say to the pope, "Thus passes the glory of the world," reminding him at this summit of his life that he too was mortal. This link between ancient Roman custom and later liturgical practice can lead to a discussion on the relation of many liturgical developments and practices to secular usages. A footnote to the discussion is that the new ceremony of investiture, which replaced the coronation, dropped the burning of the flax and the reminder of the pope's mortality. This new ceremony, without the warning of papal mortality, was first used for the installation of John Paul I, who died a month later.

The enemies of the Christians accused them of "foul and secret rites." What were these accusations in detail and how did the Christians respond to them? The patristic sources and apologies lead the student to a further investigation of this factor in the relation of Christians to the Roman state.

The liturgical celebrations in the film give a good example of anachronisms. They portray a very commonly held vision of the early Christian community at prayer. The Christians in the film meet secretly in large groups; Peter wears a garment that suspiciously resembles a chasuble, a white one at that! The ritual of baptism resembles more *The Book of Common Prayer* than early Christian practice. The presence of a cross at the service is a glaring error. These distortions present an opportunity to correct many of the students' preconceptions about the period as well as to explain how these ideas have entered the consciousness of many Christians through novels and poorly done Bible histories. From these errors also arises an opportunity to open a discussion on the current state of scholarship regarding early Christian worship. A slightly more positive aspect of this segment of the film is Peter's account of the words of the Lord. Do they represent an adequate presentation of the passing on of the oral tradition or is the presentation naive? The background illustrations of Peter's discourse provide us with the film's most glaring "howler," the presentation of the "Last Supper" as an exact reproduction of da Vinci's masterpiece.

These difficulties, anachronisms, and misrepresentations aside, the central plot of the love between the Christian Lygia and the pagan Marcus Vinicius raises several interesting issues: intermarriage, the origins of the sacrament of matrimony, and syncretism. Foremost is the perennial matter of intermarriage between Christians and non-believers. How the couple deals with it proposes several interesting questions. Was intermarriage a problem? Were there specifically Christian marriage ceremonies and regulations at this time? Within this subplot, Marcus Vinicius offers to compromise by including Jesus in his garden pantheon. The Roman practice of syncretism, welcoming gods of any origin, clashed with Jewish and Christian exclusivity, which was incomprehensible to a Roman.

Other profitable questions include whether or not the film honestly presents Paul's views on slavery or takes liberties with Scripture to accommodate to contemporary expectations; and who burned Rome and why.

The film provides a charming character in the Roman courtier, Petronius, uncle of Marcus Vinicius. Basically a good man, he reacts negatively to the amorality and excesses of Nero's person and regime. With his high ethical values, Petronius reacts to his dilemma by committing suicide. His attitudes contrast with those of the Christians, yet he is a very sympathetic character. Was he a stoic or a cynic? When Nero hears of his death he dramatically sheds a tear into a "weeping vase." Surely this is a precious detail but when one considers that numerous such tear vases have been found in Christian as well as other tombs, it too can be a teaching tool.

Glass is, after all, one of the most durable of materials and found in many archaeological sites.

No religious film of the 50s is complete without a "Dance of the Seven Veils" and a martyrdom scene of some sort. *Quo Vadis* has both. Nero's attempt to blame the burning of Rome on the Christians brings shouts of "The Christians to the lions!" But is the film's account of the lions in the circus and the burning of martyrs accurate? What do the sources say? What do the apocryphal Acts tell us? What do they tell us of Peter's death upside down on a cross, which this film vividly depicts?

Properly utilized, *Quo Vadis* can engage the student while introducing a variety of significant historical and theological issues. It can provoke lively discussion and criticism. It can educate. Best of all, it can entertain, which is why it was made in the first place.

We can use other films to engage students in the study of different periods of the history of the Church. Teacher and student can similarly introduce, dissect, analyze, and critique each. I shall briefly offer several examples.

Becket

The romantics of the last century embraced the heroes and the architecture of the middle ages. Our future-oriented culture shrinks from the word "medieval." Undoubtedly, that world differs greatly from our own. The church-state disputes of this period might fascinate professional historians and canonists but seem alien and as dry as dust to contemporary Americans. To make the richness of the church life of the middle ages come alive can be a daunting task but the film, *Becket*, based on the play by Jean Anouilh, fills the bill. This film possesses all the necessary ingredients to arouse student interest. The magnificent performances of Richard Burton and Peter O'Toole, spectacular scenery, and skillful cinematography enhance the story of a personal relationship and its intense conflicts.

Like Shakespeare's historical plays, Becket telescopes events and employs artistic freedom to alter certain details of the events. Although not perfect in every detail, it presents a fairly accurate rendering of the church-state controversies of 12th-century England. Becket's personal pilgrimage culminates in a conversion, as a fun loving courtier is transformed into an ascetic, as the king's servant and boon companion becomes the king's nemesis and the Church's advocate. He never loses the fervor of a convert, even as he receives lessons in *realpolitik* from the French king and court. Having confronted his king to preserve the rights of the Church, he then encounters a venal papal court without losing his faith in the Church it represents. This complex man becomes a martyr and is acclaimed a saint, leaving behind the lingering question, "Did he plan it all that way?"

The solemn excommunication scene in which Becket catalogues the woeful consequences, civil and religious, which will befall a baron who has killed a priest, powerfully demonstrates the inextricable links of medieval church and state. It raises the questions of whether and when to use such radical remedies and even moves us to ask about their effects in the temporal and in the spiritual realms. *Becket* allows us the luxury of involving ourselves in church-state battles as human conflicts, conflicts of laws and theology, but also of very real personalities. *Becket* helps us to put flesh on several of those in the realm of the dead and even to identify with some of their religious and personal conflicts. I venture to add that the conversation regarding the proper relation of church and state, faith and society, has not ended in our own country and that the questions presented in this film can have contemporary relevance.

In considering the medieval period, I must add another film which is neither a feature film nor a documentary nor a miniseries. It is rather a film record of a medieval event which took place in 1953. Odd as it may seem, the middle ages came to life on June 6, 1953 and were recorded in the film, *A Queen is Crowned*, the technicolor record of the coronation of Elizabeth II. England is the only nation which still crowns its monarch in a ceremony rich in medieval imagery. This documentary rings with the commentary of Lawrence Olivier (which unfortunately is inaccurate in its description of several aspects of the ceremony). In spite of the shortcomings of the narrative, it is difficult to conceive of a better way to illustrate church-state relations, the investiture controversy, and the sacral character of the monarch that to watch the robing of Elizabeth II in dalmatic, stole, and cope. Regal unction clearly has sacramental aspects; whether it possesses sacramental character is best left to the theologians of the past.

The divine origin of kingship passed on through the medium of the Church appears on the screen as the archbishop, representative of God and the Church, places the crown on the head of the queen. But the subjection of the Church of England to the state cannot be more obvious than when the Archbishop of Canterbury kneels before the queen and pledges obedience. In today's England, Henry has soundly defeated Becket. Seminarians in the classroom will quickly note that the feudal ceremonial of obeisance in which the vassal places his hands within the hands of his liege lord or, in this case, lady clearly recalls the priest's pledging obedience to his bishop in a similar rite. Tradition is alive and well.

A Man for All Seasons

In any course treating the Reformation period *A Man for All Seasons*, Robert Bolt's screen adaptation of his own play, is the ideal film to engage student interest. Paul Scofield magnificently portrays the calm, placid yet tormented Thomas More. The film tells the story of one man in the midst of the Reformation, a man who wants to keep out of the fray but cannot escape.

The personal conflict between More and Henry VIII, while not as intense as that between Becket and the second Henry, involves real intellectual and moral agony; the frictions provoked by family responsibilities bring the period to life. These very real people struggle with their principles and their demons. The theological and historical questions are played out together with personal moral and ethical dilemmas. Papal supremacy, interpretation of Scripture, and indissolubility of marriage interface with the stability of the realm, the danger of Spain, and greed for monastic riches. All these intermingle with Henry VIII's desire for a son, his friendship with More, and his glandular drives. More's family, divided by the consequences of his legal hairsplitting as well as split by theological tensions, have less concern than he for the sanctity of his conscience. They want him to stay alive. Yet the supremacy of the individual conscience as well as the difficulty of the politician reconciling his private conscience and his public duty form the major themes. Orson Welles' Wolsey, the venal Cromwell, and the ambitious Richard Rich who sells his soul "for Wales?" add ingredients which combine to hold any viewer's attention.

For our specific purposes the film presents a reasonably accurate picture of the issues surrounding the early years of the English Reformation, the "King's Great Matter," the feeble English hierarchy, the creeping Calvinism of Cranmer, the catholic attitudes of the king, the compliance of the Parliament. It raises but does not answer the question of why the Reformation moved quickly and with comparatively little opposition in England.

More's trial brings many of these questions together and his final statement to the court summarizes not only his theology but shows the strength of his beliefs. The ethical and human dilemmas provide a perfect stage for encouraging deeper investigation of the historical issues. The very human aspects of the personal struggles provide an opportunity to emphasize the complexity of judging the people involved in this and other such dramas of the past and the present.

The Mission

Unfortunately, few films treat of more recent church history as well as the preceding. *The Mission*, based on an original story by Robert Bolt, is an exception. Too often courses in the history of Christianity in the United States neglect teaching the history of the Church in other parts of the Americas. The presence of increasing numbers of Catholics from the Latin American countries makes an understanding of their cultures and heritage essential.

This film, set a few years before the papal suppression of the Jesuits in the 18th century, recounts the story of the destruction of a Jesuit-founded Guarani community in the area of Paraguay, then disputed between Spain and Portugal. It is visually appealing and rich in the symbolism of conversion, penance, and redemption. Robert DeNiro's Rodrigo Mendoza, slave trader and murderer becomes, in succession, penitent, Jesuit, and revolutionary. The cardinal legate emerges as a symbol of ecclesiastical power twisted by political necessity, a man who tries to satisfy the pope, the Spanish, the Portuguese, the Jesuits, and his own conscience. He fails and sacrifices the

Guarani people for the perceived welfare of the Church and of the Jesuits. A magnificent musical score with ecclesiastical echoes adds to the attraction of this film.

While the film takes some liberty with historical events, it remains faithful to the story of the Jesuits, the Guarani, the Spanish, and the Portuguese. It demonstrates the mixed motivations which have so often influenced ecclesiastical political decisions. Like the other films cited, *The Mission* provokes many questions, in fact, more than it can answer. The Spanish *Patronato* and the Portuguese *Padroado* have left a legacy which has affected the destiny of two-thirds of the Americas. The clash between European and Native American cultures and the role of the missionaries in this encounter continue to be debated today.

The Mission clearly reflects a support for contemporary liberation theology and clerical activism in opposition to tyranny. If this sympathy is not clear enough from the film itself, which includes Daniel Berrigan as one of the missioners, it ends with a dedication to priests still laboring and dying for justice in Latin America.

The students probably know less about the story of the "Jesuit Republics" or "Reduciones," than they do about early Christians, the middle ages and the Reformation. Most have heard of Nero and Henry VIII, some have heard of Becket and More, few have heard of these unusual Jesuit missionary endeavors; they probably know equally little about the general history of the Church in Latin America. *The Mission* provides a presentation of the shadow side of the Spanish and Portuguese colonization contrasted with the heroic activities of the missionaries. It includes ecclesiastical politics at their worst exercised by a man who is far from evil, the clash of cultures, even the suppression of the Jesuits.

The priest in the movies

A large number of students in theology schools—the seminarians preparing for the priesthood—face the major issue of "priestly identity." One way to stimulate a discussion of priestly identity is to show how the film industry and television has perceived priests. This perception and the productions resulting from it both reflect the common perception of the priest and form it for better or worse. Priests have often appeared in films as minor characters and, on occasion, as central figures.

A number of films have reflected and misrepresented, formed and deformed the image of the American Catholic priest. Their impact on the perception of priests by the American public, Catholic and non-Catholic, cannot be underestimated. Those which centered on the career of a particular priest, real or fictional, have probably had the greatest impact. These films provide a way to show seminarians how the public has seen their colleagues and how it, truly or falsely, may someday see them. They also represent with varying degrees of fidelity the ecclesiology of their time as well as the attitudes of contemporary Catholics.

In the 1930s, Spencer Tracy as *Father Flanagan of Boystown* showed Depression-era America the priest as hero and entrepreneur, confronting overwhelming odds to care for the outcasts of society. As a rugged individualist, he was doubly attractive to the audience. But he was an exception to the norm. The 1940s gave us the comforting image of Bing Crosby in *The Bells of St. Mary's* and *Going My Way*. These rather sentimental portrayals of rectory life and church environment were in many ways not totally inaccurate portrayals of the day-to-day life of many contemporary priests. The very Irish atmosphere of Catholic life and clerical life shown in this film has remained in the understanding of many Americans today who continue to see Catholicism as Irish and Irish as Catholic. Unquestioning obedience, cassocked priests, habited nuns, and lots of them, completed the portrait of a Church which no longer exists except in the reveries of some and the dreams of others.

In the 1950s, Hollywood shifted its focus to the socially involved priest portrayed by Karl Malden in *On the Waterfront*. The priest, now the rugged hero, fights the mobs and lives in physical danger. *I Confess*, starring Montgomery Clift, focused on a source of continuing interest, the seal of the confessional. The priest's determination not to break the seal, even if it might cost him his life, gave a positive portrayal of a plausible dilemma.

Spectacle once again came to the fore in the 1960s film version of Henry Morton Robinson's *The Cardinal*, starring Thomas Tryon. Here the priest resolved personal conflicts and decisions in favor of the Church's teaching no matter how painful. The protagonist was not the rugged individual Father Flanagan or the heroic priest on the waterfront, but the hero become hierarch, the perfect cleric, who climbs up the ladder, not driven by ambition but directed by ecclesiastical patrons who recognize his worthiness and move him along rung by rung.

A much less worthy character appears in the 1970s as *Monsignor*, a hardly appealing cleric who seeks to climb the same ladder. More laudable is Robert DeNiro in *True Confessions*, who would compromise principle for "the good of the Church," usually the financial good, until he reaches a point of conversion.

The 1980s gave us *Last Rites*, a rather undistinguished film starring Tom Berenger, the priest as mobster and lecher. So far the 1990s have given us *Romero*, the story of a martyred contemporary prelate, controversial within and without the Church. A made for television film shows us the priest as child abuser. Weekly television has paraded an absolutely improbable priest detective accompanied by an equally unbelievable sister sidekick. A reflection on these films and shows can give students insights into the changes in contemporary mores over the last half century, the loss of confidence in governmental and ecclesiastical institutions, and in the individual officials who represent them. At the same time they paint a portrait of how the clergy and the Church are viewed, positively, negatively, and trivially.

These examples do not exhaust the list of possibilities by any means. Imagination will prod the teacher to use other films and other media to highlight a particular moment, theme or epoch of the history of the Church. The future will bring more sophisticated means of assisting the art of teaching. The adaptation of the CD-ROM and other technology will open opportunities not now imagined. But today as we introduce theology students to the treasures of the realm of history, perhaps to them the world of the dead, we can enflesh the dry bones with the gifts which Hollywood has unintentionally placed in our hands.

12

Possibilities of Audiovisual Narrative for Moral Formation

Henk Hoekstra, O. Carm., and Marjeet Verbeek

Introduction

The very active presence of mass media, particularly the audiovisual media (cinema and television), strongly influences our contemporary culture and plays an important role in creating popular culture. Therefore, when we speak about audiovisual media, we refer not only to instruments or techniques but to important cultural phenomena. In fact, the messages in these media offer concrete models for expressions of behavior and life.

The audiovisual media "speak" a language distinct from the written language in the print media, with their own specific symbolic communicative code. This specific language is dynamic, concrete, physical, dramatic, and narrative and results from the mixing and editing of moving colorful images, speech, noises, and music, organized and supervised by electronics (Babin & Kouloumdjian, 1983). It has therefore first of all an emotional and affective logic and effect. This language has a certain congeniality with the Christian tradition, which has its own narrative and symbolic language of the Scripture and the Tradition. The audiovisual language however is a new phenomenon and has its origins in relatively recent technology and developments in electronics.

In this chapter we will give some outlines for moral formation in our mass mediated world, focusing especially on *narrative communication* and *morality*. In the formation of the ethical identity of a person or a group of persons, a receptive and dialogical attitude in narrative communication proc-

A longer version of this essay appeared in P. J. Rossi and P. A. Soukup (eds.) *The Mass Media and the Moral Imagination*. (Kansas City, MO: Sheed & Ward, 1994).

esses, mass-mediated and interpersonal, is fundamental. A story needs to be heard and watched at as a drama: The story reveals meaning to the viewer only in receiving an answer from the viewer. Moral formation in a mass mediated world, which starts with the ethical and aesthetic analysis of audiovisual stories, finally focuses on the formation of the communicative person who communicates with the audiovisual story and moves towards an exchange of stories among the members of a group. In the end the audiovisual product has primarily functioned as an inspiration for dialogical communication about moral issues.

We see narrative communication as the first objectification of the moral experience. And since we judge audiovisual media as primarily dramatic and narrative, we see them as objectifications of moral experiences and therefore as sources for an ethical reflection, which occurs not primarily in argumentative rational discourse but in narrative communication. Specifically, a narrative ethic can integrate aspects of acting and of granting identity in spoken, written, and audiovisual stories. This essay begins with an awareness of the mass mediated culture as a mainly audiovisual culture, in which narratives dominate and exercise influence on the moral formation of people, often quite unconsciously.

The Actual Situation Concerning Mass Media and Morality

Our changing communicative environment

Morality and mass media have a tangled relationship. The mass media form the symbolic environment we tend to drown in more and more. These audiovisual media create a symbolic universe, a media culture, with all kinds of messages, communications, information, announcements, and invitations concerning life and society. Thayer writes:

> People are necessarily living in three worlds at the same time: the world of their natural environment, the world of their social and cultural environment and the world of their communicative and symbolic environment. One doesn't deny the ultimate reality of the two other worlds, when one is recognizing that [hu]mans can only understand and survive in those worlds in terms of [their] communicative and symbolic world. (1973, p. 147ff.)

The prevalence of audiovisual language makes it harder to abstract from the phenomenon in order to determine how mass media and morality interact in our society. Audiovisual media do change society. The arrival of a new communication technology has always changed culture. Introduce the alphabet or typography into society and you will change perceptions, social relationships, history, religion, etc. Introduce the moving images of cinema and television and you provoke a communicative revolution (Postman, 1986, chap. 5). However, judging a contemporary development like this one runs the risk of becoming negative from a fear for the "new."

Moral fragmentation versus moral coherence

The mass mediated world has coincided with an increase of moral fragmentation, which sometimes develops towards moral relativism. Such moral attitudes can easily result from an ideologically pluralistic society (Christiaens, 1985) that has grown out of the historical development called secularization. In general, secularization rejects the normative model of ethics, which was based on obedience and was strongly influenced by the dominant ideology of the Christian Churches and Traditions. This has left us without a suitable model for moral coherence in our contemporary mass mediated society.

The information culture itself partially accounts for moral fragmentation. It is difficult to get a coherent image of human life and the world when too much (un)truthful and often conflicting information comes across the screen. But the mass media are not the only institutions that create fragmentation. They also give, like a mirror, expression to fragmentation due to other institutions in society. The mass mediated presentations of society and the pluralism in society seem to reinforce one another....[For example,] series, which use a multiperspective discourse (*Hill Street Blues, L.A. Law, St. Elsewhere, Miami Vice*) end up creating doubt through the refusal to present coherent moral concepts. These series move towards the expression of moral dilemmas (Deming, 1985) and probably present today's feelings about moral issues: They are complex and not easy to solve....

Horace Newcomb and Paul Hirsch place fragmentation in the perspective of "television as a cultural forum." They lay stress on the "collective, cultural view of the social construction and negotiation of reality, on the creation of what Carey refers to as 'public thought.' Communication is then 'a symbolic process whereby reality is produced, maintained, repaired, and transformed'" (1987, p. 457). Television plays a key role in this process.

> In its role as central cultural medium it [television] represents a multiplicity of meanings rather than a monolithic dominant point of view. It often focuses on our most prevalent concerns, our deepest dilemmas. Our most traditional views, those that are repressive and reactionary, as well those that are subversive and emancipatory, are upheld, examined, maintained, and transformed. The emphasis is on the process rather than on the product, on discussion rather than indoctrination, on contradiction and confusion rather than coherence. It is with this view that we turn to an analysis of the texts of television that demonstrates and supports the conception of television as cultural forum. (p. 459)

The concept of television as cultural forum reveals four characteristics relevant to fragmentation and coherence. First, in popular culture, "the raising of questions is as important as the answering of them." Second, television does not present firm ideological conclusions but comments on ideological problems. Third, "the rhetoric of television drama is a rhetoric of discussion" which seeks to balance ideological positions within the forum by others from a different perspective. Fourth, the pluralism of the forum corresponds to the pluralism of the wider culture and "monitor[s] the limits and the effectiveness of this pluralism" (p. 461). For moral formation it has the consequence of working to bring about a *"range* of response, the directly contradictory readings of the medium, that cue us to its multiple meanings" (p. 465). Groups may object to the same program for entirely opposing reactions (for example in the 1970s *Charley's Angels* triggered objections based on theories of sexist repression, moral decay, and feminist liberation). Interpretative strategies vary from dominance to opposition to negotiation.

The idea of the cultural forum gives us the possibility to situate and frame fragmentation in our culture. Its characteristics allow us to acknowledge both active interpretations and moral activities of the viewers. We can now raise the question, how moral formation in a mass mediated world might be realized in order to gain increasing moral coherence. Instead of searching for an answer in a normative ethic, we will take for granted the pluralism which is a value in our democratic western culture. We will elaborate a narrative-hermeneutical ethic, which reflects on values, which fulfill the human desire and form part of culture. A narrative-hermeneutical ethic aims at critically comprehending the story that people are (Dijkman, 1988). Perhaps from this point of view, moral formation can lead to moral coherence in a mass mediated world (even if this includes the recognition of a certain fragmentation as part of the coherent moral concept).

Towards a Narrative-Hermeneutical Ethic

We wish to stress the ethical meaning of narratives, in both interpersonal and audiovisual (mass) communication. People achieve their ethical identity through oral, written, and audiovisual narrative....

A story personifies on a private level what argumentative language proclaims as an abstract ideal. Rather than asserting it (as would argumentative discourse), a good story concretely and visually presents a new view on the world as a possibility for realization. This implies, first, that a story can offer a new understanding of reality to the person willing to perceive its meaning and, second, that this quality gives a dialogical character to the communication between receiver and story. Further, through dialogue the story becomes meaningful for the community.

Within narratives imagination plays a dominant role, provides image to an idea, and brings together ideas or meanings in order to give new meaning to the world to which the story refers. By metaphorically and symbolically realizing the world these stories aim not so much to truthfully reproduce reality but to express a specific attitude towards reality. Every program wants to communicate a learning process, a fable, or myth (Kuchenbuch, 1978, pp. 130-169). In audiovisual programs this occurs through the heuristic function of fiction: a presentation of new concepts that challenge our normal ways of thinking.

The interpretation of narratives

In the interpretation of the audiovisual stories viewers hermeneutically and dialectically move between the objective otherness of the audiovisual program and their self understanding (Schwartz, 1983). Audiovisual media, seen from this point of view, can reveal hidden aspects of both world and self because they consist of closed sign systems that ask questions to which viewers get the opportunity to formulate answers. These answers, in turn, the viewers transform and express in their communicative acting. This implies that audiovisual media can have a mediating function in the development of a community.

Since the audiovisual media play an important role in the personal life experiences of people, we subscribe to the thesis that the audiovisual media can act as sources of inspiration as well as fora for religious imagination and spirituality. The audiovisual narratives reveal both good and bad values of our contemporary society. In order to be able to reflect critically upon these values we think advisable an explicit moral formation which is oriented towards understanding and towards a meaningful and creative use of the mass media. In place of an obedience model of doctrine and dogma, we propose "the fantasy model" which orients people to the revealing function of narrative and drama by appealing to the imagination and creativity in the hermeneutical process. In this model people can experience audiovisual narratives as possibilities or chances for exploring new situations, relationships, and ways of life....

Spiritual Growth as Fundamental for a Moral Attitude

As we have pointed out all television programs present today's values in a narrative communication. In order to be able to critically reflect on these values we now have to decide on some principles of narrative ethic. This involves a certain image of human life and the world.

Morality in audiovisual culture

Morality and moral formation can take two forms. First, it can be unintended and implicit, almost unconscious. Most of parents' moral formation of their children follows the implicit pattern as they transmit unreflective moral values and norms to their children. Moral formation, however, can also be intended, explicit, reflected upon, and structured, as for example in courses and seminars (Fleischer, 1987). Thus we can divide morality as such into (1) morality as a way of life, habitual and implicit; and (2) morality as a result of explicit reflection, based on more abstract ideas and values. In our society we have concentrated so strongly on this second level of morality that we have forgotten that morality starts implicitly in the concrete life stories of people, that life stories are the first objectifications of moral experiences that come before the rational reflection on values. We have to take these life stories—including those which, for example, the media widely represent—seriously as one of the main sources of moral formation.

There are different levels on which audiovisual media implicitly present morality in their programs and on which viewers interact and negotiate with the audiovisual messages (van der Lans, 1989): (1) television structures reality; (2) it gives orientation, not in a systematic, but in a fragmented way (by giving signs and symbols for communicative speech; rules for communication; models for behavior; and criteria for the true, the real, and the normal); (3) it reinforces acting space of the viewer through enlarging or diminishing it; (4) it confirms the feeling of identity by presenting models and identification figures; and (5) it creates plausibility structures and collective meanings.

When we take the above mentioned functions of television and cinema seriously, we can begin to talk about a more explicit reflection on values. This more explicit moral formation occurs in groups through narrative dialogue which requires a certain moral attitude of the group members. We will try to define the required moral attitude by elaborating on the subject of spirituality.

Individuals experience life long dramas of integration (Bro, 1967). During their lives people try to realize their ideal image of wholeness but cannot because an idealized image remains imaginary. It drives and inspires people who experience this limitation permanently yet still cling to the desire to dissolve the fragmentation of existence. The way they try to do this determines the drama of integration. The desire for integration leads people to start a dialectic with the world. This dialectical movement always puts the idealized unity in the future: In order to dissolve this fragmentation, people project their desire into the future.

There are three important moments of the drama of integration: people facing towards their own limitations, towards the others who surround them, and towards the world that reaches them through symbols. Narrative communication plays an important role in the "non-imaginary" (symbolic) realization of the idealized unity.

Spirituality and the spiritual dialogue

The drama of integration however is not so "tragic" as it seems at first sight. Binding desire to the historical, contingent situation has a positive side, namely the transcendence of the self (Tillmans, 1987). The human desire to transcend oneself has two poles: self-transcendence and transcendence. Self-transcendence occurs when the individual has a liminal experience and creates a new situation, searching for (M)mystery. Transcendence, on the other hand, is the experience of the unapproachability of the other, the (M)mystery, inside and outside.

The conscious integration and ordering of liminal experiences is called spirituality (Peters, 1977) and it always takes place from a certain perspective—female, secular, atheistic, religious, Christian, Catholic, or originated by certain religious traditions as Dominicans, Franciscans, Carmelites, etc. Spirituality cultivates a mental attitude towards life, emerging out of a certain view of human life and world. Christian spirituality aims at the integration of the two poles, Self-transcendence and Transcendence. This integration determines the structure of the spirituality: transcendence which at the same time binds desire to finiteness in order to reach acceptance and responsibility for the other. Theology expresses self-transcendence positively in images of people, others and God. On the other hand, it expresses transcendence negatively as absence or longing. Films, for example, often express this as abandonment by God or as conversion of the self: One hardly recognizes the others and God anymore. The self turns to a receptive emptiness and experiences grace.

When the spiritual integration of the self occurs in a group, we speak of a dialogical spirituality. Speech has everything to do with the development of spiritual and moral identity of the speaker but also of the listeners because speech wants to be heard, asking for recognition and an answer. When it concerns a life story, this narrative speech goes beyond the rational. Communication is the key word here. Through narrative speech people try to achieve unity with themselves and with others. Rational speech is not enough to create dialogue or community. Narrative communication is more than speech because it also implies action.

Where action enters, so too do values. The normative aspects of narrative communication include what de Reuver (1987) terms some theological key words with which we can judge communication. A first set is wholeness, guilt, love, and solidarity. All of these manifest an image of human beings and the world that aims at self realization or freedom. These attitudes open up an individual towards others in solidarity and love and give meaning to human action. They give an integrated identity, a wholeness. De Reuver's second series is hope, reconciliation with death, and anamnetic solidarity. People must actively reconcile themselves with their fragmentation and failing, including death. Only having done this can they realize a free communication, a communicative acting guided by the conviction that the lives of those who have suffered under injustice in history can have a meaning. This implies not only solidarity towards the present and the future, but also towards the past. This movement is called anamnetic solidarity. One has to be aware of the conflictive reality that realizes evil and suffering and one has to protest against this in a creative way. Communicative acting requires an ongoing learning in which identity continually emerges from a fighting loose of the many forms of pressure and fear that hold the individual small and prevents an open communication with others and with the world.

Group use of audiovisual media can aid this process. This is what we mean by media and spirituality: A group looks at an audiovisual program and communicates interpersonally about the program from and towards the perspective of dialogical spirituality.

Now we can define the moral attitude required for the explicit reflection on audiovisualized morality in group dialogue. The spiritual growth of a person, which depends on a symbolic integration of life experiences, can grant a moral attitude through which the individual can realize a moral coherence based on solidarity and love towards others, without denying the fundamental fragmentation in personal existence. Dialogical spirituality, as a conscious dialogical reflection on the moral experience, grounds the development of a moral identity and a moral coherence. Sölle (1970, pp. 60-65) has defined this attitude as a free, imaginative morality, that starts from the concrete values and needs in the historical situation. She stresses the importance of a conscious and imaginative decision making that responds to needs in the concrete situation, instead of obedience to static norms. Free and imaginative people have a morality guided by the principle of care for others. It originates from a feeling for justice and solidarity.

Our view on the moral attitude required in group dialogue also gives us the opportunity to look again at audiovisual narratives as sources for morality. Often they present personalities that are involved in a spiritual process concerning ethical issues. They also constantly seem to deal with evil forces in history. By offering meaning to these and many other themes they mediate the development of a person's moral identity. As expressions of narrated values in today's situation, they can reveal meaning in our contemporary society. Audiovisual media provide a moral opportunity. But the recognition of this opportunity requires of the viewers a creative, imaginative morality.

We hope to start a learning process aimed at making people aware of this opportunity through explicit moral formation in a mass mediated world, based on dialogical spirituality. The next section describes how this conscious, goal oriented, and systematic moral formation in groups might take place.

Explicit Moral Formation in a Mass Mediated World

Objectives for explicit moral formation

Our approach to the development of the Christian community in a mass mediated world implies (1) the value in explicit moral formation of the reflection on the audiovisual stories that reveal the moral values in the life styles of our contemporary culture and (2) the value of discussion in groups about the morality in these stories and their implications for the morality of the group. Through such group dialogue, where a confrontation with media messages takes place, a new ethical identity can grow. Moral educators can only guide, confront, and question. We want people to develop a creative and active perception of what comes to them in audiovisual messages so that they become more free and imaginative. We seek a morality that is initiated from solidarity and care for others, that comes into existence as a dynamic process, not as a static, ahistorical set of values.

From this background we formulate the following objectives for explicit moral formation in a mass mediated world:

(1) to teach viewers to understand audiovisual language and its aesthetic and ethical implications (colors, music, symbols, nonverbal expressions);

(2) to sensitize viewers to the forms of implicit or explicit morality in the mass mediated culture (through the analysis of the audiovisual program);

(3) to develop a moral judgment about morality in different audiovisual programs;

(4) to stimulate and cultivate dialogue about the audiovisual programs and morality in general;

(5) to stimulate the development of a moral judgment on the mass mediated world.

The development of moral attitudes and judgments depends on spiritual growth. But not every group has the same spiritual and moral "level." Therefore, the group leader has to deal with the actual conditions of the spiritual and moral stage and development of the group members. The capability to reflect on and discuss moral issues and dilemmas depends on age, education, profession, social status, and the personal biography of the group members (Kohlberg, 1981, pp. 409-412). Therefore the choice of films and television programs for purposes of moral education should take these conditions into account....

In analyzing fiction it is important to distinguish the ideological and aesthetic moments. An audiovisual product communicates individual and collective relationships towards reality, together with emotions connected with these relationships. In fiction the characteristic dramatic performance dissolves the viewer's determination of the program's "reality" and instead presents a conceptual image of reality: a conscious reduction or styling of reality in order to effectuate a learning process.

Example 1: An Officer and a Gentleman (Implicit morality as a way of life)

In the analysis of the film *An Officer and a Gentleman* (Taylor Hackford, 1981) we focus on the ideological moments and on the concrete lifestyles that young people embody. The main characters perform the moral attitudes, behavior, conflicts, and dilemmas incarnated in these life stories.

The story. Remembering his childhood as a sailor's son, Zack Mayo decides that he wants to become an pilot in the American navy, although his father doesn't agree with his plans. Nevertheless, Zack enrolls at the training school under the sometimes harsh and humiliating leadership of Sergeant Foley. During the weekends the recruits meet with local girls to relax and celebrate. Many of these girls dream of marrying an aviator pilot, but the recruits usually just want to have fun with the girls. Sometimes the girls get pregnant, hoping that the concerned recruit will marry her.

Zack and his friend Sid meet Paula and Lynette, who both work in the local paper factory. The relationship between Zack and Paula evokes feelings they don't always have under control: Paula obviously falls in love. Lynette sees Sid as a good prospect and their relationship as an investment for a better life in the future.

Meanwhile, the training continues. Friendships develop in the midst of failures, accidents, and conflicts; even Zack and Foley develop a kind of mutual respect. At the end of the course, Zack has the clear intention not to take Paula with him and has stopped meeting her. Sid still visits Lynette, although he intends to marry Susan, a girl from his hometown. Lynette tries to gain Sid with the help of a story of pregnancy. Sid quits his training in order to marry Lynette; however, this frustrates Lynette because she wants to become the wife of a pilot. She refuses to marry him. Sid, who realizes that he loves Lynette, hangs himself. Because of this suicide Zack and Paula meet one another again. Zack tells Paula again that there is no future for them as a couple. The training is finished and there is nobody to congratulate Zack. He is alone, without family and friends. Then he takes his motorcycle and drives to the paper factory where he takes Paula in his arms and leaves the factory with her.

Reflection on the implicit and explicit morality. This film proved very popular in cinemas and video rentals all over the world. The story features moral conflicts and dilemmas; In fact the moral attitudes, implicitly embodied in the main characters, represent various kinds of moral archetypes. Although their life stories determine the moral behavior of these main characters, a development in their moral attitudes occurs. Each of them faces situations involving moral dilemmas where decisions have to be taken.

Zack is morally inner-directed but egocentric. Convinced that people are responsible for their own lives, Zack doesn't think he has any moral obligations. He also does not have much sense of them, because he was not raised with altruistic values. His strong identity, guided by an egoism based on bad youth experiences leaves him little trust in other human beings. Therefore his friendship with Sid has high value for him. Because his main goal in life is to succeed in his training, he judges his relationship with Paula as accidental, as something to finish when his training end. Confronted however with the suicide of Sid, the love that Paula feels for him, and his growing awareness of his own loneliness, he ultimately decides to give up his former moral self-centered attitude towards others and he chooses the love of Paula.

Sid is the opposite of Zack. His traditional parental background has strongly influenced Sid; moral rules come from the outside and tradition dictates his feeling of responsibility, leaving him naively altruistic. His moral behavior and thinking are only directed to moral obligations and altruism. Unlike Zack he has a weak identity. In many ways, he is a tragic figure. During the film he finds out that other people determine his life: first his parents (he has to become an aviator pilot as a replacement for his dead brother) and later Lynette (by fooling him with her pretended love). He has never chosen for his own life. Lynette's refusal to marry him triggers his suicide because he has never learned to solve his life problems otherwise.

Paula judges her love for Zack as her most important value and she shows her love in spite of all the consequences. She takes responsibility for herself and does not allow history to determine her morality (she wishes to avoid what happened to her mother when her mother once was in a similar situation). She cares for other people, like Sid. And she also respects the choices of other people, like Zack. In her moral judgment concerning the egoistic behavior of her friend Lynette, however, she is very negative. In this film Paula's moral attitude develops most strongly. Involved in a spiritual process where self transcendence plays a major part, she reaches a certain coherence between altruism and egocentrism. Lynette, like Paula, comes from a lower social class and has few prospects for her future but thinks she can change her situation through Sid. All her strategies are oriented towards this option. Her strategy changes, however, when Sid decides to leave the training school. Because opportunism guides her, she instrumentalizes her moral attitudes to reach her goals. All her moral decisions, her relationship with Sid, her pretended love and pregnancy, have to be seen in this egoistic perspective. In the end she (together with Sid) loses all. She is the most unsympathetic character.

The film in general works out two themes: the love story, including its moral dilemmas, and the pilot training which highlights options for authority, discipline, and competition. (This story, which we do not discuss here, takes personal form in Sergeant Foley and his group of recruits.)

Example 2: Bronski Beat, "Small Town Boy" (Audiovisual aesthetics as carriers of moral values)

In this music video the symbolic character of the nonverbal expressions, the music, and the *mise-en-scene*—in other words, the audiovisual language and the aesthetic moments—determine the ideological moments and the moral values presented. We will start, therefore, with an analysis of the aesthetics in order to determine the ideological moments.

The story. A boy in a train remembers events from the recent past which the video clip dramatizes: his situation at home, where there is a lack of understanding; his situation on the streets where he has been beaten up and which leads to his decision to leave home. In the end we see the train going further.

Symbols. The boy sits in a train that passes through switching points. This symbolizes that the boy faces choices; he is on his way, but still searching. At the end of the video the train leaves the switches behind: The boy continues on his way, but not searching nor as confused as he was five minutes before. He now has a new perspective for his future. By going through his memories again, he has integrated his past. The camera symbolizes the reminiscences through a close up of his expressive eyes. We then see the events passing through his memory. At a breakfast at home hardly any communication takes place between the members of the family. Next we see a scene in the local swimming pool where he watches some boys that are diving. From the slow motion pictures of one particular boy he watches extensively and from the scene where the same boy beats him up it becomes clear that the main character is a homosexual. Later on a police officer brings him home. His father wants to hit him; his mother is crying. In the next scene the boy leaves home: His mother embraces him, his father just gives him some money. The bird's eye camera shows a lonely, small boy in a rainy street on his way to the railway station.

From the analysis of the symbols in this music video the content becomes clear. The message consists of the problems homosexuals encounter when they are confronted with heterosexuals, like the parents and the local boys. The video uses cliché images and symbols so that it can present the story without speech beyond the text of the song.

Ideological aspects. At first sight the video deals with homosexuality and the problems heterosexuals have with them. This does not mean that only homosexuals can identify with the story. Young people in general can project themselves in the video because the deeper structure of the story carries the message that young people have to say goodbye to their childhood. Each young person must search for autonomy. From the point of view of spirituality, as the conscious integration and ordering of life experiences, this video is very interesting. In the compartment of the train the boy integrates his experiences through reminiscing. But his end remains open because his future is still unclear. The viewer gets a place in such an ending because the viewer, too, must decide what the future can be. A dialogue about such a music video can reach the soul of viewers....

Our discussion of these audiovisual products illustrates the possibilities for a dialogue with the mass media. Although interpersonal communication has a strategic priority over mass communication for moral formation, mass communication offers narratives to the viewers and draws attention to them so that the viewers dialogue about, reflect on, comment on, evaluate, and decide about the audiovisual narratives. A media dialogue can offer moments of (self)recognition through identification or alienation. In this sense audiovisual narratives can initiate a dialogue with the viewpoints, options, and preferences of the producers. Second, audiovisual narratives can provoke interpersonal communication between the receivers in a group, engaging them in a dialogue about their own viewpoints, options, preferences. The group dialogue about their own morality grows from the audiovisual narratives. Third, the group can (re)order and integrate their life experiences, see new perspectives, and find new orientations. In this sense audiovisual narratives can develop a reorientation of life.

This dialogue about audiovisual narratives has importance for moral formation in a mass mediated world because it is possible to organize in a goal-oriented and systematic way what quite often happens spontaneously between people. Furthermore, it is possible to realize these narrative moral dialogues about audiovisual narratives from a Christian viewpoint. Anything (news programs, advertisements, documentaries, drama series, films, talk shows, video clips, religious programs, etc.) can function as a starting point.

People might tell about the way they feel and experience these messages. They can discuss the content and composition of the audiovisual narratives. They might search for and reflect on the implicit or explicit viewpoints, values, norms, options, lifestyles in the audiovisual messages. They can analyze the intentions and interests of the producers. And last but not least, they might reflect on all these questions from the Christian point of view....

All media narratives create a kind of ordering and integration of life experiences from a certain point of view. In this sense all media narratives have a certain spirituality. As viewers we look with our own spiritual eyes and hear with our own spiritual ears. The media dialogue becomes an expression of dialogical spirituality: the spirituality *in* the media narratives and *in* the viewers. [One could also use audiovisual materials in which spirituality and moral growth predominate, as they do for example in the film *Choices of the Heart*.]...

Conclusions

We wish to summarize the main thoughts of this chapter in the form of some theses.

(1) The audiovisual media and culture can work as a site and source for religious inspiration and imagination, for morality and spirituality.

(2) In terms of moral formation, the audiovisual media should not be isolated from the communication of people with themselves (intrapersonal) and with their fellows (dialogical communication). Interpersonal communication has a strategic priority over mass communication.

(3) The intended, goal oriented, and systematic dialogue about audiovisual narratives in a group can lead to an explicit moral formation. Audiovisual narratives initiate this moral formation which interpersonal communication sustains and deepens. This media dialogue implies an active and creative interaction of the viewers with the mass mediated messages.

(4) This dialogue about media messages is or should be at the same time a spiritual dialogue which deals with the ordering and the integration of life experiences from a Christian viewpoint.

(5) Media dialogue and spirituality function as answers to the questions of moral coherence/fragmentation and pluralistic cultural forum and help create moral coherence in the mass mediated world.

(6) In the development of moral coherence through dialogical spirituality, the acceptance of a certain fragmentation in our world and in ourselves nevertheless is inevitable.

(7) The cultivation of the media dialogue should have a priority in the perspective of the development of the Christian community in a mass mediated world.

13

Formation of Church Leaders for Ministering in the Technological Age

Angela Ann Zukowski, MHSH

The 1990 Unda-OCIC World Congress held in Bangkok, Thailand, concentrated on designing effective communication plans for all levels of Church ministry. **Unda,** the International Association of Catholic Broadcasters and Communicators, has chapters on each continent, as does **OCIC,** the International Catholic Association of Cinema and Film. Every three to four years Unda and OCIC sponsor a joint international congress. In 1990 Cardinal Carlo Martini of Milan, a keynote presenter, described in detail the importance pastoral communications planning has in his overall archdiocesan plan.

In Milan parish and diocesan personnel utilize every available means of communication to address the needs of the local church. Each year the diocese selects a ministry and educates the personnel associated with that ministry to imaginatively apply communication resources/technologies to their ministry. Church and lay Catholic professional communicators work in a collaborative effort to support this diocesan pastoral communications endeavor.

In discussing his insights on pastoral communications planning, the Cardinal stated the plan should be identified with all ministries in the diocese; utilize all the means of communications; not change frequently since it takes time to implement and become a core element of the Church's activities; engage priests, educators, and pastoral leaders as well as lay Catholic communication professionals in the design, implementation, and evaluation phases (1990, p. 48).

The local Church rarely considers pastoral communication plans "because the Church is lazy and suspicious of media. The Church is weak in her public relations skills and integrating communications into her works of education, administration, evangelization, and catechesis." The real problem, he said, "is the Church is not at ease with communications in our own Church; therefore, we are not at ease with media in general." The irony is "the Church itself is all about communications" (p. 48). In the spirit of *Communio et Progressio*, the Cardinal called for a renewed commitment to incorporating the advancement of communication skills and pastoral commu-

171

nication plans into the design and service of our parishes and dioceses. He concluded by stating, "If we do not address our own communication failures, we project these failures onto the media" (p. 50).

In 1986 the Congregation for Catholic Education produced the *Guide to the Training of Future Priests concerning the Instruments of Social Communications*. This document outlines the importance of communications to the mission of the Church; it also sketches proposals and directives for each level of the training of priests in order to make them media literate and creative applicants of communications in their ministry. The document states:

> The social communications training...which is specifically pastoral, is to be given to all students without distinction during their philosophy and theology courses. It has three aims: (a) to train those concerned in the correct use of the instruments of social communication (and in general, of every technique of expression and communication) in their pastoral activities, when the circumstances permit it; (b) to train them to be masters and guides of others (receivers in general, educators, all those who work in the mass media), through instruction, catechesis, preaching, etc., and as consultants, confessors, spiritual directors; (c) and above all, to get them into a state of mind in which they will be permanently ready to make the necessary adjustments in their pastoral activity, including those demanded by the inculturation of the Christian faith and life in the different particular cultures, in a world psychologically and socially conditioned by the mass media and even already by telematics and informatics. (pp. 20-21)

It is difficult to imagine the Church educating priests, religious educators, and pastoral ministers for the 21st century yet failing to take into consideration the interpersonal and technological communication skills required to engage in dialogue with contemporary culture. Personal computers, computer networking, the World Wide Web (Internet), faxes, interactive multimedia, videocassettes, CD's, audio/video/computer teleconferencing, radio, cable television, and a variety forms of print media are accessible to all diocesan and parish ministries. How to access these technologies and use them in an effective manner to enhance the Church's administration and educational ministries is key. The Church has encouraged seminaries, Catholic colleges and universities, and diocesan formation programs to integrate communication courses into their curriculum.

> Training should include a practical consideration of the special nature of each medium and of its status in the local community and how it can best be utilized. (No. 123)

> It is the mission of those with responsible positions in the Church to announce without fail or pause the full truth, by the means of social communications, so as to give a true picture of the Church and her life. Since the media are often the only channels of information that exist between the Church and the world, a failure to use them amounts to "burying the talent given by God." (Pontifical Council, 1971, No. 64)

Thus, it hopes that church ministers and leaders will become innovative and creative in identifying ways to reveal the Church to contemporary culture and foster internal and external dialogue. *Communio et Progressio* states, "the Church has been ordered by God to give people the message of salvation in a language they can understand and to involve herself in human concerns" (Pontifical Council, 1971, No. 125).

"A New Era" (*Aetatis Novae*, Pontifical Council, 1992) offers Church leaders, communicators, educators, and ministers a foundation for reflecting on the new trends in social communications and communication technology, as well as guidelines for designing integrated pastoral communication plans to support the mission of the Church in the 21st century.

Aetatis Novae is a timely document whose message comes at a time when new diocesan structures are beginning to evolve. The message of *Aetatis Novae* is directed not only to bishops but to all persons who serve in ministry and education leadership positions in the Church. The document states,

> Catholic media work is not simply one more program alongside all the rest of the Church's activities: Social communications have a role to play in every aspect of the Church's mission. Thus, not only should there be a pastoral plan for communications, but communications should be an integral part of every pastoral plan, for it has something to contribute to virtually every other apostolate, ministry, and program. (1992, No. 17)

The idea of an integrated pastoral plan for social communications is the heart of *Aetatis Novae*. Even though found in an appendix, it does not stand as an afterthought but as the key for implementing the vision of the document. It presents the basic steps and elements to be considered in designing an effective, integrated pastoral communications plan.

What does *Aetatis Novae* mean for Church leadership? I believe there are several important challenges which are based on collaborative efforts in communications (No. 30) of all ministries in a diocese. They invite us to reflect on the new media culture and to determine our role and relationship to this new culture within a Catholic Christian context (No. 4-6). Finally, these challenges encourage us to identify practical steps to prepare church leaders and the Christian community to be able to listen, dialogue and respond to the gospel message in the 21st century (No. 8).

The five key challenges are: (1) equipping church leaders to understand, interpret and speak the "new language" of the new media culture (No. 1, 2, 8, 11); (2) equipping all church ministers with media literacy skills (No. 4, 7, 8, 9, 12); (3) comprehending and responding to the social justice significance of the new media age and its impact on the development of peoples and cultures (No. 4, 7, 8, 9, 15); (4) equipping church leaders and ministers with skills to use mass media and new technologies as a means to "offer meaningful proposals for removing obstacles to human progress and the proclamation of the Gospel" (No. 8, 11, 13, 14); and (5) designing an integrated pastoral communications plan central to all the ministries of the Church (No. 21-33).

In closing, *Aetatis novae* reminds us that

> As the Spirit helped the prophets of old to see the divine plan in the signs of their times, so today the Spirit helps the church interpret the signs of our times and carry out its prophetic tasks, among which the study, evaluation, and right use of communications technology and the media of social communications are now fundamental. (No. 22)

A Rationale for Pastoral Communications

Traditional classrooms and seminaries, however, form only one site for the Church's pastoral formation. The growth and development of adult religious education, various forms of pastoral ministry, and the explosion of interactive multimedia distance education opportunities also mark out a sign of the times. This results from, I believe, the expansion of new educational opportunities and the enriched understanding for the renewed apostolate of the Catholic laity in the marketplace.

We watched the laity's enthusiasm build like a tidal wave through the '70s. They formed new ministries. Dioceses and parishes created new offices and structures to meet rising expectations and needs of the people of God. Religious education provides a simple case in point. It has mushroomed into a variety of sub-divisions. We saw youth ministry, young adult religious education, adult religious education, new forms and approaches to catechesis and evangelization, and programs like RENEW and RCIA all blossom forth. As new arenas of interest emerged and developed, so did new staff to support and address these interests. As dioceses and parishes moved through the '80s, however, the local Church faced growing financial concerns. How can the Church support the explosion of ministry and services with limited funds?

Now in the '90s we see a consolidation and centralization of ministries and services. News reports call our attention to the dilemma dioceses and parishes face throughout the United States as they cut back staff and services. Dioceses must consolidate parishes and may not assign full-time priests to many more by the end of the '90s. Yet, the enthusiasm and involvement of an enlightened laity within the Church encourages the Church to continue to support and nurture their faith commitment. How does the Church move forward with limited staff and personnel services? Integrating pastoral communications into the Church's mission provides one solution to the problem.

How Pastoral Communication Supports our Ministries

Twenty years ago I was responsible for coordinating adult religious education and catechist formation courses for 60 parishes in our diocese. The demand for courses far exceeded both the number of hours in a day or week available to any one individual on the diocesan staff. The day a parishioner approached me to consider placing my core adult religious education courses on cable TV began the advent of a new perspective for integrating educational technology within my ministry. In three years over 10 cable systems aired our diocesan core adult religious education courses in 13 communities each week. I found I had become more effective and efficient in my use of time to serve the specialized needs of parishes and small faith communities.

Eleven years ago the Center for Religious Telecommunications at the University of Dayton installed a satellite downlink on campus. Following the installation of the system, I received comments such as, "Now what do you plan to do with it?" "Don't ask me to change my methodology." "The one-on-one personal classroom relationship is the only authentic methodology—especially for higher education!" "All of this technology is just a trend. In due time this will all pass away." I did not deny the value of face-to-face educational experience. I firmly believed, however, that educational technology would enhance our course offerings on campus and at our satellite locations. Today a significant amount of my time is dedicated to the design and implementation of interactive multimedia distance education courses for graduate credit.

Another frequently-posed question asked, "Is technology cost effective for higher education?" I believe we have never understood that term, and I am not sure whether those who ask fully comprehend the complexities associated with it. Overall, we might make the argument that education itself is not cost effective, whatever that means. A better question might be: Can a price tag be computed for ignorance and its impact on Church and society?

Some of these negative attitudes regarding educational technology related to the shortcomings of educational television in the 1950s and '60s. Then people misunderstood its capabilities and purpose. In certain instructional settings, for example, administrators treated it as an instrument to increase productivity in terms of faculty-teacher ratios, rather than a way to improve learning. One would frequently find classrooms with students listening to a TV lecture by a teacher. In terms of such productivity, it achieved a rousing success. However, a combination of students' satisfaction and learning marked those early educational television days as a dismal failure.

I believe the scene has changed. In *Megatrends* (1982), John Naisbitt indicates how thinking about change can evolve within an individual. He identifies three stages in the development and acceptance of new technology. In the first stage, new technology follows the line of least resistance; persons accept it if it enters their lives in a non-threatening manner. In the second stage, technology is used to improve previous technologies; people realize that improvements can facilitate the quality of their work and learning experiences. A good example of this would be how word processors replaced the typewriter in our work, research, and learning environments. New uses grow out of the technology in the third stage and create new applications and interactions in ways previously unimagined. This is realized, for example, as multimedia distance education via CU-See-Me conferencing where graphic, audio, active images are creating alternative learning environments. If we accept Naisbitt's stages for the introduction of technology into society, we begin to visualize not only new opportunities for the classroom but realize the classroom no longer is limited to four walls. We already speak about Global Classrooms where students are communicating with other experts and students from around the world each day.

Twelve years ago I participated in a telecourse on "The Impact of Telecommunications on the Development of Culture." Once a week for eight weeks 50 persons from 10 states participated in the interactive (one-way video/two-way audio) class. Each participant could ask questions, make comments, and seek clarification from the instructor. Within a few sessions a sense of familiarity developed among most of the participants, encouraging participants to ask questions of one another, thus adding peer education to the experience. This first-hand experience reinforced for me the value of educational technology. As I continue to observe the presence of satellite downlinks in communities and in more and more parishes and Catholic schools I wonder, why hasn't the Church come to grips with the technological age? Why was it so difficult for the Church to enable the Catholic Telecommunications Network of America (CTNA) to become a dynamic reality of communications within the Church? Why have others succeeded while we failed to succeed in this telecommunications initiative? Although we invested significant funds in making the technology available, we did not invest equal amount of funds in educating our leadership to know how to apply the technology to our mission. In every situation I have studied in the past 15 years, the lack of equal investment in formation and training in media/technology has resulted in a failed adventure.

Today laboratories and classrooms all over the world develop revised modes of instruction based on applications of new technologies. It is conceivable that one of these innovations will exert as significant an impact upon education and society as did the printing press, film, television, or computers.

Education itself is in flux. However, a consensus has emerged that teaching and learning will indeed be different in the 21st century: More individualized, computer assisted instruction will be available; lifelong learning will be firmly established; the distinctions between formal education and work-related experience will become blurred; learning in the home and other non-classroom environments will increase; the individual learner will be a more proactive participant in the learning process. Since education is itself essentially a communication process, educators can expect both its efficiency and its palatability to improve as a result of new communication resources available to it.

Futurists have predicted a technological revolution in education ever since motion pictures and then radio broadcasting appeared in the first quarter of the century. Now many perceive the presence of videocassettes, satellite systems, fiber optics, laser video-disc systems, audio/video teleconferencing, and computers as innovations that have already brought fundamental changes in the teaching/learning process.

Certainly it appears that many equate innovation in teaching with the quantity and complexity of new technologies. Teachers often believe that in buying and using overhead projectors, tape recorders, VCRs, laser video disks, CD's, computers, or multimedia systems they contribute to technological advancement; and conversely if they lack these technologies, they feel they have missed out on technological progress. Unfortunately, nothing in the nature of the new technologies guarantees improved educational outcomes. Instructional television, for example, frequently does nothing more than transmit what happens in the classroom. As a result, the televised lesson usually combines the worst aspects of both the classroom experience and television, without the benefits of either form of instruction.

There are few periods in history that deserve the label of transforming eras. Yet, ours is one. Thomas Kuhn (1970), the historian of science, has pointed out that major change takes place only occasionally, in what he called paradigm shifts, when the working assumptions on which people have depended become so inappropriate that they break down, to be replaced by a more appropriate set. Those who recognize the entrance into the "transforming era" realize that it requires a leap of imagination and faith. There are no immediate forecasts, futures, or advanced guarantees that we can offer our colleagues that the new communications age is no longer a luxury for the few but a necessity for the many.

The information superhighway is the smallest part of this new beginning within our educational environment. Knowledge banks, virtual communities, and artificial environments will dominate much of society a generation from now and will make the global village either a healthy or unhealthy place to be, depending on the kind of content that we put into these new channels. Today I firmly believe that if the Catholic Church and especially Catholic education would have embraced the dawning of cable television in the 70's, cable television would have a different function within our culture. Therefore, we can not take any of today's new technologies or media resources passively or for granted. We need to be at the table in the design and development process of each new technology. If we are not, we will end up being either passive recipients of the new communications revolution or committees of counter-cultural revolution fighting for either our access rights or protesting the content and penetration of negative human value messages into our culture.

Advancing Paradigm Shifts

The rapid advancement of communication technologies and their impact on our educational environment requires our full attention. New paradigms are emerging. What are some of the paradigm shifts? Virtual communities, customized knowledge banks and virtual experiences are but a few.

Virtual communities deal with telepresence and tele-mentoring. This is the ability to cross distances to form new relationships. High performance computing and communication technologies will make this possible. We will be able to look over the shoulders of experts who are engaged in research and share their discoveries and insights. In one sense we will be telecommuting and tele-existing from within our seminaries, homes, and schools.

Customized knowledge banks is a type of multimedia serving multiple learning styles. It shifts the balance between in-classroom and out-of-school work. One of the problems with classrooms now is that the professor/teacher spends so much time presenting information instead of interpreting information. But if we can have rich presentational sources that routinely are available outside of class, then we can make better use of our time in an interpretive interactive role with our students. Our growing sophistication about the nature of learning points inevitably to the virtues of individualized learning and to the creation of customized learning environments that accommodate the diverse learning styles of our students.

Harvard's Howard Gardner in his book *Frames of Mind: The Theory of Multiple Intelligences* (1983) suggests that there are at least seven human intelligences, two of which—verbal/linguistic and logical mathematical—have dominated the traditional pedagogy of Western societies. The five non-traditional intelligences—spatial, musical, kinesthetic, interpersonal, and intrapersonal—have generally been overlooked in education. We can develop ways to teach and learn by engaging all seven intelligences through the new communication revolution.

Virtual experiences is not just a new medium. What virtual experiences will create is a place to live and to be and to experience, instead of just a communications channel. You may have heard this expressed as "virtual reality" which uses computerized clothing to create the subjective impression of being inside a virtual world instead of looking through a window into some kind of an artificial reality. And that subjective feeling is very powerful. It influences people emotionally as well as intellectually and it is going to lead to some very interesting kinds of outcomes for society. Imagine how it could be to teach church history, Scripture, world religions, etc., via virtual reality?

Educational technology holds out the promise of an opportunity to develop models of education far different from the dominant one(s) we may presently use. Perhaps the most pervasive issue facing Catholic educators and Church leaders is how they can effectively apply each new technology to the growing educational needs and expectations of the local Church.

If communication lies at the heart of the Church's life, and society has undergone a communications revolution, then the Church must enter in a decisive way into this new age. Its mission, therefore, will be threefold: (1) to articulate and demonstrate on all communication levels through word, sacrament, witness, and service the meaning of Church; (2) to identify the most effective medium and format of communications to proclaim the mission of the Church in contemporary society; and (3) to integrate a variety of communication courses in our seminary, university, and pastoral ministry formation programs. We can begin by a careful reflection and application of recommendations found in the Church documents referred to earlier in this chapter.

The Church's Current Use of Educational Technology

In 1979, the National Conference of Catholic Bishops engaged in a lengthy dialogue on the application of satellite communication/networking in the Church. The research and study resulted in the establishment of CTNA. Initially the NCCB hoped that every diocese would join as an online affiliate within five years, resulting in national distribution of religious and educational programming for narrowcasting and use in parishes, colleges/universities, seminaries, and Catholic hospitals.

While this exciting concept offers many possibilities for the Church, it requires the support and implementation of CTNA in all 183 dioceses. By 1995, CTNA could not attract the religious imagination of either our Church leadership, ministers, or Catholic educators. In June 1995, CTNA ceased to exist after millions of dollars of investment.

What could CTNA have offered our seminaries and other academic institutions? CTNA could have connected all our Catholic institutions of higher learning across the United States. Outstanding theologians, liturgists, educators, homiletics teachers, etc. could have been brought into our learning environments through a press of a button. Imagine bringing together 10 or 15 classes via video or audio teleconference to share ideas and insights on new liturgical, theological, or pastoral issues! Instead of transporting 100 or 300 students, they could remain on their own campus. For example:

In the spring of 1991 CTNA carried two telecourses for graduate credit. One telecourse consisted of a 26-part series, *Introduction to Scripture*, sponsored and taught by faculty from Catholic University. The University of Dayton sponsored the second, *Vatican II Vision 2000: The Teaching Church*. This six-part series brought together eight leading Catholic Bishops and 12 theologians to discuss current theological issues for the '90s. Each one hour program involved a panel dialogue on the topic plus opportunities for the audience to call in and ask questions. Notre Dame University through Golden Dome Productions hosts a variety of teleconferences and special high powered television programs directly related to our ministries. The National Catholic Educational Association and the University of Dayton continue to sponsor the New Frontiers for Catholic Schools Telecourses bringing over 60-70 sites around the country to discuss innovative approaches to enhancing our curriculum via technology.

If seminaries and Catholic colleges/universities could only identify an imaginative way to establish an electronic distance education network, the opportunities of sharing research, teaching courses, and engaging in national and international dialogue would be limitless. In general this is not a radically new idea: Universities around the United States have already established state, national, and international networks to offer graduate and post-graduate courses and degrees via various educational technological networks.

Factors Influencing
the Church's Pastoral Communications Efforts

In the fall of 1986, the Center for Religious Telecommunications distributed a national survey entitled "Diocesan Profile of Communication Ministry in the Town and Country Church" to the 183 Catholic dioceses in the United States. The survey had three purposes: (1) to identify the availability and frequency of diocesan ministry services to small town and rural parishes; (2) to identify knowledge of diocesan personnel about existing telecommunication resources available to small town and rural parishes; and (3) to identify the educational opportunities for supporting small town and rural parishes application of telecommunications for parish enrichment. A similar survey entitled "Parish Profile of Communication Ministry in the Town and Country Church" was sent to a sampling of parishes in three states: North Carolina, Kentucky, and Ohio.

The results of the study from 90 responding dioceses indicated that 88% of those dioceses have access to the use of television and radio, 69% have cable television, and 49% have access to a satellite downlink. Further, 23% of the dioceses offer courses or workshops in the use of communication resources and technologies; 44% offer courses in communication skills; 60% of the dioceses had some access to CTNA; and 92% have a diocesan media center. The study also indicates that over 50% of the small town and rural parishes who responded have access to a computer, over 95% have access to a telephone, and 70% have access to television and video-cassette recorders. Simply combining any of these technologies offers the diocesan Church a rich resource for interfacing with the local parishes in a personal and effective manner. However, a study commenced in the winter of 1994 is demonstrating a decline by dioceses in the use of radio and television for evangelization, catechesis, and mission outreach.

In 1989 the Center commenced a five-year study to monitor the development of parish video libraries (PVL). The project has identified over 500 parishes whose PVLs vary in size from 25 to 700 videocassettes. PVLs exist to encourage family faith development, support adult religious education, and offer alternative quality media opportunities to parishioners. Of the group, 35% have special budgets to maintain the PVL. Budgets range from $200 to $2000 per year. Several parishes have combined to establish regional PVLs. These regional libraries' budgets range from $3,500-$8,000 per year. The remaining 65% of the parishes indicated that their parishes have no special budget; they purchase videocassettes when needed, or as money is available (Zukowski, 1990).

Catholic elementary and secondary schools are moving ahead in educational technology. A project entitled New Frontiers for Catholic Schools, sponsored by the National Catholic Education Association and the Center for Religious Communications, works with Catholic Schools from across the United States and Canada to design integrated interdisciplinary technology plans to enhance the curriculum within their schools. The project has inspired a powerful network of innovative Catholic educators who share success stories and ideas of how computers, computer networking/conferencing, multimedia education, video-production, and communication courses enhance the core curriculum of the schools (Zukowski, 1992)

What if the Catholic Church could design an infrastructure to network each of their schools, parishes, and dioceses? This infrastructure of technology would enable dioceses to offer quality education and service for collaborative and distance education on all levels. Special strengths and skills in one school or diocese could be shared with another. Our rural schools and/or parishes could have access to educational opportunities not presently available because of distance, cost, personal resources, and time. Such a project took shape in May 1992 in Ohio. The Ohio Catholic School superintendents spent a day reflecting on new approaches for enhancing the curriculum. The result of their day of reflection was a decision to form the Ohio Interdiocesan Telecommunications Task Force (OITP) to explore new paradigms for Catholic Education. The project is based on principles of collaboration, empowerment, ownership, and networking all Catholic School institutions within the State of Ohio. The OITP's mission statement focuses their vision:

> With Jesus, the Great Communicator, and in the spirit of our Christian tradition, we recognize that we live in a new media age, immersed in a new culture with an evolving new language. We propose to make use of the most effective, most powerful means to communicate the integration of faith and culture which is at the center of Catholic values and education. (1993)

Every two months the OITP Task Force meets in Columbus. While reflecting on the process individual schools and dioceses are engaged, the task force is laying the foundation for the infrastructure within the state. At the present time the task force is in dialogue with the Public Television Stations (OHIO) via SOITA (Southwestern Ohio Instructional Television Association) in planning teleconferences and telecourses to network all of the Catholic Schools in Ohio. They are also working with Ameritech to pilot networking seven Catholic High Schools throughout the State with schools in Mexico through computer-on-line distance education for teaching Hispanic language and culture. Each diocese has set a goal that all their schools will have integrated interdisciplinary technology plans in place by 1997. Every Catholic school administrator and teacher will have entered into educational opportunities to develop multimedia communication skills.

The students coming out of these schools are the future leaders in the Church and ministry. As Church, we have a responsibility to understand this new culture which has been formed. We need to explore how we can reengineer our teaching and learning experiences in our seminaries and higher education if our education is to have any meaning or relevance in the 21st century.

Identifying and Overcoming Barriers

The research and studies described above indicate that communication resources and technologies do exist in and around local Church communities and Catholic schools. Although many Catholic schools and some parishes have advanced in integrating educational technology into the learning experiences, we have just begun to step onto the threshold of the future. The perplexing issue is how to educate our priests, educators, and pastoral ministers in the application of these communications technologies to support the Church's mission.

The Center for Religious Telecommunications staff interviewed priests, Catholic school educators, and pastoral ministers regarding their perception of communication resources and technologies and their reluctance to use them. Their comments were not much different from those identified in related research with academics in higher education.

Basically, the Center found three key barriers to be addressed and overcome: (1) insufficient knowledge to understand the meaning and role of communication resources and technologies for ministry in the Church; (2) lack of fundamental skills for applying communication resources and technologies in the design of adult learning projects and administration in the parish; and (3) absence of a supportive environment both to introduce and then to apply communication technologies and resources within the parish experience.

Barrier one: Insufficient knowledge and understanding

The primary resources and tools for parish communication, administration, and adult religious learning have changed little over the years. Although educators and pastoral leaders have attempted to introduce 16mm projectors, filmstrips, records, and more recently the video-cassette recorder into the adult learning environment, the methodology for applying these resources has continued to be quite teacher-directed. That environment remains the gathering of adult learners in a formal place, at a sometimes inconvenient time with the teacher assuming responsibility to transmit the insights of leading theologians or other Church representatives. Communication technology functions as a support system to back up theological ideas related to the theme of the lesson.

But we must also consider the impact which communication resources and technologies have on the roles of the learner and the teacher, roles altered by such technological innovations as distance learning via satellite communication, audio/video teleconferencing, television, radio, interactive laser video disc systems, multimedia, and computers. The teacher becomes a facilitator and a resource person to the learning experience; learners take the initiative, with or without the help of others, in diagnosing their learning needs, formulating learning goals, and identifying the type of programs they will utilize to achieve these specific personal learning goals.

Priests, pastoral ministers, and adult religious educators surmount this first barrier when they identify the existing communication resources and technologies that exist in their communities; when they change their attitudes toward the potential these technologies have for communicating within and outside the faith community; and when they support and encourage the production of quality programs that address the needs and concerns of their adult faith community.

Barrier two: Lack of skills

The lack of fundamental skills for using communication resources and technologies results to some degree from our existing educational system. Traditional approaches to training priests, pastoral ministers, and religious educators have emphasized content, with minimal experiences in designing alternative methodologies for adult religious education or improving Church administration. Many academics and Church leaders believe that formation programs have as their primary goal transmitting content concerning the latest trends, insights, and developments in scriptural and theological thought. Other than homiletics, communications (interpersonal or technical) appears not relevant or trivial.

I have studied pastoral ministry and religious education brochures and syllabuses which come across my desk. The absence of courses, workshops, and seminars to support the development of skills in applying educational technology and/or communications to ministry is quite obvious. To date only two Catholic universities offer pastoral communications summer programs for diocesan and parish personnel: the Institute for Religious Communications at Loyola University (New Orleans) and the Pastoral Communications Institute at the University of Dayton (Dayton, Ohio). Marquette University has frequently offered seminars, conferences, and symposiums in these areas over the years also. Perusing most ministry, church administration, and religious education textbooks confirms this absence. Elaborated references to educational technology and/or communications seldom appear.

Few have single chapters dedicated to the area. The decision to ignore these technologies not only prolongs the Church's fundamental relationship to the print culture, but also prevents the Church from integrating these technologies into its mission. Thus, the Church destines itself to be ill-prepared for communicating in the 21st century.

Barrier three: Lack of supportive environment

The absence of a supportive environment that will enable priests, pastoral ministers, and adult religious educators to introduce new communication innovations into the parish experience forms the final barrier. Neither the parish nor the diocese places any expectations on our Church leaders or educators to find innovative ways to use communication resources; no one gives special rewards for designing new patterns of thinking and planning related to these resources. In most cases, Church leaders and educators resist communication resources and technology.

The potential initial cost for investing in either the hardware or the software for the communication technologies creates the first resistance. The second resistance appears when one considers the amount of time required to begin to reorient oneself to thinking in new patterns. The third resistance deals with change itself; once educators have found a comfortable niche it is often difficult to encourage them to move out of it (Naisbitt, 1982).

My hope is that when enough academics, parish leaders, and adult religious educators begin to hear an ongoing parade of success stories related to the use of communication resources and technologies, we will see a change in attitude. Those of us who avidly believe in the present and future implications of multimedia and distance education for education and ministry have the challenge of making every use of these technologies demonstrate their impact on and value for church ministry.

A Sample Case Study

In order to begin the process of finding innovative ways to not only encourage parishes to incorporate communications effectively but also design creative models for application, the Center for Religious Telecommunications introduced a pilot project, "Telecommunications in Ministry," to parishes in three dioceses. The inherent flexibility of the process allowed the participating parishes to adapt it to their own specific situations. The methodology, an application of systems design theory to the small town and rural context, provided a pattern for working out an idea from conception through implementation to evaluation in relation to an initial goal or purpose of the organization. In applying systems thinking to this case study, we attempted to design and evaluate a process that challenged the traditional planning and communication procedures of both parish and diocesan programs.

The process for the case study involved five phases: (1) the analysis phase, (2) the design phase, (3) the development phase, (4) the implementation phase, and (5) the evaluation phase.

Once we identified the participants we invited them to an orientation session held at a central location within the diocese to hear an explanation of the entire process. We assured them that their involvement should relate to current needs in their parishes. We asked them to reflect on this key question, "How can our parish's involvement in this project assist us in the present and future enrichment of our parish life?"

The communications application did not attempt a panacea. It offered an alternative to assist parishes in reaching out and touching many people's lives via the available communication resources and technologies. Most of the basic communication technologies are no longer foreign to home environments. Telephones, video-cassette recorders, audio-cassette recorders, radios, and computers appear almost everywhere. Applying these technologies in new and innovative ways for parish ministry challenged the participating parishes.

Several audio-conferences joined the participating sites during the nine month project, either within each diocese or among all the groups. The dioceses of Owensboro (Kentucky), Raleigh (North Carolina), and Cincinnati (Ohio) engaged in the project. Each diocese had seven to 10 parishes participating for an approximate total of 21 parishes. A commercial conferencing service provided the connections for the audio-conference calls with the 21 parishes several times during the nine month period. These conference call meetings demonstrated to the participants the value and impact of audio-conferences for parish planning and enrichment.

As parishes shared their various models, an inter-diocesan support system emerged. Gradually participants were energized and motivated to think of communications in new contexts. They began to believe in their ability to identify new communication opportunities for parish administration, evangelization, public relations, and catechesis.

Praxis in action

Holy Trinity parishioners in Williamston, North Carolina, found an effective way to apply the telephone for parish ministry. They purchased two speaker phones (approximately $70 each), and on Sunday they now place one speaker phone on the altar and deliver the other to the home of a parishioner who cannot be present with the worshipping community. During the sign of peace, individuals come up to the speaker phone and extend words of friendship and compassion to the person at home.

One parishioner decided that it would be a good idea to audio-tape the Sunday liturgy. During the week, parishioners make copies, which they delivered to the local nursing homes or private homes where individuals are confined. This ministry outreach sustained the concept that communications is for enhancing community. Distance was not a barrier for this parish.

In Ft. Loramie, Ohio, St. Michael's parish used audio-conferencing and videocassettes to design a three hour in-service training program for its high school teachers. The parish could not bear the expense of bringing in a consultant for only four or five teachers. By using videocassettes and speaker phone, the author of the series "appeared" in the parish from Minnesota. The teachers benefitted from a rich educational opportunity for the cost of a one hour telephone call; in fact, the textbook author had a toll free 800 number.

Holy Trinity parish in Coldwater, Ohio, chose the model of the development of a video library. They acquired their videocassettes either from religious production houses or though the archdioceses affiliation with CTNA. For Lent, the parish decided to encourage families to utilize its video library as a resource for home religious enrichment programs. The Director of Religious Education and the teachers designed discussion questions and activities to accompany the videocassettes. The number of families who participated in the Lenten project exceeded the parish's dreams.

St. Henry's parish in St. Henry, Ohio, discovered that one of their parishioners had a camcorder. The parish decided to recruit the parishioner's services to assist in developing a one-hour video program to celebrate the parish's 150th anniversary. Through interviews with people of all different ages about how the parish had affected their faith life, the video tells the parish's story and preserves it for the future. The parish will continue to use this excellent program for introducing the parish to new parishioners, encouraging students in confirmation classes, and inspiring people to get in touch with the traditions of their faith community.

A Raeford, North Carolina, faith community took a different approach. St. Elizabeth of Hungary parish wanted to invite everyone "To Come Home For Christmas." By using radio spots, ads in the local newspaper, and hand delivered letters, they filled the church for the Christmas liturgy. Some individuals expressed interest "to once again be part of the family."

There are many more stories that could be told. Some of the comments of the participants regarding their involvement in project TIM tell their own stories.

"I became more convinced that media opportunities must be taken more seriously in religious education."

"When I first started on this endeavor I asked myself, 'What am I doing here?' But as time went on, I started to use our parish equipment with more knowledge and assured myself I would continue to learn more."

"It has opened the door to awareness of the many possible uses of telecommunication technologies for small parishes like ourselves."

"It has developed a bond with the Catholics in our community and created an interest in all the surrounding communities."

"I feel this project has precipitated the necessary sparks for firing up the imaginative, realistic, and possible profitable uses of the latest technology for parish enrichment."

New Developments in Catholic Schools

How can our Catholic schools address the problems of declining enrollments, teacher shortages in critical areas, limited curricular resources, and increased state academic requirements and guidelines? A group of Catholic educators met to explore these issues. The shortage of teachers in critical curriculum areas concerned superintendents the most. The financial situation of the schools prohibited hiring personnel to teach the same subject in five or 15 locations. A few educators indicated their schools shared programs through busing students from one school to another—a situation with problems of its own, especially the time factor. Gradually it became apparent that an interactive telecommunication system, with its promise of an enhanced curriculum through sharing of teacher expertise, could provide a better alterative.

The technology of two-way interactive television gives a convenience and flexibility for both the instructor and the student. It allows two (or more) participants to respond to each other. Simultaneous feedback does not necessarily increase the amount of information, but it makes for a more natural environment. By allowing people to talk as they do when face to face, the system itself becomes less noticeable to the users. Designers call this the "transparency" of a system.

Basically, a two-way interactive television system, or computer conferencing CU-See-Me system, provides the opportunity for an instructor at one geographic site, the "home site," to teach students located in other "remote sites." The students in each remote site can see and hear the instructor at the home site. The instructor can see and hear all students at all sites. This is accomplished in "interactive classrooms," equipped with microphones, at least two cameras, and as many monitors (television sets) as there are sites on the system. The signal from the home site and back again travels via microwave, coaxial cable, or fiber optics.

In one successful interactive system, located in Cheboygan, Michigan, the local cable television company wires together four schools, one in each public school district. Each school has its own channel, so students and teachers at participating schools can tune into each other's broadcasts. Each classroom is equipped with color cameras, four monitors, a special effects generator, and microphones. Students from all locations can participate simultaneously in discussion just as they would in a standard classroom.

Jack A. Keck, coordinator of the project, which began in 1986, stated in a telephone interview that "Planning, implementation, and evaluation are critical to the success of the program." Initial in-service workshops offered teachers an excellent transition from teaching in a regular classroom to teaching via telecommunications. The areas of training presented to the teachers included equipment operation, interactive teaching techniques, cooperative management techniques, curriculum concerns, and evaluation strategies.

All students completed tests at the beginning and end of the interactive television courses to compare cognitive training. The evaluation results of the first two years have encouraged the staff. Students not only learned as well or better than those with "live" teaching but also indicated above average satisfaction with the courses.

Teleconferencing—audio, video, or computer—has emerged as a significant resource for educators and education administrators. It offers the capability to bridge together two or more persons in different locations through an electronic media system.

Several years ago the Diocese of Raleigh (North Carolina), began using audio-teleconferencing for teacher in-service. In the past, the 26,000 square miles of the diocese meant for some teachers a two-to-five hour drive for a two-hour program. Audio-teleconferencing removed the roadblock and elicited a refreshing receptivity towards in-service days. With the assistance of the diocesan communications office, the education office planned two effective audio-teleconferencing days for 17 elementary schools wanting to improve their reading program.

Audio-teleconferencing uses a communication technology which we all know—the telephone. By means of a conference bridge, two or more remote locations can participate. Although bridging can be accomplished in a number of ways, most schools use either their long distance telephone company conference operator or a conferencing service.

I integrate audio-conferencing into all my own graduate classes. Theologians, scripture scholars, and expert pastoral ministers from all over the United States come in this way into my class to dialogue with the students. Students read a theologian's research, discuss their insights on the research with their classmates, and via audio-conferencing bring in the expert. In every instance, I find the students begin to take a more in-depth interest in further reading the research and insights of experts in a particular field.

At times national presentations or board meetings may take me away from my class. Physical absence, however, does not mean total absence. In these instances, I package my lesson by producing one or two video-cassette tapes on the lesson and plan an audio-conference call with the class from my location in the States. A student is selected to facilitate the class. He/She begins the class discussion, shows the video-cassette taped program, and then calls me at a designated time. I can manage a 30-45 minute class discussion from any location. Sometimes I can even invite experts into the discussion if they are participating in the same meeting or conference with me at my location. This approach also demonstrates to students how technology may be used in an educational setting in their future ministry.

As technological developments rapidly expand in all forms of electronic media, and specifically in audio, today's classroom can literally reach almost anywhere. Quite feasibly, with the help of the audio medium, no place is "outside the classroom" anymore.

Summary

The practical communication stories shared in this chapter attempt to illustrate where parishes and Catholic schools are headed in educational technology. I also hoped to demonstrate the importance of equipping our future church leaders with the knowledge to move into these parishes and classrooms of the future. Seminaries and Catholic colleges/universities need to identify the types of communications courses which will enable our church leaders to effectively communicate. These courses include topics such as theology of communications, interpersonal communications, public relations, pastoral communications, introduction to radio/video production, computer networking, Internet (World Wide Web), communications and administration, effective use of the print media, and emerging multimedia technologies and Catholic education. If schools do not offer these courses, the faculty—at least—should be knowledgeably efficient for integrating these skills into their classroom environments and learning experiences.

The social and organizational dynamics of the new educational technologies create new alliances of decision makers, new organizational communication patterns, new ways to evaluate performance and knowledge, new institutional consortia, and new budgetary requirements. In a sense we can say the new communication technology creates a new renaissance in educational interests. As educational technology becomes more popular and widely accepted, the issues surrounding its control, design, use, and implementation will increase. The test for the future will be to use the new electronic bridges made possible by modern technology to respond to the learner's needs, thus expanding the physical boundaries of the classroom, the psychological boundaries of student-teacher interaction, and the curricular boundaries of traditional education.

The primary factor most educators consider in using technology in the classroom is its effectiveness in the teaching-learning environment. Because nearly all technology will require an investment of time and effort on the part of the teacher, he/she must be thoroughly convinced that this is worthwhile for students. Technology never exists independently of people. It merits our concern only because it touches our lives as we create, understand, and use it. Therefore, true study of technology in religious education, Catholic education, and parish ministry is the study of its relationship with those who create and use it. The instructional designs described in this chapter are as information rich as our culture. Empowering people to understand and use information resources and technology challenges the education and pastoral leadership formation centers of the Catholic Church today.

Technology will move ahead quickly with or without the planning of dioceses, Catholic schools, and parish ministries. If, in their preoccupation with day-to-day responsibilities, Church educators and leaders fail to recognize the pervasive impact of the technological revolution and to actively plan for its proper utilization in the Church, they will neglect their mission to find innovative ways to reveal the Good News in the 21st century. It is a mind-boggling challenge.

Cardinal Martini's remarks invite us to re-visit the meaning and role of communications in the Church. More than simply a matter of using the communication resources and technologies, such a task means strategic and long-range planning on all levels of ministry. It means preparing our future leaders of the Church to be media literate and technologically savvy for the 21st century. *Communio et Progressio* supports the forward thrust:

> The People of God walk in history. As they, who are, essentially, both communicators and recipients, advance with their times, they look forward with confidence and even with enthusiasm to whatever the development of communications in a space-age may have to offer. (Pontifical Council, 1971, No. 187)

Those seminary and academic professors who have a vision beyond the learning environment of today, a receptive attitude to change, and a pioneering spirit to persevere will have the privilege of preparing our future Church leaders and educators to be well-equipped to integrate communication resources and technologies into their ministries in imaginative new ways. The proclaiming of the Good News will not be limited to physical space but can transcend time and space through the new telecommunications media.

As we have seen in this chapter, more and more of our Catholic schools and parishes have moved beyond the threshold of initial integration of educational technology into their ministry. If our future leaders are to be adequately prepared, they must be able to move forward without fear, insecurity, or anxiety in the face of the opportunities and communication skills required for communicating the faith in a technological age.

14

Forums for Dialogue: Teleconferencing and the American Catholic Church

Frances Forde Plude

An essential component of human organization, from religious communities to constitutional democracies, public opinion depends on public expression and public assembly. Today we speak and assemble in ways unknown to past generations of theologians, political leaders, and social theorists. Our *forums* have changed: Some have disappeared; others have arisen. Our small Town Hall debates and even our faith communities have given way to TV and radio talk shows, world-wide news analysis, satellite and telephone hookups, and the Internet.

I offer the ideas proposed here—about *the value of forums for dialogue*—with the hope that new, interactive, technological modes of speech and assembly will enrich public discourse. Such forums, I believe, increase in importance as churches, nations, and communities of all kinds, attempt to move beyond serious divisions toward collaborative solutions. We have seen, in Bosnia for example, the cost of such division.

Here I examine one specific kind of technological forum—the teleconference—reflecting on its history and its future potential as a mode of "assembly" within the Catholic Church. These concepts have new meaning as use of the Internet and the World Wide Web explodes.

For more than a decade we heard predictions of an imminent burst of growth in teleconferencing but it didn't happen. In spite of this track record, I begin here with a prediction that the boom is beginning to happen now and teleconferencing will see remarkable growth in *this* decade.

This chapter treats three aspects of teleconferencing: (1) its current status, along with examples; (2) the special fit with church goals and needs; and (3) the deeper contextual issues raised by such dialogue.

Essentials of the Technological Forum

The three main types of technical conferences differ according to their links: computer links, audio links, and audiovisual links, i.e., videoconferencing. Each one constitutes a *forum*—a technical bridge by satellite or telephone lines—which enables people in different places to "be" together. Teleconferences are *meetings*. Although people tend to think of videoconferences as TV programs, they are essentially meetings. The key factor differentiating teleconferencing from television is its interactive nature: People can "talk back."

In computer conferencing people interact with others through their computers. Much of the time this occurs not in "real" time but in a delayed manner. In other words, people can sign on to the conference whenever they like, retrieve existing messages or text, and then leave a response for the other conference participants to pick up at their convenience. Most electronic mail (e-mail) works like this. Of course, one can also link up to on-going conversations.

Audio conferences "bridge" or connect people from varied sites so they can talk together. Such meetings have a feel about them that "the meter is ticking" so organizers plan them well ahead of time, with materials distributed in advance. This format requires a certain amount of courtesy and verbal name-tags throughout the meeting so people can identify correctly among themselves the individual speaking; this helps because one has only audio cues to sort out individual input.

In both of the above conferences, interaction obviously occurs. When we turn to videoconferences, we will similarly assume a forum with feedback. (A conference isn't really a conference without interaction.) Conferences differ from satellite-connected video programs hooking various sites together simply for information distribution, such as a corporate show to unveil a new product. Instead, here we speak only of video meetings with two-way interaction. Up to now feedback to the distribution site usually takes place from the field via telephone calls because of the expense of two-way video. However, one can now predict the long-expected growth in videoconferencing because prices have dropped dramatically due to technological breakthroughs. A recent invention allows people at computers to be seen at other sites, using a small video camera the size of a golf ball.

In the past all three conferencing modes utilized analog (electromagnetic wave form) message transmission but now digital (computer bit pattern) transmission has replaced much of it. Once this change occurred it became possible to speed up the transmissions through time-sharing, compression, and other techniques. A concomitant technological change, the switch from copper wires to optical fibers, has allowed "space" for more messages. More and more information travels over these fiber highways, with satellites helping to make global distances irrelevant.

Since the demand exists for so much information transfer, developed nations are racing to construct the global interconnected networks to carry the data load. The European Union (EU) nations have made this a key priority and predict that 12% of the gross national product of the EU will be in this telecom sector. Similarly, Congress has proposed the development of an "information highway" as part of the plan to update America's infrastructure. Even without government help, telephone and cable companies are major players in this growth. And in an unregulated market, major corporate and institutional groups have built their own local area networks (LANs), providing even more highways for messages.

Videoconferences will become more economical because of several specific changes:

- signals can now utilize public-switched telephone networks instead of dedicated lines
- technical standardization emerges as public and private networks and various long-distance carriers develop compatibilities for easier interface
- engineers have improved compression techniques so video no longer needs as much transmission space (bandwidth)
- the manufacture of *desktop* video communication systems simplifies interaction which has required large TV studio settings in the past
- the development of new video processor chips has meant cost savings and allows the insertion of computer graphics into video conferencing

This decade thus offers mobile (or desktop) videoconferencing units which can be wheeled from room to room, making video forums possible—an easy technical "freedom of assembly" at much less cost. These may become as common as fax machines for interaction.

Teleconferencing and Church Goals and Needs

Pioneers in Catholic Church teleconferencing

Much creative conferencing already occurs within the American Catholic Church. Historically, the San Francisco Archdiocese pioneered teleconferencing techniques for the entire nation, using a NASA satellite in their early experiments. For this overview, though, I have selected three types of current teleconferences as examples: one forming a university-family community (Notre Dame); one linking a prayerful community (Contemplative Outreach); and one building a pastoral community (the National Pastoral Life Center). All three types utilized the facilities of the Catholic Telecommunications Network of America (CTNA). For many years this satellite network provided the infrastructure for helpful forums within the American Catholic community.

When its planners first conceptualized CTNA, they saw it as a significant intra-institutional communications system; the satellite system could facilitate internal communications through lower-cost telephone transmission,
fax transmission, and intra-messaging of all kinds—internal meetings/brief-
ings and training conferences, for example.

About a decade ago, having recently completed doctoral studies at
Harvard and MIT, I accepted a consultancy to travel to many Catholic universities throughout America and confer with them about how a satellite
system could service their needs. Monsignor Michael J. Dempsey, a telecommunications pioneer, coordinated this research phase for CTNA. I remember arriving in South Bend to suggest that Notre Dame might find it
helpful to interconnect with their Alumni Clubs through CTNA satellite facilities. I suggested to then President, Father Ted Hesburgh, that he could
speak to Notre Dame graduates throughout America with a satellite hookup.

And Notre Dame had the vision to do both. When Father Hesburgh
retired as President of Notre Dame he gave a farewell address to graduates
throughout America on a satellite teleconference. Dr. Kathleen M. Sullivan,
Director of Alumni Continuing Education at the university, told me recently
that with 200 Alumni Clubs in this country, they have a university community just waiting to be linked.

After consulting their alumni, Notre Dame decided to focus their teleconferences on family life—a continuing challenge to their graduates and to the
nation-at-large. One live-interactive teleconference, for example, helped parents
(and grandparents!) understand preschooler needs. A panel of experts from
Notre Dame and St. Mary's College offered ideas and answered questions.

One of the most significant decisions made by the university was to
link up with diocesan family life offices throughout the country in the teleconference planning and marketing. Notre Dame also distributes special
guidebooks for local facilitators and provides information packets for all
audience participants. The packets contain promotional ideas and locales
participating, materials well planned to aid local networking.

For example, a teleconference on elementary education had links to
Catholic school personnel; through the use of area zip codes tags, the Catholic
school principals in every locale with an alumni club received notification of
the broadcast. This local networking is vital to interactive televised meetings.

Part of the on-going celebration of Notre Dame's Sesquicentennial
year involved a satellite teleconference. Alumni clubs were urged to participate in community service outreach in their areas—giving back to society
what the university gave to them. The celebratory satellite teleconference
highlighted some of the local community service projects and allowed a forum for the university to share its past history and its future mission.

I don't believe any other university in America has the systematic educational outreach to its alumni that Notre Dame has. The fact that a significant part of this community-building and service occurs through satellite

teleconference forums provides a rich model of dialogic enrichment for churches and other institutions in America.

The support offered to modern contemplatives by satellite interconnection exemplifies another valuable forum. Trappist monk Thomas Keating founded Contemplative Outreach, Ltd. as a national service organization to facilitate the growth of centering prayer. The many works of Basil Pennington, a member of the same religious order, have popularized this contemplative approach to prayer. Hundreds of prayer groups meet regularly throughout the country and many participants attend centering prayer retreats or conduct workshops in how to pray in a contemplative manner.

The organization linked these scattered groups through a teleconference with two goals: (1) to facilitate a sense of national support among the communities, and (2) to permit various local groups to hear a talk by Abbot Keating and enter a dialogue with him. Most locales either began or concluded the satellite meeting with a 20-minute period of centering prayer—thus providing a technologically-linked prayer group throughout the country. The organization conducted an extensive evaluation process, with participants giving reactions; these suggestions were distributed widely so the organizers could make improvements in subsequent televised meetings. This studied evaluative procedure is a significant aspect of successful teleconferences.

In addition to interactive prayer gatherings, other pastoral practice benefits from special interactive training in televised meetings. The expert in this field is Father Phil Murnion, Director of the National Pastoral Life Center in New York City. When I asked him whether this forum represents a participatory church he said: "Absolutely! When I was first asked to do TV programs, I said no because that's not what we do. But when I was told it would be a forum, with dialogue, a meeting-on-the-air, then I said sure, we will do that."

These teleconferences have focused on a range of topics: the drug crisis; the Church as seen through media; teaching sexual morality; what's really working in adult religious education; the Church and rural communities; dwindling priests and church finances; and many other topics. Some people may say this panders to the trendy. However, Murnion senses from his feedback in the field that the topics are "timely."

Assembling a live audience in many locales represents a major challenge for these meetings. Father Murnion and his staff distribute press releases and fliers to local affiliates and specific constituencies for each teleconference topic. The sessionis were videotaped and many requested taped copies; for example the teleconference discussion on the parish council continues to be requested. The number of telephone calls received by the teleconference can sometimes act as a barometer of how many people are out there. Sometimes no calls come in.

The fact that many folks prefer to view programs later (on tape) indicates that we still tend to think of these conferences as video programs instead of meetings. Teleconferencing best occurs as an extension of the telephone, however, rather than a form of television show; it is a dialogic forum.

The Church in the modern (telecommunications) world

During the Second Vatican Council the Church re-cycled its view of interaction with the world. In the *Church in the Modern World* document we see the recognition of the value of dialogue with the world (while retaining the obligation to critique it in terms of higher—gospel—values).

If the theology of Church now endorses dialogue (with other churches, with laity, with women, with modern society), then systematic forums to facilitate this dialogue will aid the work of the Spirit in a postmodern world. We use automobiles in this work; we use modern medical science in this work; we can also use communication technologies in this same work. One of the first things required is that we stop thinking of all media as *programs*. Many media are simply tools, connecting links—just like letters, like telephone calls, like mediated meetings.

Many factors should assure a comfortable fit between teleconferencing and the Church. In fact, an institutional infrastructure in the American Catholic Church already exists in its system of schools, diocesan structures, parish communities—all awaiting linkages or networking that communication systems provide.

The American Catholic Church first developed a communications network in connection with its system of schools. The Catholic Television Network consists of more than a dozen dioceses with closed circuit microwave broadcast systems to service their schools. This network still exists, and many affiliates now lease some channel space, thus earning income to support their work. In one of these dioceses, San Francisco, they have recently celebrated the 20th anniversary of the establishment of their closed circuit system. Here the earliest satellite teleconferencing experiments began, under the direction of the man who is now Bishop of the San Jose (Silicon Valley) diocese: Bishop Pierre DuMaine.

In their educational television studios located in St. Patrick's Seminary in Menlo Park, a user-controlled teleconference studio was constructed before 1980. Marika Ruumet, the creative woman who directed that studio operation, later convinced the heads of the Hewlett Packard Corporation to develop one of the corporate world's most innovative satellite teleconferencing operations.

Another early staff member in this teleconferencing history was a Sister of Notre Dame, Jeanette Braun. Jeanette later organized many international teleconferences for corporate clients.

Jeanette served a staff role in an historic early satellite project in San Francisco called "Project Interchange." This teleconference permitted teachers in public and private schools in northern and southern California to "meet" regularly to discuss their individualized instruction curricular work.

The project utilized the Canadian/American Communications Technology Satellite (CTS), under the direction of NASA engineers.

Over 20 years ago, Bishop Pierre DuMaine wrote in an unpublished document entitled "Notes on an Electronic Information/Communications System to Support Individualized Instruction":

> The "economy" of computer-supported information systems depends, of course, upon a sufficiently large number of users to optimize the capacity of the computer and to achieve economy of scale necessary....This is possible if remote users can be linked to the information source by telephone line, cable, or communications system. (1972, p. 1)

Conceptual Communications Issues

As I struggle to delineate the larger contextual issues emerging in a tele-connected Church (and world), many, many things come to mind. In these remaining paragraphs I can only point readers and practitioners toward some of the basic questions and hint at ways to seek answers to these questions. I will reflect here on (a) broad context questions, (b) selected concepts in relation to the Church, and (c) emerging needs.

As background, we should reflect upon certain facts. For one thing, we regularly see, even hear, teleconferencing in our evening news. Satellite linkages regularly interconnect various geographic sites into a program like the evening network news or Ted Koppel's *Nightline*. So, in a sense, our news/analysis TV programs are already forums. The *MacNeil-Lehrer NewsHour* on PBS developed into one of the most substantive and in-depth news forums in America. This is a model for the dialogic approach to problem-solving; sometimes it works better than others.

Another background factor for our reflection is that infrastructures in America (the "information superhighway") require planning and development if we are to keep pace with telecommunications growth in Japan and Europe. A $2.9 billion High-Performance Computing Act, passed in Congress, will provide funding for systems to link government, university, and library computers in a National Research and Education Network (NREN). Such networks will provide the infrastructure supplied by roads, railroads, and canals of previous eras. Moreover, the news media document almost daily that Internet use is spreading to citizens everywhere; it is no longer just for researchers.

Broad context questions

We have already become aware that interactive communications technologies have altered the process of decision-making. In *Computer Message Systems*, Jacques Vallee states, "In conferencing, the messages themselves are not as important as the group process which they support" (1984, p. 70). Vallee adds that interactive message systems have many benefits in strategic planning, in group dynamics for better tactical decisions, and in the faster resolution of routine issues. We have consultants like Peter Drucker warning us that the intra-group interactive tools will drive structural changes within organizations. Major effects include decentralization and a flattening out of hierarchical structures, with fewer mid-management staff.

In an essay entitled "The Churchification of Christianity," German theologian Hermann J. Pottmeyer examines the Church in the light of modern societal change and reflects on the "structural differentiation" of society identified by the theorist Talcott Parsons.

> [This] consists of the disintegration of the old multifunctional forms of life in[to] "social partial systems" which then take on functional specialization and tend toward autonomy. Examples of such partial systems are the economy, transportation systems, politics, the state, the nuclear family, and the Church. (1990)

I would add *the partial system of telecommunications* to this list. Pottmeyer cites the difficulty:

> The tendency of these partial systems toward autonomy creates many problems. Since each individual is seen only as a participant in the operation of those partial systems, it becomes more difficult for the individual to find his own identity....The connecting horizon of a consensus of values which links all members of the society continues to disappear. (1990)

This sociological phenomenon contributes to our discord; it calls for new modes of linking and overlapping partial systems if we are to dialogue and collaborate effectively on today's (and tomorrow's) challenging issues. Interactive forums will serve such challenges if we thoughtfully create the forums in our strategic planning and include telecom-infrastructure planning and use.

Two final broad dynamics: technologies are *converging* while communities are *dispersing*. Communication and computer technologies have become so integrated that one cannot see boundaries any longer. Telephones are computers; and computers communicate with each other. However, as these technologies integrate, communal groups disintegrate. Individuals seek hookups with each other through phones, computers, electronic churches, and want ad personals. We must conceptualize and implement new forms of forums for a postmodern world where traditional borders have disappeared.

Selected concepts in relation to the Church

Obviously churches have an interest in communal groups. Christian churches are supposed to be communities of faith linked to one other. Today we see examples of walls coming down throughout the world—between nations, occasionally between religious groups, sometimes among ethnic enclaves. Dialogic tools and forums can facilitate these unions if we learn how to use them; they require new kinds of *interactive* communication habits—with a lot of listening to one another. When we are used to thinking that we have the right answers, it requires communication re-learning to listen more and to work through legitimate differences.

The Church, along with the rest of society, faces enormous *training* and *re-training* needs. According to *Via Satellite* magazine (November, 1991, p. 32), business teleconferencing to reach and train members was a $195 million business by 1990. The training task is a major focus of teleconferencing in American corporations. The American Catholic Church already uses teleconferencing for training, but needs to plan and coordinate much, much more in this area. Part of the goal, ultimately, is to provide means for people to have on-demand access to the information they need to develop themselves.

The question of *access* is another major church-related issue. As communication/information technologies become the coin of commerce in the decades ahead, those who do not have access to the tools and the content (software) will find themselves closed out. Access has clearly become a justice policy issue for today's Church. The accompanying training question—learning to *use* modern communication technologies—connects to the access question. This involves encouraging local initiative, creating incentives, and fostering other human development strategies.

Distribution of resources will also continue to play a vital role in modern society. As emergency-aid needs arise throughout the world, people see that *systems of distribution* often hold the key to getting help through to the right people quickly. Communication systems will help to meet this need more and more. And within the institutional Church, the allocation of resources (people, funds, etc.) will continue to be a challenge. We need to become expert in using technologies to achieve economies.

For the American Catholic Church, the focus for most families remains the local parish community. Our infrastructures should serve and support this local community, not dislodge it. One of the most interesting new communication tools in this arena—the parish video library (PVL)—benefitted from research by the Center for Religious Telecommunications at the University of Dayton. The Center also studies models of collaborative planning among church organizations, so such collaborative models can be duplicated elsewhere.

Emerging needs

No one doubts that modern telecommunications present challenges to churches. We have long realized the need for media literacy. We know, without being told by experts, that our communication habits are changing us. Similarly, we are learning more about the impact of mass media. We are now aware that people *identify* with the stories they see on TV—fictional stories, news stories, and human interest (witness) stories, as well as advertising stories. This bonding with oral and visual narrative creates a whole new hearth for humanity to gather around and to evaluate.

Now we need to focus more on the intra-group communication mechanisms and the role of telecommunications tools in these interactive forums.

We need a long-term and systematic strategy over this decade so we can approach the millennium with confidence. I propose a two-lane highway approach.

On the one hand we need to bring theologians and communication scholars together for continual "think-tank" interaction—doing the communications research and development work for the Church. Existing professional organizations should have structures (special sections) to accommodate this thinking-together at their organizational conventions. The Catholic Theological Society of America (CTSA) does this annually in a forum on communication theology. The national offices in Washington (for schools, the bishops' conference) should all facilitate such forums. Many, many week-long conferences need to be scheduled over the decade, so these thinkers can spend time together sharing ideas, stimulating the development of new conceptual models. Universities should link their theology and communication faculty in systematic planning forums.

Alongside of this work, however, in the second lane, should be much, much collaborative strategic planning among practitioners, the communications personnel in the trenches, who meet the daily, continual challenges (and crises) where Church and society interface and "reach out and touch" each other. This on-going practical planning needs to utilize teleconferencing and other tools to get the day-by-day jobs done. There needs to be much interconnection and collaboration. And both groups—the think tank types and the daily practitioners—need to sustain and enrich each other as the decade progresses.

It is right there on the horizon. Karl Rahner called it our "global epoch."

References

Abbott, W. (Ed.). (1966). *The documents of Vatican II*. New York: Herder & Herder.

Administrative Board, U.S. Catholic Conference. (1986). *In the sight of all—Communication: A vision all can share*. Washington, DC: USCC.

Aronowitz, S. (1981). *The crisis in historical materialism: Class, politics, and culture in marxist theory*. New York: Praeger.

Babin, P., & Kouloumdjian, M. F. (1983). *Les nouveux modes de comprendre: La génération de l'audiovisuel et de l'ordinateur*. Paris: Le Centurion.

Bainton, R. H. (1966). *Christendom: A short history of Christianity and its impact on western civilization* (Vols. 1-2). New York: Harper & Row.

Baragli, E. (1974). *Comunicazione e pastorale: sociologia pastorale degli strumenti della comunicazione sociale*. Rome: Studio Romano della comunicazione sociale.

Barthes, R. (1981). *Camera lucida: Reflections on photography* (R. Howard, Trans.). New York: Hill and Wang. (Original work published 1980)

Baumgartner, C. (1953). Tradition et magistre. *Recherches de science religieuse, 41*, 161-187.

Bellah, R. N. (1985). The sociological implications of electronic media. In M. L. Schropp (Ed.), *The electronic media, popular culture, and family values: A proceedings report* (pp. 13-21). Washington, DC: United States Catholic Conference.

Bellah, R. N., Madsen, R., Sullivan, W. M., Swidler, A., & Tipton, S. M. (1986). *Habits of the heart: Individualism and commitment in American life*. New York: Perennial Library, Harper & Row.

Benz, E. (1963). *The eastern orthodox church*. New York: Anchor.

Berchmans, B. M. (1988). *Proposal for a Catholic youth magazine: A uses and gratifications study of religious media use by Catholic teenagers*. Unpublished master's thesis, Marquette University, Milwaukee, WI.

Berger, P. (1970). *A rumor of angels*. Garden City, NY: Doubleday.

Bevan, E. (1940). *Holy images: An inquiry into idolatry and image-worship in ancient paganism and in Christianity*. London: George Allen & Unwin.

Bevan, E. (1957). *Symbolism and belief*. Boston: Beacon Press.

Bishops' Committee on the Liturgy. (1978). *Environment and art in Catholic worship*. Washington, DC: United States Catholic Conference.

Bishops' Committee on the Liturgy. (1983). *Music in Catholic worship* (rev. ed). Washington, DC: United States Catholic Conference.

Bishops' Committee on Priestly Life and Ministry. (1982). *Fulfilled in your hearing: The homily in the Sunday assembly*. Washington, DC: United States Catholic Conference.

Bloom, A. (1987). *The closing of the American mind*. New York: Simon and Schuster.

Borg, M. J. (1994). *Meeting Jesus again for the first time*. San Francisco: Harper.

Boyle, M. O. (1977). *Erasmus on language and method in theology*. Toronto: University of Toronto Press.

Braddock, R. (1958). An extension of the "Lasswell formula." *Journal of Communication, 8*, 88-93.

Bro, B. (1967). De mens en de sacramenten: De antropologische onderbouw van de christelijke sacramenten. *Concilium*, 35-52.

Brueggeman, W. (1977). *The Bible makes sense*. Winona, MN: St. Mary's College Press.

Brueggemann, W. (1989). *Finally comes the poet: Daring speech for proclamation*. Minneapolis: Fortress Press.

Burghardt, W. J. (1951). The Catholic concept of tradition. *Proceedings of the Catholic Theological Society of America*, 42-76.

Burke, J. (1978). *Gospel power*. New York: Alba House.

Burke, K. (1961). *The rhetoric of religion: Studies in logology*. Boston: Beacon Press.

Carey, J. W. (1989). *Communication as culture: Essays on media and society*. Boston: Unwin Hyman.

Chaffee, S. (1986). Mass media and interpersonal channels: Competitive, convergent, or complementary? In G. Gumpert & R. Cathcart (Eds.), *Inter/Media: Interpersonal communication in a media world* (3rd ed.) (pp. 62-80). New York: Oxford University Press.

Christiaens, M. (1985). De moraal van de zelfontplooiing: een illusie. *Kultuurleven*, 824ff.

Coleman, J. A. (1982). *An American strategic theology*. New York: Paulist Press.

Comstock, G. (1978). The impact of television on American institutions. *Journal of Communication, 28*(2), 12-28.

Congregation for Catholic Education. (1986). *Guide to the training of future priests concerning the instruments of social communication.* Rome: Tipografia Poliglotta Vaticana.

Craddock, F. B. (1978). *Overhearing the Gospel.* Nashville: Abingdon Press.

Craddock, F. B. (1979). *As one without authority.* Nashville: Abingdon Press.

Day, T. (1990). *Why Catholics can't sing: The culture of Catholicism and the triumph of bad taste.* New York: Crossroad.

de Reuver, G. J. (1987). *Schoolkathechese en communicatie.* Kampen: De Reuver.

Deming, C. (1985). Hill Street Blues as narrative. *Critical Studies in Mass Communication, 2,* 1-22.

Denny, J. P. (1991). Rational thought in oral culture and literate decontexualization. In D. R. Olson, & N. Torrance (Eds.), *Literacy and orality* (pp. 66-89). Cambridge: Cambridge University Press.

Denziger, H., Bannwart, C., Umberg, J. B., & Rahner, K. (Eds.). (1947). *Enchiridion Symbolorum* (31st ed.). Barcelona, Freiburg-im-Breisgau, and Rome: Herder.

Dijkman, J. H. (1988). Integratie van het verhaal in de ethiek: Mogelijkheden en grenzen van het narratieve binnen een theologischethische handelingstheorie. *Tijdschrift voor theologie, 28,* 50-73.

Dionysius the Areopagite. (1972). *The divine names and the mystical theology* (C. E. Rolt, Trans.). London: S.P.C.K.

Dulles, A. (1972). The church is communication. *Multimedia International, 1.*

Dulles, A. (1974). *Models of the Church.* Garden City, NY: Doubleday.

Dulles, A. (1988). *The reshaping of Catholicism: Current challenges in the theology of church.* San Francisco: Harper & Row.

Dulles, A. (1989). Vatican II and communications. In R. Latourelle (Ed.), *Vatican II: Assessment and perspectives* (Vol. III, pp. 528-547). New York: Paulist Press.

DuMaine, P. (1972). Notes on an electronic information/communications system to support individualized instruction. Position paper for the Archdiocese of San Francisco.

Eisenstein, E. L. (1979). *The printing press as an agent of change: Communications and cultural transformations in early-modern Europe.* Cambridge: Cambridge University Press.

Flannery, A. (Ed.). (1992). *Vatican Council II: The conciliar and post conciliar documents.* Northport, NY: Costello Publishing Company, Inc.

Fleischer, H. (1987). *Ethik ohne Imperativ: Zur Kritik des moralischen Bewusstseins.* Frankfurt a/M: Fischer Wissenschaft.

Fore, W. F. (1987). *Television and religion.* Minneapolis: Augsburg Press.

Funk, V. C. (1990). Do it with style. *Pastoral Music, 14*(4), 25-28.

Gadamer, H.-G. (1975). *Truth and method* (G. Barden & J. Cumming, Eds.). New York: Crossroad. (Original work published in 1960)

Gallagher, M. P. (1988). *Help my unbelief.* Chicago: Loyola University Press.

Gans, H. J. (1979). *Deciding what's news: A study of CBS Evening News, NBC Nightly News, Newsweek, and Time.* New York: Pantheon Books.

Gardner, H. (1983). *Frames of mind: The theory of multiple intelligences.* New York: Basic Books.

Garside, Jr., C. (1966). *Zwingli and the arts.* New Haven: Yale University Press.

Gerbner, G., & Connolly, K. (1978). Television as new religion. *New Catholic World, 221,* 52-56.

Gerbner, G., Gross, L., Hoover, S., Morgan, M., Signorielli, N., Cotugno, H. E., & Wuthnow, R. (1984). *Religion and television: A research report by the Annenberg School of Communications, University of Pennsylvania and the Gallup Organization, Inc.* New York: National Council of Churches.

Gerbner, G., Gross, L., Morgan, M., & Signorielli, N. (1986). Living with television: The dynamics of the cultivation process. In J. Bryant & D. Zillmann (Eds.), *Perspectives on media effects* (pp. 17-40). Hillsdale, NJ: Lawrence Erlbaum Associates.

Gilson, E. (1940). *The mystical theology of Saint Bernard* (A. H. C. Downes, Trans.). New York: Sheed & Ward. (Original work published 1934)

Godschmidt, R. C. (1940). *Paulinus' churches at Nola: Texts, translations and commentary.* Amsterdam: N. V. Noord-Hollandsche Uitgeuers Maatschappij.

Greeley, A. M. (1990). *The Catholic myth: The behavior and beliefs of American Catholics.* New York: Scribners.

Habermas, J. (1971). *Knowledge and human interests* (J. J. Shapiro, Trans.). Boston: Beacon Press. (Original work published 1968)

Hall, E. T. (1959). *The silent language.* Greenwich, CT: Fawcett Publications.

Haughey, J. C. (1973). *The conspiracy of God: The Holy Spirit in men.* Garden City, NY: Doubleday.

Havelock, E. (1963). *Preface to Plato.* Cambridge, MA: Harvard University Press.

Heidegger, M. (1977). The age of the world-picture. In *The Question Concerning Technology* (W. Lovitt, Trans.). New York: Harper and Row. (Orignal works published 1952-1962)

Hirsch, E. D., Jr. (1987). *Cultural literacy: What every American needs to know.* Boston: Houghton Mifflin.

Hoffman, L. A. (1988). *The art of public prayer: Not for clergy only.* Washington, DC: The Pastoral Press.

Holt, E. G. (Ed.). (1957). *A documentary history of art: Vol. 1. The middle ages and the renaissance.* Garden City, NY: Doubleday.

Hovda, R. W. (1980). *Strong, loving and wise: Presiding in liturgy.* Collegeville, MN: The Liturgical Press.

Hynds, E. C. (1987). Large daily newspapers have improved coverage of religion. *Journalism Quarterly, 64,* 444-448.

Innis, H. A. (1951). *The bias of communication.* Toronto: University of Toronto Press.

Jensen, J. (1990). *Redeeming modernity: Contradictions in media criticism.* Newbury Park, CA: Sage.

Katz, E., & Lazarsfeld, P. (1955). *Personal influence.* Glencoe: Free Press.

Keifer, R. A. (1980). *To give thanks and praise.* Washington: National Association of Pastoral Musicians.

Kennedy, E. (1987, May 1). Want the truth? Turn over a myth and look under it [interview with Joseph Campbell]. *National Catholic Reporter,* 7-8.

Kidson, P. (1987). Panofsky, Suger and St. Denis. *Journal of the Warburg and Courtland Institutes, 1.*

Kitzinger, E. (1980). *Byzantine art in the making: Main lines of stylistic development in Mediterranean art, 3rd-7th century.* Cambridge, MA: Harvard University Press.

Kohlberg, L. (1981). *The philosophy of moral development: Vol. 1. Essays on moral development.* San Francisco: Harper & Row.

Kracauer, S. (1965). *Theory of film: The redemption of physical reality.* New York: Oxford University Press.

Kraeling, K. H. (1967). *The Christian building.* New Haven: Dura-Europos Publications.

Kuchenbuch, T. (1978). *Filmanalyse: Theorien, modelle, kritik.* Koeln: Prometh Verlag.

Kues, C. (1990). The art of the silent interview. *Graduating Engineer, 11*(4), 39-40, 42.

Kuhn, T. S. (1970). *The structure of scientific revolutions* (2nd ed., enlarged). Chicago: University of Chicago Press.

Kuhns, W. (1969). *The electronic gospel.* New York: Herder & Herder.

L'Orange, H. P. (1965). *Art forms and civic life in the late Roman empire.* Princeton: Princeton University Press.

Lasswell, H. (1948). The structure and function of communication in society. In L. Bryson (Ed.), *The Communication of Ideas* (pp. 37-51). New York: Harper and Bros.

Leclercq, J. (1961). *The love of learning and the desire for God* (C. Misrahi, Trans.). New York: Fordham University Press. (Original work published 1957)

Leo XIII. (1981). *Satis cognitum.* In C. Carlen (Ed.), *The papal encyclicals, 1878-1903* (pp. 387-404). [Wilmington, NC]: McGrath Publishing Co. (Original work published 1896)

Lichter, S. R., Amundson, D., & Lichter, L. S. (1991). *Media coverage of the Catholic church.* New Haven: Catholic League for Religious and Civil Rights and the Knights of Columbus.

Lonergan, B. J. F. (1972). *Method in theology.* New York: Herder & Herder.

Lourdeaux, L. (1990). *Italian and Irish filmmakers in America: Ford, Capra, Coppola, and Scorsese.* Philadelphia: Temple University Press.

Luke, T. (1983-1984). From fundamentalism to televangelism. *Telos, 58,* 204-210.

Maletzke, G. (1965). *Psychologie der Massenkommunikation.* Hamburg: Verlag Hans Bredow-Institut.

Mann, P. (1980). Spirituality and innervision. *Studies in Formative Spirituality, 1*(1), 103-114.

Mann, P. (1983). *Through words and images.* New York: CTNA.

Mann, P. (1984) Journey into the image: Religion, the arts, and telecommunication. In E. C. Lange, (Ed.), *Reflections on a theology of telecommunications: Image, model, and word,* pp. 27-40. Dayton, OH: Center for Religious Telecommunications.

Mann, P. (1987a). Media and the common good: The search for justice. In O. F. Williams & J. W. Houck (Eds.), *The common good and U.S. capitalism* (pp. 364-374). Lanham: University Press of America.

Mann, P. (1987b, May-June). A way of life shaped by death and resurrection: Memories of Karl Rahner. *New Catholic World,* 136-139.

Marcuse, H. (1964). *One-dimensional man: Studies in the ideology of advanced industrial society.* Boston: Beacon Press.

Martín-Barbero, J. (1993). *Communication, culture, and hegemony: From the media to mediations* (E. Fox & R. A. White, Trans.). Newbury Park, CA: Sage. (Original work published 1987)

Martini, C. (1990). Let's organize hope: Situations, priorities, methods. *The new media age: Meeting the challenge, Unda/OCIC study days, Bangkok 1990.* Brussels: Unda/OCIC.

Marty, M. (1967). *The improper opinion: Mass media and the Christian faith.* Philadelphia: Westminster.

McCombs, M., & Gilbert, S. (1986). News influence on our pictures of the world. In J. Bryant & D. Zillmann (Eds.), *Perspectives on media effects* (pp. 1-15). Hillsdale, NJ: Lawrence Erlbaum Associates.

McLuhan, M. (1962). *The Gutenberg galaxy: The making of typographic man.* New York: New American Library.

McQuail, D., & Windahl, S. (1981). *Communication models for the study of mass communication.* London: Longman.

Mechling, J. (1988). The mass-mediated pope. *This World, 20,* 92-103.

Memorial Volume of the Diamond Jubilee of St. Louis University. (1904). St. Louis: Press of Little and Becker Printing Co.

Metz, J. B. (1981). *The emergent church: The future of Christianity in a postbourgeois world* (P. Mann, Trans.). New York: Crossroad. (Original work published 1980)

Meyrowitz, J. (1985). *No sense of place: The impact of electronic media on social behavior.* New York: Oxford University Press.

Miles, M. R. (1985). *Image as insight: Visual understanding in western Christianity and secular culture.* Boston: Beacon Press.

Mische, P. (1985). *Star wars and the state of our souls: Deciding the future of planet earth.* Minneapolis: Winston Press.

Moberg, D. (1984). *The church as a social institution.* Grand Rapids: Baker Book House.

Mueller-Vollmer, K. (Ed.). (1988). *The hermeneutics reader.* New York: The Continuum Publishing Company.

Naisbitt, J. (1982). *Megatrends: Ten new directions transforming our lives.* New York: Warner Books.

Newcomb, H., & Hirsch, P. M. (1987). Television as a cultural forum. In H. Newcomb (Ed.), *Television: The critical view* (pp. 455-470). New York: Oxford University Press.

Ohio Interdiocesan Telecommunications Task Force. (1993). Mission statement.

Ong, W. J. (1965). Oral residue in Tudor prose style. *PMLA, 80,* 145-154.

Ong, W. J. (1967). *The Presence of the Word.* New Haven: Yale University Press.

Ong, W. J. (1969). Communications media and the state of theology. *Cross Currents, 19,* 462-480.

Ong, W. J. (1982). *Orality and literacy: The technologizing of the word.* London & New York: Methuen.

Ouspensky, L., & Lossky, V. (1983). *The meaning of icons.* Crestwood, NY: St. Vladimir's.

Pannenberg, W. (1961). Dogmatische Thesen zur Lehre von der Offenbarung. In W. Pannenberg, R. Rendtorff, U. Wilckens, & T. Rendtorff (Eds.), *Offenbarung als Geschichte* (pp. 91-114). Göttingen: Vandenhoeck und Ruprecht.

Panofsky, E. (1979). *Abbot Suger on the abbey church of St. Denis and its art treasures.* Princeton: Princeton University Press.

Paul VI. (1982). *Evangelii nuntiandi.* In A. Flannery (Ed.), *Vatican Council II: More postconciliar documents* (pp. 711-761). Collegeville, MN: Liturgical Press. (Original work published 1975)

Peters, J. (1977). Religie en spiritualiteit. *Speling,* 18ff.

Pontifical Council for the Instruments of Social Communication. (1971). *Communio et Progressio.* In A. Flannery (Ed.). *Vatican Council II:*

The conciliar and post conciliar documents (pp. 293-349). Northport, NY: Costello Publishing Company, Inc.

Pontifical Council for Social Communications. (1992). *A new era, aetatis novae: Pastoral instruction on social communications on the 20th anniversary of* Communio et progressio. Rome: Libreria Editrice Vaticana.

Postman, N. (1986). *Amusing ourselves to death: Public discourse in the age of show business.* New York: Viking Penguin.

Pottmeyer, H. J. (1990). The churchification of Christianity. Paper presented to the Faculty of Theology, Notre Dame University, South Bend, IN.

Ricoeur, P. (1970). *Freud and philosophy* (D. Savage, Trans.). New Haven, CT: Yale University Press.

Ricoeur, P. (1974). *The conflict of interpretations: Essays in hermeneutics* (D. Ihde, Trans. and Ed.). Evanston: Northwestern University Press.

Riley, M. W., & Riley J. W., Jr. (1951). A sociological approach to communications research. *Public Opinion Quarterly, 15,* 445-460.

Riley, J. W., Jr., & Riley, M. W. (1959). Mass communication and the social system. In R. K. Merton, L. Broom, & L. S. Cottrell, Jr. (Eds.), *Sociology today: Problems and prospects* (pp. 537-578). New York: Basic Books, 1959.

Roberts, N. (1984). *Dorothy Day and the* Catholic Worker. Albany: SUNY Press.

Rostovtzeff, M. (1938). *Dura-Europos and its art.* Oxford: The Clarendon Press.

Sacred Congregation for Divine Worship. (1974). General instruction of the Roman missal. In *The Sacramentary* (pp. 17*-48*). New York: Catholic Book Publishing Co.

Sacred Congregation of Rites. (1964). Instruction on the proper implementation of the constitution on the sacred liturgy. In A. Flannery (Ed.). *Vatican Council II: The conciliar and post conciliar documents* (pp. 45-56). Northport, NY: Costello Publishing Company, Inc.

Schapiro, M. (1977). On the aesthetic attitude in romanesque art. *Romanesque Art: Selected Papers* (pp. 6-10). New York: George Braziller.

Schramm, W. (1954). How communication works. In W. Schramm (Ed.), *The process and effects of mass communication* (pp. 3-26). Urbana, IL: University of Illinois Press.

Schudson, M. (1982). The politics of narrative form: The emergence of news conventions inprint and television. *Daedalus, 111,* 97-112.

Schwartz, S. (1983). Hermeneutics and the productive imagination: Paul Ricoeur in the 1970s. *Journal of Religion, 63,* 290-300.

Senior, D. (1986). Not by exegesis alone: From scholarship to preaching. *Church, 2*(3), 16-20.

Smolarski, D. C. (1982). *How not to say Mass.* New York: Paulist Press.

Sölle, D. (1970). *Fantasie en gehoorzaamheid: Toekomst en christelijke ethiek.* Baarn: Bosch & Keuning.

Sontag, S. (1973). *On photography.* New York: Farrar, Straus and Giroux.

Soukup, P. A. (1983). *Communication and theology: Introduction and review of the literature.* London: WACC.

St. Louis Post-Dispatch. (April 30, 1903).

Stein, B. (1979). *The view from Sunset Boulevard: America as brought to you by the people who make television.* New York: Basic Books.

Steiner, G. (1980). *On difficulty and other essays.* (New York: Oxford University Press).

Steinfels, P., Wycliff, D., Marin, C., Neff, D., Lehmann, D., & Marty, M. (1995). Religion and the media. *Commonweal, 122*(4), 13-52.

Stevens, W. (1954). Anecdote of the jar. *The collected poems of Wallace Stevens.* New York: Knopf. (Original work published 1923)

Stock, B. (1983). *The implications of literacy: Written language and models of interpretation in the eleventh and twelfth centuries.* Princeton, NJ: Princeton University Press.

Tannen, D. (1990). *You just don't understand.* New York: William Morrow and Co.

Thayer, L. (1973). Massamedia in de moderne samenleving. *Massacommunicatie,* 147ff.

Thorn, W. (1990). The history and role of the Catholic press. In B. J. Hubbard, (Ed.), *Reporting religion: Facts and faith* (pp. 81-107). Sonoma: Polebridge Press.

Tichenor, P., Donohue, G. A., & Olien, C. (1980). *Community conflict and the press.* Beverly Hills: Sage.

Tillmans, W. G. (1987). Theologische impulsen voor een werkzame samenhang van spiritualiteit en tv/film. In J. G. Hahn, H. Hoekstra, & F. Tillmans (Eds.). *Over religieuze films gesproken* (pp. 76ff.). Hilversum: Gooi & Sticht.

Tracy, D. (1978). *Blessed rage for order: The new pluralism in theology.* New York: The Seabury Press.

Tracy, D. (1981). *The analogical imagination: Christian theology and the culture and pluralism.* New York: Crossroads.

Troeger, T. H. (1990). *Imaging a sermon.* Nashville: Abingdon Press.

Vallee, J. (1984). *Computer message systems.* New York: McGraw Hill.

van der Lans, J. (1989). Zingeving onder invloed van het televisie-medium: een conceptueel kader. In *Televisie en zingeving.* Nijmegen: Katholiek Studiecentrum Nijmegen.

van Driel, B., & Richardson, J. T. (1988). Print media coverage of new religious movements: A longitudinal study. *Journal of Communication 38*(3), 37-61.

Virt, G. (1994). The life of the spirit in a mass-mediated culture. In P. J. Rossi & P. A. Soukup (Eds.), *Mass media and the moral imagination* (pp. 52-67). Kansas City, MO: Sheed & Ward.

von Simson, O. G. (1948). *Sacred fortress: Byzantine art and statecraft in Ravenna.* Chicago: University of Chicago Press.

Vorgrimler, H. (Ed.). (1966). *Commentary on the documents of Vatican II.* New York: Herder & Herder.

Weakland, R. (1991, February 27). Herald of hope. *Catholic Herald.* [Milwaukee: Archdiocese of Milwaukee].

Weitzmann, K. (Ed.). (1980). *Age of spirituality: A symposium.* New York: The Metropolitan Museum of Art, published in association with Princeton University Press.

Whalen, J. (1967). "The press opens up Vatican II." *Journalism Quarterly, 44,* 53-61.

White, D. M. (1950). The "gatekeeper": A case study in the selection of news. *Journalism Quarterly, 27,* 383-390.

White, R. A. (1994, December). *Media reception theory: Emerging perspectives.* Paper presented at Le Programme Pluriannuel en Sciences Humaines Rhone-Alps: Societe et Communication, Lyon, France.

Woodstock Letters. (1903).

Woodward, K. L. (1990). *Making saints: How the Catholic church determines who becomes a saint, who doesn't, and why.* New York: Simon and Schuster.

Yates, F. A. (1966). *The art of memory.* Chicago: University of Chicago Press.

Zagano, P. (1987). Equality before the press: Media coverage of the Vatican birth technology statement. *Crisis 5*(5), 29-34.

Zukowski, A. A. (1990). Parish video libraries. *Catholic Library World, 61*(4), 160.

Zukowski, A. A. (1992). Trends in technology [Quarterly Column]. *MOMENTUM.* Washington, DC: National Catholic Education Association.

Index

About the Authors

Gregor T. Goethals is the author of *The TV Ritual: Worship at the Video Altar* and *The Electronic Golden Calf: Images, Religion, and the Making of Meaning*. She is professor of art history at the Rhode Island School of Design, a free-lance designer, and the lead designer for the American Bible Society's Multimedia Translation Project.

Andrew M. Greeley is a Professor of Sociology at the University of Arizona and a visiting professor at the University of Chicago. A priest of the Archdiocese of Chicago, he has published widely both as a sociologist chronicling religious attitudes and as a novelist. His recent books include *Religious Change in America* (Harvard University Press) and *The Catholic Myth: The Behavior and Beliefs of American Catholics* (Scribner).

Born in the north of Holland in 1932, **Henk Hoekstra** is a Carmelite priest. He studied philosophy and theology in Holland and communication sciences at the Catholic University of Louvain (Belgium). Now a member of the Catholic Theological Faculty of Amsterdam teaching mass media and group dynamics, he has served as a member of the Study and Research Department of the KRO (Catholic Broadcasting in Holland). He is president of OCIC (Organisation Catholique Internationale du Cinema et Audiovisuel), member of the Pontifical Council for Social Communications in Rome, and president of CAMECO (Catholic Media Council). He teaches and conducts training courses at several Universities and Institutions around the world. He is the co-author of *Media and Religious Communication*, *The Media Dialogue about Film and Television*, and many articles about media education.

Robert F. Leavitt, S.S., teaches at St. Mary's Seminary and University in Baltimore.

Based in New York, **Peter Mann** works as the international coordinator for World Hunger Year (WHY) and research editor of *Why Magazine: Challenging Hunger and Poverty*. Before joining WHY in 1986, he had a wide experience in media, having produced more than 200 television programs based on his conversations with leading activists and thinkers on world development, poverty, and religion. In addition to his own reflections on the impact of the media (*Through words and images*, CTNA), he has translated the works of the German theologian, J. B. Metz.

Walter J. Ong, S.J., is University Professor emeritus of Humanities and Professor emeritus of Humanities in Psychiatry at Saint Louis University, Missouri. His work on orality and literacy and the impact of printing has won wide acclaim. The more recent of his hundreds of books and articles are *Orality and Literacy: The Technologizing of the Word* (Methuen); *Hopkins, the Self, and God* (University of Toronto Press); and three volumes of collected essays, *Faith and Contexts* (Scholars Press).

Frances Forde Plude is Associate Professor of Communication at Notre Dame College in Cleveland. She earned a doctorate at Harvard University and studied satellite communications at MIT. She has directed a network of wireless cable stations and has authored studies on direct broadcast satellites, U.S. private schools, telecommunications careers, and microwave technology. She recently coauthored *Communication Ethics and Global Change* (Longman). Dr. Plude served as communications consultant for the American Catholic bishops in the development of their national satellite system. She has also done communications strategic planning with other groups including the Amish, the American Methodist Church and B'Nai B'rith International. As director of a research project on the telecom markets of the European Community, Dr. Plude is developing new planning concepts involving the use of collaborative systems.

Dennis C. Smolarski, S.J., received M.Div. and S.T.M. degrees from the Jesuit School of Theology at Berkeley and holds a Ph.D. in computer science from the University of Illinois at Champaign-Urbana. He is presently on the mathematics faculty at Santa Clara University. Fr. Smolarski has had a long-time interest in Western and Eastern rite liturgy and worship. He is the author of *Eucharistia: A Study of the Eucharistic Prayer, How Not to Say Mass, Liturgical Literacy* and *Sacred Mysteries* (Paulist Press).

Paul A. Soukup, S.J., has explored the connections between communication and theology since 1982. His publications include *Communication and Theology* (World Association for Christian Communication); *Christian Communication: A Bibliographical Survey* (Greenwood Press); and *Mass Media and the Moral Imagination* with Philip J. Rossi (Sheed & Ward). In addition, he and Thomas J. Farrell have edited three volumes of the collected works of Walter J. Ong, SJ (Scholars Press). A graduate of the University of Texas at Austin (Ph.D., 1985), Fr. Soukup teaches in the Communication Department at Santa Clara University.

William J. Thorn, Ph.D. (mass communication, University of Minnesota) is the Director of the Institute for Catholic Media and the chairman of the Department of Journalism at Marquette University. He has worked as a newspaper reporter and editor, in broadcasting, and in public relations. His research specialty has been the Catholic press and religious communication. He has been an invited guest professor at the Pontifical Gregorian University, the Pontifical Salesian University, and Santa Clara University. His books include *On The Edge of the Millennium: the Catholic Press of Europe and the United States*, *The Future of the Catholic Press*, *Newspaper Circulation: Marketing the News*, and *The Handbook of Diocesan Communications*. Dr. Thorn has been a consultant to the Pontifical Council for Social Communications and was a member of the drafting committee of *Aetatis Novae*. His past research includes studies of American Catholics' use of media, audience studies for various newspapers and magazines, and Church access to commercial broadcast and cable.

Dr. Marjeet Verbeek studied pastoral theology and mass communication (film and television) in Amsterdam, the Netherlands. Since 1986 she has worked in media education, specifically addressing the question of how to integrate the audiovisual media into religious education and spiritual guidance. Her main activities in this area include training theology students, catechists, and lay people on the subject; lecturing; writing journal articles; and writing handbooks for using specific film and television programs in teaching. From 1986 to 1992 she worked at the Catholic Media Center in Amsterdam; since 1992 she has continued her teaching and writing on a free-lance basis.

Robert P. Waznak, S.S., is a Sulpician priest who is Professor of Homiletics at the Washington Theological Union. He holds a Ph.D. in Rhetoric from Temple University. He was the first elected president of CATH (Catholic Association of Teachers of Homiletics). He is the author of numerous articles. His latest book is *Like Fresh Bread: Sunday Homilies in the Parish* (Paulist Press).

Robert J. Wister, a priest of the Archdiocese of Newark, NJ, is associate professor of Historical Studies at the School of Theology of Seton Hall University in South Orange, NJ. He holds a doctorate in Church History from the Gregorian University and was Executive Director of the Seminary Department of the National Catholic Educational Association from 1988 to 1993.

Phyllis Zagano received her doctorate with a dissertation on the priest-poets Gerard Manley Hopkins and R.S. Thomas at the State University of New York (Stony Brook). She has served as program officer of the National Humanities Center, an advanced research institute, and as a research for the Roman Catholic Archdiocese of New York. Since 1988 she has been an associate professor of communication at Boston University, where she is also director of the Institute for Democratic Communication, a research institute focused on communications and culture. She also teaches at the Boston University School of Theology, and is co-chair of the American Academy of Religion's Roman Catholic Studies Group. She holds graduate degrees in theology, literature, and communications and writes widely in academic and popular journals. Her books include *Religion and Public Affairs* (edited, Rockford), *Woman to Woman: An Anthology of Women's Spiritualities* (The Liturgical Press), and *On Prayer* (Paulist Press).

Angela Ann Zukowski, MHSH, directs the Center for Religious Telecommunications at the University of Dayton. Extensively involved in Church communication, she has served as president of Unda-USA; she is currently president of Unda International and a member of the Pontifical Council for Social Communications.

www.ingramcontent.com/pod-product-compliance
Lightning Source LLC
Chambersburg PA
CBHW021812270326
41932CB00007B/155